T0078432

GROWING TREES IN URBAN KINSHASA

SHRUB VEGETATION IN RESIDENTIAL
PLOTS IN KINSHASA

GUTU KIA ZIMI, PhD

authorHOUSE®

AuthorHouse™
1663 Liberty Drive
Bloomington, IN 47403
www.authorhouse.com
Phone: 833-262-8899

Published by AuthorHouse 01/07/2021

ISBN: 978-1-6655-1263-3 (sc)
ISBN: 978-1-6655-1262-6 (e)

EDITORIAL

One can resist the invasion of armies;
one cannot resist the invasion of ideas
Victor Hugo

Our African cities in general and particularly those of the Democratic Republic of the Congo have followed two distinct types of settlement. The first is where urbanization followed industrialization and the second is where industrialization followed urbanization. In the first situation, the predominant culture remains more that of a market economy based on the capitalist principle. The population is in search of well-being and is adapting to the requirements of industrialization. It is in this social construct that there are great waves of migration leading to social maladjustment. Everything is then for sale and living conditions are deteriorating daily. In the second case, where industrialization comes after urbanization, the culture of the already settled population influences the conduct of business. The problem with this system is the presence of an excessive unemployment which is the basis for a low level of workers' wages

In both cases, the City of Kinshasa did not escape the culture of both migratory settlement and industrialization. It is at this point that the work of Dr. Gutu Kia Zimi on "GROWING TREES IN URBAN KINSHASA", a reflection on SHRUB VEGETATION IN RESIDENTIAL PLOTS IN KINSHASA, is of paramount importance insofar as this well-researched and rich in conceptual as well as statistical information, brings a plus in the understanding of this culture in relation to the developmental evolution of our African cities in general. Kinshasa did follow this same form of transformation from a small non-urbanized town to a large city with a population of around 16,000,000. People.

Living conditions change every day. The tree has become, in this culture, not only a source of food and social protection but also of marketing. Dr. Gutu eloquently demonstrates how this third larger city in Africa, which is dying by erosion, encloses a hope and a model of development for our African cities.

In line with the work of the Botanist, Francis Hallé, specialist in primary forests, Dr. Gutu demonstrates in his interdisciplinary the essential role that trees play at the level of the City Province of Kinshasa. The current reforestation of the environment of our cities after their deforestation clearly shows the social as well as the economic importance of "the tree in our plots". If one could take a step back to get a proper idea of the importance attached to the presence of a tree, he would, indeed, notice that forty years ago, approximately, there were still many forests on the surface of the globe. Today, only scraps remain, in the loop of the Congo River, in Australia, in the Canadian Far North, in Siberia… Only the very difficult climate or the total lack of access still protect them from the human destruction. In the Amazon, it's too late. Trees are cut down to replace them with transgenic soybeans and livestock.

Dr. Gutu forcedly demonstrates, how trees play decisive roles in the survival of humanity. Trees purify the atmosphere by absorbing carbon dioxide and releasing oxygen. Cutting down a tree is destroying a natural purification plant. Trees attract rain. Their foliage and root system filter water. They also play a role of stabilizers for the soil. And of course, they are home to exceptional flora and fauna. They are our allies, our protectors. They are a major asset for promoting the climate. Each tree planted makes it possible to reduce the pollution of a space and to find a land seine and wild. Trees produce moisture that turns dry, uncultivable land into wetlands suitable for growing food.

The reforestation of the city of Kinshasa allows "Kinois" (inhabitant of Kinshasa) to rebuild a better future from an environmental, social and economic point of view.

This work by Dr. Gutu, which is added to many other works from the same author, should be considered not only as information conducive to human development but also for our political decision-makers on the role of human protection of environment. No social and economic development will be possible apart from improving the environment in which people live.

ALPHONSE KASONGO, DBA; PHD.
Professor
PhD in Business Management
PhD in Conflicts Analysis and Resolution
Department of Business Management and Work Organization
School of Psychology
UNIVERSITY OF KINSHASA (DRCONGO)
DEVRY UNIVERSITY (USA)

Photo GKZ
Shrub vegetation in a residential plot of Kintambo commune

I have always believed that hope is that stubborn thing inside us that insists,
Despite all the evidence to the contrary,
that something better awaits us so long as we have
the courage to keep reaching,
to keep working, to keep fighting
OBAMA
November 6, 2012

DEDICATE

To

Mom Fannie D. Garnes
and
Dad John L. Hudson

For your love and affection

CONTENTS

GENERAL INTRODUCTION

Change is never easy, but always possible
OBAMA
May 1, 2005
Change will not come if we wait for some other person or some other time.
We are the ones we have been waiting for.
We are the change that we seek
OBAMA
February 5, 2008

The city of Kinshasa compared to many other Congolese cities is a city, which once looked like a wooded city. When we contemplate it from the top of its hills, it offered us the spectacle of a green city. However, we note in the behavior of the "Kinois" (Kinshasa resident) a certain predisposition to plant a tree in his plot. The reasons for this behavior are many and varied, as we will have to explain in this study. It is important to note that this behavior of the resident of Kinshasa ("Kinois") gave birth to an urban arboriculture, which is at the base of the urban vegetation of Kinshasa, mainly of anthropic origin since the original vegetation has completely disappeared. Before urbanization, Kinshasa's vegetation was dominated by shrub savannah. Different plant elements such as fruit and ornamental trees, flowers and vegetables, as well as other crops in the vicinity and around of their homes, can be observed in the different residential plots of Kinshasa. This study falls within the framework of urban ecology[1]. According to Grimm N.B, Faeth

---

[1] Urban ecology is stricto sensu a field of ecology, which focuses on the study of the ecosystem: the city. Today, by popularization and with the aim of raising awareness of environmental issues, it can bring together the consideration of all environmental issues concerning the urban or peri-urban environment. It aims to articulate these issues by inserting them into territorial policies to limit or repair the environmental impacts and improve the living environment and the quality of life of the inhabitants.

S.H (2008), urban ecology is a concept that brings ecological issues closer to urban life, including from the perspective of global changes. It defends a transversal approach on all the themes relating to the promotion of a sustainable way of life in urban areas: transport, town planning, housing, and fight against pollution, vegetation, democracy and local economy...[2]. In approaching this study, we would like to know the underlying reasons for this behavior of city dwellers; what are the motives that drive them; what is the goal; why the preference to plant one species of tree than another. This study focuses on shrub vegetation in residential plots in Kinshasa. This means that we have deliberately excluded herbaceous vegetation and the like. This urban vegetation performs various functions including: purifying the air, regulating the microclimate, creating the physiognomy of ecosystems and improving the fertility of urban soils, at the same time as it provides households with vegetables and fruits. Some of this vegetation has already been the subject of a number of studies[3]. However, it should be noted that the shrub plant species cultivated in residential plots have been little studied. The vegetation in the city is often assimilated to that of public spaces: parks, flowerbeds, rows of trees. However, a large part of the urban vegetation is found

---

[2] GRIMM N.B, FAETH S.H, GOLUBIEWSKI N.E, REDMAN C.L, WU J, BAI X, BRIGGS J.M (2008) "Global change and the ecology of cities [archive]", Science, Vol.319, 756-760.

[3] KABEYA M., LUKEBAKIO L., KAPENDA K. & PAULUS J. Sj. (1994). Inventaire de la flore domestique des parcelles. Cas de Kinshasa (Zaïre). Revue Méd. et Pharm. Africaine, 8 (2), 38-66
- MINISTERE DU PLAN (1998), Agriculture et Elevage, Education Nationale, Environnement Conservation de la Nature et Tourisme, 1998. Sécurité alimentaire, production et commercialisation, ville de Kinshasa. Plan d'action triennal 1998-2000, pp. 296-297.
- PAUWELS L., (1982). Plantes vasculaires des environs de Kinshasa. Ed. Luc Pauwels, Bruxelles.
- PAUWELS L., (1993). N'Zayilu N'ti. Guide des arbres et arbustes de la région de Kinshasa/ Brazzaville. Ed. Jardin botanique national de Belgique. Meise (Belgique), pp. 3-16
- PAULUS J., KABEYA M., MUTUBA N., MUSIBONO E. & F. MBEMBA, (1989). Rôle des jardins et élevages de parcelles dans l'alimentation urbaine. Le cas de Kinshasa. Les 4es journées scientifiques internationales du GERM. SPA/Belgique, 22-29 avril. Karthala Paris, pp. 45-49

in private spaces (delimiting hedges, shrubs, fruit trees). Private properties abound in plants, which are not counted in the urban public inventories, for lack of data. This is the case with the urban vegetation of Kinshasa.

1. We approach this study with an interdisciplinary approach on the one hand, and a systemic (global) approach on the other. Interdisciplinary is necessary to better understand a subject in its global reality. This approach is essential as soon as we tackle a concrete problem, a project, a subject, or a concept. "Interdisciplinarity also means starting from a project, from a problematic, to make people perceive and promote research into the interactions of knowledge and their complementarity, in a spirit of openness", since the understanding of the functioning of 'an urban space like the city of Kinshasa immediately calls upon many factors (physical, historical, sociological, cultural, political, economic, ecological, environmental, ...

   The study integrates space (plots), vegetation (trees) and population (communities), this requires the following two approaches:
   - On the one hand, it is an interdisciplinary approach, because we cannot study the urban vegetation of Kinshasa without worrying about the space (plot) where this tree is planted and where it lives in interaction with various elements. The plot where the tree is planted is an ecosystem where various biotic and abiotic elements can be observed, including humans. The interrelation of all these elements has a real impact on vegetation, people and space. It determines their development, as well as their quality of life.

- On the other hand, to be able to understand this complex problem of shrub vegetation in residential plots of Kinshasa, the systemic approach is also adopted. Indeed, the solution to the problem of this urban vegetation in residential plots requires the integration of various elements, which influence this vegetation, including in particular: demographic growth, urban growth, population density, household size, poverty, housing and habitat crisis, urbanization, development and settlement of neighborhoods, education of the population, cultural influence of populations, etc. ...

2. To carry out this study, we proceeded by a direct survey in the various plots of our sample. It was a question of investigating in each plot and counting the trees, which are planted there, to determine their number and their species, finally to interview the owner on the year of plantation and the reasons which pushed him to plant such tree rather than any other. The size of the tree was retained when it was considered normal (+/- 1 meter), that is to say from a young plant except seedlings and young shoots.

3. The objective of this study is:
   - To know the species of trees, which make up the vegetation in the residential plots of Kinshasa;
   - To know the factors, which contribute to the growth or decrease of urban vegetation;
   - To determine the reasons which motivated the owners to plant these species of trees rather than others;
   - To know the use or functions of these trees in their plots;
   - Assess the impact of population growth on urban vegetation;
   - Finally, to estimate the evolution of this vegetation in future years.

4. The city of Kinshasa does not cease to attract a great deal of research on various academic and scientific themes. We cannot claim to be doing a pioneering work here with regard to the study of urban vegetation in Kinshasa. However, if several studies have already been carried out in this area, this did not prevent us from contributing through an environmental study to a better knowledge of this urban vegetation of Kinshasa. However, despite these intellectual productions, we note that, very few if not none of these authors has mainly and globally focused, following an interdisciplinary and global approach, a study on the whole of the urban vegetation of all the neighborhoods of the municipalities of the town of Kinshasa. Indeed, "there is no endogenous development without endogenous research". This is undoubtedly the interest of our study. We believe that the solutions to the various problems that arise in the town of Kinshasa must come from the population themselves, using their genius on the one hand, and their intellectual imagination on the other. The intellectual is not the graduate, but it is the man, who studies around him and who seeks answers to the various problems, which arise in his community and, which hinder or block the development of his community and his nation. It is absurd that other people can find solutions to the various problems facing the town. This is the case with refuse collection. Since the start of cooperation with the European Union, the rubbish problem in the town of Kinshasa has become unsolved. Awareness is needed on the part of the population and its leaders. Demographically, Kinshasa is now home to more than 16 million inhabitants after Cairo and Lagos, but at the expense of its environment.

In 1960, its urban area was made up of 46% forest, to gradually decrease to 36% in 1982 and to 15% in 1987. In addition, in 1960, the wooded and grassy savannah occupied 48% of its urban area and gradually increased in 1982 to 56% and to 64% in 1987 (Tshibangu et al, 1987)[4]. Today, Kinshasa's vegetation cover has shrunk considerably by several kilometers. However, the town is covered with countless fruit trees. Kinshasa is a town in full urban and demographic growth. We assume that these two factors have a negative impact on urban vegetation.

5. From the above, we hypothesize that the shrub vegetation in the residential plots of Kinshasa is declining as a result of rapid population growth. Analysis will allow us to affirm or refute this hypothesis.

6. Regarding the structure of this study, in addition to the introduction, our study is subdivided as follows:

   – Chapter 1 explains the role and importance of urban vegetation in Kinshasa

   – Chapter 2 describes the urban environment of Kinshasa, that is to say its physical, socio-economic, socio-cultural environment. This is in fact the presentation of Kinshasa

   – Chapter 3 gives us a description of the urban residential space of Kinshasa, that is to say the organization and birth of neighborhoods, the important role of plots and streets as ecological entities. We cannot talk about urban vegetation without being interested in the support that shelters this urban vegetation.

   – Chapter 4 analyzes the results of our survey, that is to say the species counted, the vegetation, the number of trees and its distribution by neighborhood and study area.

   – Chapter 5 analyzes the relationship between urban growth and population growth with urban vegetation, more precisely,

---

[4] FRANCIS LELO NZUZI, Les bidonvilles de Kinshasa, L'Harmattan/RDC, 2017, p.19.

the impact of population growth on urban vegetation: size of households, type of habitat, urban densification and extension, etc…

– Chapter 6 explains the fundamental role of urban vegetation on our urban environment.

– Finally, the general conclusion.

CHAPTER I

KINSHASA TREE VEGETATION

❖

If you work hard and meet your responsabilities,
you can get ahead, no matter where you come from,
what you look like, or who you love
OBAMA
February 12, 2013

I. STATE OF THE QUESTION AND THE PROBLEMATIC

George Orwell in his book "1984"[5] said "Who controls the past controls the future; who controls the present controls the past". Since 2007, humanity has reached a milestone, with more than half of the world's population recognized as urban. The urbanization process has a translation in demographic terms, translation all the more remarkable as the phenomenon occurred in a context of strong global population growth: 10% of the world population lived in cities at the beginning of the 20th century., there could be more than two-thirds of them in the years 2020-2025, which would represent 5 billion urban dwellers out of the 8 billion inhabitants that the planet should have[6]. Today, increasing urbanization, global warming, climate change and the phenomenon of urban heat islands are contributing to the deterioration of the quality of life of city dwellers. Since the turn of the millennium, humanity has changed from a predominantly

---

[5] GEORGE ORWELL (2017), 1984, Barnes and Noble, 2017; Penguin Publishing Group, 1950
[6] FREDERIC ALEXANDRE, ALAIN GENIN (2012), Géographie de la végétation terrestre, pp.179-192

rural species to a predominantly urban species. In 1810, London was the only city of one thousand inhabitants[7]. Professor Joel E. Cohen predicts, "virtually all population growth in the next 45 years is expected to occur in economically less development regions"… This means that, despite higher death rates, the populations of poor nations will outpace those of richer nations. More people, more poverty[8]. Today, there are over 35 cities, including the city of Kinshasa, with a population of over five million, and most of them are located in developing countries (Girardet, 1996)[9]. What are the implications of this urban explosion? Can the cities of the world accommodate so many people in a sustainable way? Will people find these urban environments welcoming enough? What will be the impact of such demographic growth on the urban natural environment? As more and more people move from rural environments to the man-made urban steel and concrete environment of cities, it is increasingly recognized and sensed for this urban population the need for some form of vegetation present in their homes everyday life. Nevertheless, the condition of a viable city must simultaneously respond to many challenges in social, energy, ecological, resilience… terms involving transversal and integrated approaches, still largely to be invented[10]. Whether it's shrub vegetation in residential plots, a shaded urban park for recreation, a tree line for noise reduction or a wetland for flood

---

[7] GIRARDET HERBERT (1992, 1996), The Gaia Atlas of cities: new directions for sustainable urban living. London: Gaia Books Ltd.

[8] MARIE D. JONES (2008), 2013 The end of days or a new beginning, Envisioning the world after the events of 2012, New Page Books, NJ, 2008, p.121

[9] TJEERD DEELSTRA AND HERBERT GIRARDET (2000), Urban agriculture and sustainable cities, https://www.researchgate.net/publication/284992045_Urban_agriculture_and_sustainable_cities.

[10] FRANÇOIS BERTRAND ET GUILLAUME SIMONET (2012), Les trames vertes urbaines et l'adaptation au changement climatique: perspectives pour l'aménagement du territoire, *VertigO - la revue électronique en sciences de l'environnement* [En ligne], Hors-série 12, Mai 2012, mis en ligne le 04 Mai 2012, consulté le 05 septembre 2020. URL: http://journals.openedition.org/vertigo/11869; DOI: https://doi.org/10.4000/vertigo.11869.

control, etc…, the concept of urban vegetation or urban greening quickly becomes a reality but also a requirement[11].

While urban arboriculture generally refers to the planting and maintenance of groups of trees and urban agriculture, the food grown by people in cities and suburbs, this includes a holistic approach to urban greening. Urban greening comes from the recognition that these urban green spaces can and should be used in an integrated and holistic manner for many other environmental and social benefits beyond recreational and aesthetic use. For the purposes of this study on shrub vegetation in residential plots of Kinshasa, we affirm that urban vegetation or urban greening refers to any revegetation effort, including the planting of trees, shrubs, or agricultural plots of which the design aims to improve the environmental quality, economic opportunities or aesthetic value associated with the landscape of the town of Kinshasa.

Photo GKZ

[11] MILLER, R.W. (1988). Urban forestry: planning and managing urban green spaces. New Jersey, E.U.-A., Prentice Hall. The term urban greening is derived from Millers' (1988) definition to denote "an integrated, city-wide approach to planting, maintaining and managing all vegetation in a city in order to guarantee multiple environmental and social benefits for city dwellers.

3

Urban greening, which encompasses urban vegetation, is seen as a comprehensive strategy to simultaneously make our cities more pleasant, livable and sustainable. Urban parks and other green areas are traditionally considered primarily as facilities and spaces for recreation. As a living and leisure space, this must also include residential plots. This is the case of the city of Kinshasa, where urban parks and other green spaces are non-existent. As a result, in Kinshasa, the living and leisure space is essentially in the plot. For that, in Kinshasa, residential plots are not only housing and living spaces, but also leisure and economic spaces. In the city of Kinshasa, the residential plots are home to a large number of socio-economic and leisure activities such as bars, dancing clubs, churches, cinema, shops, dispensaries, etc., unlike the residential area in the West, which does not only concerns the dwelling. These include improving basic sanitation, providing potable water, controlling floodwater, treating wastewater, reducing air pollution, eliminating solid waste, moderate macro and microclimates, increase biodiversity and reduce poverty.

The political future of most developing countries will be influenced by their success or failure in managing their cities (Porritt 1991)[12]. In view of the immensity and complexity of urban needs, many provincial governments in the DRC do not know what to do with their cities or do not have effective action plans to clean up cities on the one hand and '' helping the poor urban dwellers on the other hand. Even some of the urban projects in the city of Kinshasa, which in fact have enormous difficulties on the ground to be successful, in fact only deal with symptoms rather than causes.

---

[12] PORRITT J. (1991), The Common Heritage: What Heritage? Common to Whom? Environmental Values Vol. 1, No. 3, pp. 257-267, Published By White Horse Press

Photo GKZ

This is the case of the "Kin Bopeto" project for the sanitation of the city and the *"Saut de Mouton"* project (sheep jump) which is supposed to solve the problem of traffic jams in the city of Kinshasa. Regarding this project initiated by the President of the Republic in his 100-day program. We know that the real solution lies in the construction of new roads, which must meet the demands of urban growth. On the one hand, each year the vehicle fleet keeps increasing and on the other hand, there is population growth. Thus, a new rail-based transport system is necessary and urgent, because we cannot efficiently transport an urban population of more than sixteen million inhabitants and still growing by road (bus, taxis, moto-taxis, etc.).

The urban train called *"Kibola bola"* that left Tshangu district for the central station of Gombe commune is non-existent, although this mode of transport is expected to expand into other urban and peri-urban areas. As paradoxical as it may seem for the same trip, a bus going from the central station of Gombe to Masina commune can only carry around 50 people. While for the same trip, the urban train carried thousands of passengers. It will be necessary to invent and imagine other modes of urban transport in the city of Kinshasa. The same is true of the housing framework and urban environment to improve the quality of life of "Kinshasa" citizens. Hence, also the need for an urban greening program, or better still urban revegetation, to recreate a new healthy and clean living environment for the urban population of Kinshasa. The study reveals that urban vegetation is in marked decline in the neighborhoods of the old municipalities of Kinshasa, while it is growing and young in the new neighborhoods of the outlying municipalities. Unfortunately, the balance that we observe in the young neighborhoods of peri-urban municipalities is threatened by the very strong demographic growth. The owners of the plots prefer to build so-called "annex houses" on spaces formerly reserved for trees in the plots to meet the needs of tenants.

Photo GKZ

We also note the phenomenon of parceling out plots to respond to the housing crisis. As Léon de Saint Moulin (2001) underlines: "The city of Kinshasa was built more by its population than by its leaders. Most of the neighborhoods developed since 1960 have been without intervention from higher authorities, and it is often the residents who themselves carry out the necessary environmental protection and erosion control works. The urban authority, on the other hand, had the merit of designing the city's primary network on a very large scale. Kinshasa has not only grown demographically and in terms of social media. We also think about it more and more. The conclusion is that, despite the poverty and the more often highlighted decay, Kinshasa is a large city in full expansion.

If its future also depends on world developments, it lives above all on the strength of its inhabitants and on the exemplary dedication of a number of its agents, in whose eyes it is a city of hope "[13]. The growing human population in the city of Kinshasa poses enormous challenges for urban and municipal authorities, but also for town planners and other municipal leaders, in meeting the demand for infrastructure. Population growth and high human densities impose a heavy toll on the fragile natural and environmental resources of the city province of Kinshasa where squatter communities are widespread and resources are scarce.

---

[13] LEON DE SAINT MOULIN S. J., Kinshasa, ma ville... Etat des lieux et perspectives, Magazine LA JAUNE ET LA ROUGE, MAI 2001, https://www.lajauneetlarouge.com/wp-content/uploads/2013/03/565-page-035-038.pdf

Photo GKZ

Given that the city is weakening day by day, nevertheless, the preservation of a system of vegetated spaces, or green spaces, can improve the quality of life of the "Kinshasa" by offering the inhabitants a natural environment for them, leisure activities, and preserving the quality of precious invigorating resources such as air and water, etc. We note that the green space in the city of Kinshasa is sacrificed for the benefit of housing construction of economic interest. Urban vegetation and green spaces also have the potential to offer citizens the possibility of obtaining direct economic benefits through agriculture or urban forestry. Yet none of these commodities happens in the same way. Careful planning and thoughtful thinking are the keys to ensuring that the city of Kinshasa has healthy natural resources for today and tomorrow.

Because urban vegetation, which also includes green spaces, are ultimately for the enjoyment and benefit of citizens. This requires that, urban authorities must involve local communities and the population in the decision-making process of urban planning of the city. This means soliciting the opinion of the public, which is to say of the Kinshasa population on the location and design of green spaces to establish a priority ranking of the desired environment. Today, in Kinshasa we are building everywhere, even on spaces intended for schools, public gardens, playgrounds, etc ... Cooperation also includes the participation of the private sector, as well as community groups, local and national non-governmental (NGOs), and even the International Communities.

Photo GKZ

Ultimately, it is the population of Kinshasa (*Kinois*) who should benefit most directly from a project to revegetate or green the city of Kinshasa. Our study on the urban vegetation of Kinshasa aims to provide the reader with a solid experience of the advantages, challenges and approaches of developing a sustainable urban greening program. This study is intended to be applicable to a wide audience, ranging from government officials and town planners, to local business owners, to members of the relevant urban community, and to staff of organizations such as national and international NGOs. Although, the objective is not exhaustive on any part of the subject studied, the aim is to make the Kinshasa population aware of the challenges of its current and future urban environment. At this time of the problem of global warming, the study on shrub vegetation in residential plots of Kinshasa is important insofar as it reveals the importance of a green space in an urban environment, in this case the city of Kinshasa.

CHAPTER II

THE URBAN ENVIRONMENT OF KINSHASA

— •◉• —

People don't progress in a straight line.
Countries don't progress in a straight line.
OBAMA
April 6, 2010

The urban environment of Kinshasa, does it conform to the definition of a sustainable city. Girardet (1995) gives us the definition of a sustainable city: So what is a sustainable city: "A 'sustainable city' enables all its citizens to meet their own needs and to enhance their well-being without damaging the natural world or endangering the living conditions of other people, now or in the future"[14]. According to this definition, one can ask the question whether Kinshasa, it complies with this condition of a sustainable city[15]? The city of Kinshasa is very badly off. Its inhabitants do not have access to any quality green space, while the World Health Organization (WHO) recommends a ratio of 10 m$_2$ [16] of unfinished open green spaces (unpaved) for each inhabitant in an urban area. Kinshasa has a zero ratio. WHO also suggests designing networks of green spaces so that

---

[14] HERBERT GIRARDET (1999), Creating Sustainable Cities, Green Books, Darlington.
[15] What is a quality green public space? A friendly, safe place where there is a high proportion and a variety of plants, public facilities for walking, picnicking, games or rest, water access devices or even a reduction the grip of the car and an absence of breaks in the cycle-pedestrian paths.
[16] BOTOLISAM POLORIGNI ET AL (2014), Perceptions, tendances et préférences en foresterie urbaine: Cas de la ville de Lomé au togo, European Scientific Journal February 2014 edition vol.10, No.5 ISSN: 1857 – 7881 (Print) e - ISSN 1857- 7431

all residents live within a 15 minutes' walk of an open space. The other proposed objectives are: the development of a biodiversity index used to classify green spaces according to the number and percentage of composition of native species; keeping a permanent record of changes in air and water quality; encourage the use of native species and their management for biodiversity objectives. While urban green spaces are traditionally designed for recreational and aesthetic value, their utility far exceeds these functions. With proper design, both urban vegetation and green spaces can also improve air and water quality, protect biodiversity, reduce the risk of erosion and flooding, provide agricultural production, etc. In Kinshasa, for example, many fruits like papaya, mango, etc… are produced by urban vegetation. However, all of this requires urban green space planning. It also requires intersectional communication with the different sectors of the city. The best chance for urban vegetation and other urban green space to remain a viable source of multiple amenities for urban communities, not only should provision be made for the development and maintenance of urban green space, but also in the participation of citizens in the development of their residential plots. It is essential to reflect today on the characteristics of the Kinshasa city of tomorrow, in order to improve the quality of life of its inhabitants and offer them a healthy, comfortable and sustainable environment. To address this issue, research must be initiated, among other things, on the effects of urban vegetation. What can be the benefits of shrub vegetation, through their physico-chemical and biological properties or their landscape function? Is urban vegetation a relevant area of work to contribute to the development of sustainable cities?

TITLE I: PHYSICAL ENVIRONMENT

1. GEOGRAPHICAL LOCATION

The city of Kinshasa is the capital of the Democratic Republic of the Congo. It is located between latitudes 4° 19' 39' South and between longitudes 15° 18' 48" East. It is a city, but it has the administrative status of a province. The city of Kinshasa is limited:

– to the east by the provinces of Mai-Ndombe, Kwilu and Kwango;
– to the West and North by the Congo River thus forming the natural border with the Republic of Congo;
– in the South by the province of Kongo Central

2. RELIEF

The city of Kinshasa covers an area of 9,965 km² [17] or 0.42% of the national territory, of which 2,500 km² constitute the agglomeration. Its relief is formed by a continental shelf to the east, a chain of steep hills to the south, a plain and swamps on the banks of the Congo River, along the southern shore of the "Pool Malebo" and constitutes a huge crescent covering a low flat surface with an average altitude of about 300m. In general, the relief of the city of Kinshasa can be characterized by four main elements:

---

[17] MARC PAIN (1984), Kinshasa: la ville et la cité, mémoire O.R.S.T.O.M. d'études urbaines, Vol.105, Éditions IRD, 267 p.

Photo GKZ

–   Pool Malebo: vast lake expansion dotted with islands and islets corresponding to the widening of the river bed between Kinshasa and Brazzaville. It stretches over 35 km with a maximum width of 25 km. On the Kinshasa side, it is surrounded by the Commune of Ngaliema to the west, that of Maluku to the east and crosses the municipalities of Gombe, Barumbu, Limete, Masina and Nsele.

–   The Kinshasa plain: the most urbanizable area in the city, not very sensitive to erosion, it is however exposed to a serious problem resulting from poor water drainage. The plain is shaped like a banana surrounded by hills facing west east. This configuration gives the site the shape of an amphitheater. This plain extends over nearly 20,000 hectares with low sandy alluvial masses located between 260 and 225 m above sea level, penetrating to a depth of nearly 10 km on average.

It stretches from Maluku Commune in the east, to the west where the feet of the Ngaliema hills stop its extension. The same plain receives the Congo River as soon as it enters

Pool Malebo in the east and accompanies it to Ngaliema Bay in the west. She lets go of him before he begins to tackle Kinsuka Falls in Ngaliema.

– The terrace: set of low ridges surmounting the plain from 10 m to 25 m. It is the vestige of a surface, which only survives in the western part of the city, between N'djili and Mont-Ngafula, at the foot of the hills of which it constitutes in a way the first step. Like the plain, this terrace is made up of a stony deposit of soft sandstone blocks mixed with sandstone with silica covering a yellow clay and topped with brown silt.

– The hilly area: the hills start a few kilometers from the Malebo pool. If in the East, we can consider some of them as witness mounds of the Batéké Plateau in the West and in the South, in the West as in the South, nothing clearly indicates their origin. They extend over a very great depth and peak at over 700 m. They are rounded with soft shapes, shaped and modeled by the local rivers, which hollow out numerous valley heads in the shape of circuses. In this area, normal phenomena such as sheet runoff or the evolution of circuses by regressive erosion are accentuated by human activity. They then take on a catastrophic appearance[18]. The relief of Kinshasa is made up of a large plateau, a chain of hills, a plain and swamps on the edge of the Congo River. In fact, the Plateau du Kwango massif, at an altitude of 600 to 700 m, completely dominates the eastern part of the city of Kinshasa. Its portion located in the city is called "Plateau des Bateke". It totals an area of approximately 7,500 km2, or 75.3% of the entire extent of the city of Kinshasa. The

---

[18] SHOMBA KINYAMBA S. et all, Monographie de la ville de Kinshasa, ICREDES, Kinshasa, 2015, p.10

population density is very low there. Indeed, this part of the city is occupied by more or less 2% of the total population of the city. The chain of hills, not very steep (350 to 675 m of altitude) where one finds the Ngaliema, Amba and Ngafula mountains, constitutes the common border with the province of Kongo Central and forms the southern part of the city, until to the Southeast, where the Bateke Plateau is located. These hills, including the heights of Binza and Kimwenza, would have resulted from the dismantling of this Plateau. The Kinshasa plain follows the bed of the Congo River and is enclosed between the Congo River, the Bateke Plateau and the hills. It is only an average of 5-7 km wide and shaped like a crescent. This plain is between 300 and 320 m above sea level and has an area of approximately 100 km2. It is divided into two parts: the Lemba plain west of the Ndjili river, slightly wavy; and the Ndjili plain in the east, towards the Nsele River, which has a flatter shape, interspersed by several rivers, which flow almost parallel from the South-East to the North-West, to empty into the Congo River. This is where the largest portion of the population of the city of Kinshasa is concentrated.

3. CLIMATE

The city of Kinshasa has a humid tropical climate according to the Köppen classification. It is located in the area where a rainy season and a dry season alternate. There is an average annual precipitation of 1,200-1,400m, an average annual humidity of 80% and a temperature of 24 °C - 25 °C. The monthly absolute maximum temperatures exceed 35 ° C. The lowest temperatures of the year are observed in the dry season in July in the range of 17.1 ° C - 17.5 ° C. March is the hottest month of the year. Throughout the day, for most of the year, relative humidity is above 70%. Its annual average calculated over 24 hours is 81%: it fluctuates from 76% during the day to 86% at night. The average annual water balance of the soil calculated in relation to precipitation is 1,362 mm. It becomes loss-making in the course of June. Soil moisture reaches its maximum holding capacity (200mm) at the end of October[19]. Located on the shore of a vast river lake that is the Malebo Pool, the local breezes and the proximity to the water determine its mesoclimate. As described, the plain of Kinshasa thus experiences a heavy and hot climate reinforced by the nakedness of the ground due to deforestation and by construction materials (galvanized sheets, etc.) not suited to the climate. On the other hand, in the hills of Binza, Mount Amba, the climate seems a little milder and cooler because of the somewhat high altitude[20]. The City-Province of Kinshasa experiences a tropical climate, hot and humid. This is made up of a large rainy season lasting 8 months, from mid-September to mid-May, and a dry season which runs from mid-May to mid-September, but also, a short rainy season and a short dry season, which runs from mid-December to mid-February. As for the temperature, two large wind currents blow over the city all year round, both at altitude and at low levels.

On the heights, there are two main wind currents: on the one hand, the trade winds, very hot and dry, from the North-East which come from Egypt and on the other hand, a very humid equatorial current, almost permanent in the above 300 m altitude, coming from the east. The lower layers of the city of Kinshasa constantly receive the Benguela current, a very wet current coming from the southwest.

---

[19] LOKAKAO ILEMBA THEODORE et all, Monographie de l'eau de la ville de Kinshasa, Document Inédit, p.2

[20] MARC PAIN, Kinshasa, Ecologie et organisation, Thèse de doctorat, Université de Toulouse, 1979, p.30

The temperature differences are generally established as follows: more than 18 ° C for the daytime temperature of the coldest month of the year on the one hand, and about 22 ° C for the night temperature of the hottest month, on the other hand.

AVERAGE TEMPERATURE OF KINSHASA

	Jan	Feb	Mar	Apr	May	Jun	Jul	Aug	Sep	Oct	Nov	Dec
Max°C	30	31	32	32	31	28	27	28	30	30	30	30
Min °C	23	23	23	23	23	21	20	21	22	23	23	23

Source: World climate guide[21]

4. RAINFALL

From the pluviometry point of view, during the last three decades, the average annual pluviometry observed in the City-Province of Kinshasa is 1,529.9 mm and the monthly minimum is below 50 mm. November has the highest volume of precipitation, averaging 268.1 mm. About 40% of precipitation falls between October, November and December, which are the wettest months of the year. Peak rainfall amounts to 203.3 mm in April and the number of rainy days reaches the annual average for the period of 112 days, with a peak of 17.8 rainy days in April.

AVERAGE RAINFALL OF KINSHASA

	Jan	Feb	Mar	Apr	May	Jun	Jul	Aug	Sep	Oct	Nov	Dec
mm	2	4	3	2	3	0	0	0	7	4	6	9

---

[21] https://www.climatestotravel.com/climate/democratic-republic-congo
https://www.holiday-weather.com/kinshasa/averages/

PRECIPITATION (MM / DAY)

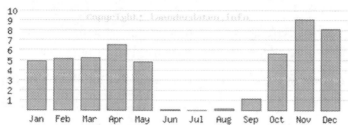

HOURS OF SUNSHINE

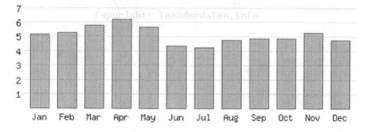

RAINY DAYS PER MONTH

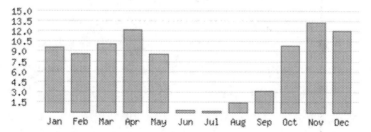

RELATIVE HUMIDITY (%)

Source: Worlddata.info[22]

---

[22] Source: https://www.worlddata.info/africa/congo-kinshasa/climate-kinshasa.php.

5. SOIL

The soil of Kinshasa is of the Arénoferrasol type, made up of fine sands with a clay content generally less than 20%. They are characterized by a low content of organic matter and a low degree of saturation of the absorbent complex[23]. The city of Kinshasa develops on a sandy substrate. On this layer of slightly clayey sand is found everywhere a polymorphic sandstone bank above the red and soft sandstone of the Lubilash system and below it around 275m, the Inkisi red sandstone[24]. As for the basement, Marc Pain (1979) notes that a Precambrian base characterizes it. This comprises finely stratified and often feldspathic red sandstone rocks. It constitutes the upper part of the Schisto-sandstone system and outcrops at the level of the rapids at the foot of Mount Ngaliema and to the south of the Ndjili river. This condensed rock is resistant to erosive action[25]. The characteristics of the soils of the City-Province of Kinshasa depend on the geomorphological structure of the place where one is located. Thus, they are different on the massif of the Plateau des Bateke, on the hills, in the plains or in the swamps. In general, these soils are mainly sandy with some particular elements. They have low water retention capacity and therefore have marginal utility for agricultural activities.

6. VEGETATION

The Kinshasa region is home to different types of vegetation: forest, grassy, ruderal and aquatic. Each type of vegetation is linked to a certain number of ecological parameters. The urban landscape of

---

[23] SYS, C., La cartographie des sols au Congo. Ses principes, ses méthodes, INEAC, Série Sciences. Techniques, N°66, Bruxelles, 1961.
[24] CRABBE M., Le climat de Kinshasa, Bruxelles, 1980.
[25] MARC PAIN, op.cit.

Kinshasa seen from its hills presents a plant cover of anthropogenic origin mainly consisting of fruit trees and a few rare ornamental trees. The original vegetation of Kinshasa, which still survived in rare places such as in the perimeters of the parish and the Canisius Institute of Kimwenza, of the rectorial residence of the University of Kinshasa (UNIKIN) is described as follows: "Dense humid, semi-deciduous-subequatorial and Periguinean forests in galleries or as massifs, isolated in the Guinean savannas". The initial vegetation, in several areas of Kinshasa, was made up of gallery forests on the one hand and grassy formations on the other. The gallery forests along the main watercourses, being in the humid valleys and of the Guinean-Congolese shade-loving type, are no more than pre-forest fallows that are highly degraded, intensively exploited and appear in the form of forest recruits of various ages. In addition, a small typically ruderal plant group runs along the tracks of the railway on a strip a few meters wide[26]. The types of soils in the city of Kinshasa condition the types of vegetation, which grow there and, which generally consist of savannas dotted with shrubs and interspersed with steppes and forest galleries of low density and dimensions. Overall, field observations reveal discontinuity and repetition of vegetation cover.

7. HYDROLOGY

The hydrography of the city of Kinshasa includes the Congo River, rivers that flow into it and small lakes. The Congo River, at the level of the City-Province of Kinshasa, is expanding and in some places reaches more than 20 km in width. This is his last game in the Cuvette Centrale, before the Kinsuka rapids west of Kinshasa.

---

[26] HABARI M. JP., Etude floristique, phytogéographique et phytosociologique de la végétation de Kinshasa et des bassins moyens des rivières Ndjili et Nsele en République Démocratique du Congo, Thèse de doctorat en biologie, Faculté des Sciences, Université de Kinshasa, 2009.

The hydrographic network is made up of rivers of various sizes, which take their sources mainly from the hills, flow from the South to the North, and bathe the plain and flow into the Congo River, especially at the Pool Malebo. Kinshasa is crossed by two types of rivers, on the one hand, local rivers, which are the drains of the hills, which frame the lower parts of the site[27]. These are either local sources of rivers such as Kalamu, Gombe, Makelele and Funa, or allogeneic sources of rivers such as Ndjili, Nsele, Maïndombe and Bombo-Lumene. Some very small lakes are located here and there in the City of Kinshasa including the Lake of Ma Vallée. In addition, the municipality of Nsele has several lakes, which are tourist sites. These are the following lakes: Nainke, Inye, Masia, Ngalu, Boo, Monumburu, Banganza, Muiri, Bambiembie, Banalemie, lac vert, Matshubu and Mantere.

8. GEOLOGY

The Bateke Plateau, which is a two hour drive from the city center to the east, is covered with arenoferalsols, with an AC type profile, a soil structure that is also found on the hills and with podzols, such as in flat areas and in dry ponds. In other words, the surface of this Plateau is made up of silicified rocks or polymorphic sandstone. Towards the hills of the southwest, there is, in places, a mixture of arenoferalsols with other soils with a kaolinitic or ferralitic tendency. Overall, they are recent mineral soils, developed on Kalaharian sand. They are characterized by a clay content of less than 20% over at least 100 cm of depth, a low reserve of weathering minerals and a low water retention capacity.

---

[27] MARC PAIN, op.cit., p.30

TITLE II. HUMAN ENVIRONMENT

1. DEMOGRAPHIC SITUATION

It can be said with certainty that Kinshasa is the largest city in Central Africa and one of the third largest cities in Africa. However, the certainty fades when one has to put forward figures on its population. There are several sources for estimating the current population of Kinshasa: the projections established by the National Institute of Statistics (INS) following the 1984 census and the administrative counts carried out annually within the municipalities and summarized by the 'City Hall. They do not come to the same conclusions, and both have their supporters and detractors. Being two official sources, they should be discussed. In the absence of censuses since 1984, the size of the Congolese population in general and Kinshasa in particular varies according to the sources. On this subject according to Lututala et al, for the year 2003 alone, estimates range from 57 million inhabitants (INED, 2004) to 64.6 million inhabitants (RDC-PEV-LMTE, 2002). As for the population of the city of Kinshasa, it has experienced tremendous growth in the 20th century. From 17,825 inhabitants in 1923, it rose to 400,000 inhabitants when the country gained independence in 1960. After independence, it was estimated at 901,520 inhabitants in 1967 and 1,323,039 inhabitants in 1970 (Houyoux, 1973). In the 1984 scientific census, it was estimated at 2,653,558 inhabitants and later at 4,870,000 inhabitants in 1995 (Ngondo et al, 1991). This population growth is therefore beyond the projections of the EDOZA (République du Zaïre et al., 1978, p. 157) which forecast for the year 2000 a population of 4,410,000 inhabitants (number exceeded in 1984) from a workforce of 1,725,000 inhabitants on January 1, 1976 with a natural growth rate of 39.9 ‰. In 2004, PNLS (2005) estimated the population of Kinshasa at nearly

6 million inhabitants. Like other African countries, the population of the Democratic Republic of Congo is predominantly young. With a population estimated in 2018 at 13.2 million inhabitants, its urban agglomeration, Kinshasa is the third most populous in Africa after Cairo and Lagos[28], and constitutes the largest French-speaking agglomeration in the world, having overtaken that of Paris in the 2010s[29], and is one of the most populous cities in the world. The rapid increase in the population of the city of Kinshasa is a result of the combined effect of high fertility, declining mortality and heavy immigration[30]. The United Nations estimates that Kinshasa, the capital of the Democratic Republic of Congo (DRC) will welcome 4 million new inhabitants in the next 10 years. In 2020, Kinshasa could therefore, with more than 16 million inhabitants, become the most populous city in Africa. For the UN, these figures are a source of concern for the living conditions of the future inhabitants of the Congolese megalopolis. According to this UN Habitat report, the strongest population growth in the decade will be that of Kinshasa, which already accounts for 13% of the country's population. A city that is already struggling to manage the influx of many migrants in 2010. Kinshasa is now home to many "informal neighborhoods", slums, still further from the city center and from minimum services (roads, water, school, etc. electricity, health, etc.). "The urbanization of poverty is a dramatic development on the African continent, because it generates alarming contrasts between the wealth of business districts or residential areas for high-income social strata,

---

[28] ONU, The World's Cities in 2018 https://www.un.org/en/events/citiesday/assets/pdf/the_worlds_cities_in_2018_data_booklet.pdf

[29] According to Pierre Magnan, France info Afrique, June 7, 2017. Kinshasa has more than 12 million inhabitants. With an annual demographic growth of 4.2% on average over the period 2000-2016, the "Kinois" population now exceeds that of the Paris area, estimated at 10.9 million. This ranking has just been confirmed by the United Nations report on cities.

[30] LUTUTALA et all, op.cit.

on the one hand, and the mass of miserable people languishing in vast slums". Totally left behind, the people of Kinshasa thus live 95% of their resourcefulness and the majority below the poverty line, "according to the United Nations.

The influx of new poor and rural populations is unfortunately not expected to improve the daily lives of Kinshasa in the years to come[31].

TITLE III. POLITICAL-ADMINISTRATIVE ENVIRONMENT

Kinshasa has the administrative status of city-province and is one of the 26 provinces of the country. Its inhabitants are called the "Kinois". Kinshasa is subdivided into 4 districts, 24 communes and 365 neighborhoods (quarters), 595,069 plots, 14,389 streets, (Bienvenu Bolia Ikoli, 2014). The administrative subdivision of the city of Kinshasa meets the requirements of Decree-Law n ° 081 of July 22, 1998 on the territorial and administrative organization of the Democratic Republic of Congo, which in its articles 3 and 5, gives the quality of City-Province to Kinshasa and the country's capital status by its article 4. This Decree-Law confers on the municipalities of the City of Kinshasa the status of Decentralized Administrative Entities (DAE), with legal personality. Burgomasters and Deputy Burgomasters administer them. Administratively, Kinshasa is managed by a Provincial Government headed by a Governor assisted by a Vice Governor, both elected by the Provincial Assembly. The 24 burgomasters (mayors) who administer the municipalities assist them. The Provincial Government has 10

---

[31] CHRISTOPHE RIGAUD (2010), RDC: Kinshasa, plus grande ville d'Afrique en 2020, www.afrikarabia.com, https://blog.courrierinternational.com/afrikarabia/2010/12/15/rdc-kinshasa-plus-grande-ville-dafrique-en-2020/

Provincial Ministers appointed by the Governor of the province and leading the following ministries: Plan and Reconstruction, Economy and Finance, Population, Security and Decentralization, Agriculture and Rural Development, Transport, Mines and Energy, Education, Information, Status of Women and Family, Health and Social Affairs, Urban Public Service and Employment, Sports, Culture and the Arts, Tourism and Youth and Land Affairs, Town Planning and Housing. A President seconded by a Vice-President, both elected by their peers, heads the Provincial Assembly. It is made up of 48 provincial deputies elected by universal suffrage and representing the municipalities where they were chosen. The Urban Director manages the Administrative Services, the civil servants and the agents of the City Hall of Kinshasa. These are assigned to Urban Divisions which represent the Ministries of Central Power. It also includes Special Services such as the National Intelligence Agency (ANR), the General Directorate of Migration (DGM), etc ... The Governor and Vice-Governors as well as the Burgomasters and their Deputies currently manage the City of Kinshasa and the municipalities, with the collaboration of the "Security Councils" attached to their levels. These Councils are structures made up of heads of certain urban services, which have public order, justice, peace, the safeguard of territorial integrity and socio-political security in their attributions. In addition to the Governor, the Vice-Governors and the Urban Director, the Burgomasters and their deputies, the main officials who sit on the "Urban or Communal Security Council" are the following: the Commander of the Military Region; the Urban Commander of the Congolese National Police; the heads of ANR and DGM; the First Presidents of the Courts of Appeal; the Attorneys General near the Courts of Appeal. There is the Governor of the City; the latter is assisted by three Vice-Governors, who in the current political configuration are responsible for one of Political, Administrative and Socio-Cultural Questions, the other of Economic and Financial Questions and the third of Reconstruction and Development[32].

A. MUNICIPALITIES AND DISTRICTS OF KINSHASA

The 24 Communes (municipalities) are grouped into 4 districts:

1. Tshangu District

    It is bounded to the North by the Congo River, to the South by the province of Bandundu and that of Kongo Central, to the East by the province of Bandundu, and the commune of Ndjili constitutes its western limit. It is made up of the following municipalities: Ndjili, Masina, Kimbanseke, Nsele and Maluku.

2. Lukunga district

    It is bounded to the North by the Congo River to the South by the Kongo Central province, to the East by the district of Funa and Mount Amba, and to the West by the Kongo Central Province. It includes the following municipalities: Gombe, Ngaliema, Kintambo, Mont Ngafula and Selembao.

3. Funa District

    The district of Funa is bounded to the North by the Congo River, to the South by the district of Lukunga, to the East by the district of Mount Amba, and to the West by the district of Lukunga. It includes 7 municipalities below: Bumbu,

---

[32] https://www.congovirtuel.com/page_province_kinshasa.php

Ngiri-Ngiri, Kasa-Vubu, Makala, Lingwala, Kalamu and Bandalungwa.

4. Mount Amba District

The districts of Funa and Lukunga constitute its northern and southern limit respectively. While to the East and West we have the Ndjili river and the Funa district respectively. It includes the municipalities of Lemba, Matete, Ngaba, Limete and Kisenso.

TITLE IV. SOCIO-ECONOMIC ENVIRONMENT

Kinshasa's preponderance over the country as a whole is particularly evident in the sector of non-agricultural processing industries, services and trade. The origin of this importance lies in its role as a transshipment port for industrial products intended for hinterland consumers and agricultural products for Kinshasa. Kinshasa is the first consumer center of the Democratic Republic of the Congo and the heart of its industrial, commercial and financial activities. The main industries of Kinshasa concern the food industry and the production of consumer goods, generally intended for the national market. Buildings and services also play a major economic role there. However, the political turmoil that has rocked the country since the fall of President Mobutu's regime in 1997 has weakened the city's economic fabric. The eighteen-year reign of President Kabila, who succeeded the Mobutu regime, is characterized above all by impunity, which is the basis of significant tax evasion. The consequences of this impunity have further worsened the socioeconomic situation of the country, as it deprived the country of a substantial investment budget.

1. Social conditions of the population

    Moreover, the living conditions of the "Kinois" (Kinshasa resident) are an expression of the poverty experienced by the country. The history of the economic situation of the DRC and the city of Kinshasa, from the colonial period until the end of the 1960s, is well described by Houyoux (1973)[33]. After ten years of economic prosperity (late 1960s to early 1980s), the DRC is today one of the poorest countries in the world. It is among the last ten countries in terms of the human development index (HDI) in 2002. It occupies the 168th place out of 177 countries with an HDI evaluated at 0.365, a slight regression compared to its situation for the year 2001 where it occupied 167th place out of 175 countries with an HDI of 0.363 (UNDP, 2003; 2004). According to the Human Development Report (DRC, Ministry of Planning, 1999), the national income per capita rose from US $ 250 in 1981 to US $ 110 in 1999, roughly one fifth of the African average. According to the Central Bank of Congo (2002), in 2001, GDP/h was estimated at nearly US $ 74. The level of per capita income per day rose from US $ 1.31 in 1973 to US $ 0.91 in 1974, to US $ 0.30 in 1998. This poverty is notably attributed to the "Zairianization" policy of at the beginning of the 1970s, the failure of the stabilization and structural adjustment programs of the 1980s, the two looting in the 1990s as well as the two wars of 1996 and 1998 (DRC-Ministry of Plan, 2002)[34]. To these causes must be added corruption, fraud, embezzlement of state public

---

[33] LUTUTALA et al, op.cit.
[34] LUTUTALA et al, ibid.

funds[35]. These causes explain the State's resignation from its social obligations, thus generating unemployment, the rise of the informal sector, the unpaid and underpayment of a few people, who may still have jobs, dropping out of school, etc. Households in Kinshasa are not immune to the poverty experienced by the DRC. In this city, "... the population is struggling to order chaos, to secure insecurity, to protect themselves from uncertainty. It develops different kinds of mechanisms to respond to the crisis: prayer, resourcefulness, laughter, fatalism, bluffing, discretion..." (Maréschal, 2004, 13). Already in 1993, 95% of "Kinshasa"/kinois households lived below the poverty line, a threshold set at US $ 1 per person of daily expenditure (Mususa and Ntangoma, 1994), whereas it normally took US $ 20 for consumption daily for a household of 8 people. Under these conditions, we are far from being able to establish adequate supervision of children.

To survive, households set up several strategies, in particular hospitality, which further inflates the size of households, selective schooling, entrusting or looking after children to other family members, informal and early child labor., nuptiality,..[36].

TITLE V. SOCIO-CULTURAL ENVIRONMENT

Kinshasa's socio-cultural environment is characterized by various important social phenomena[37]. It is mainly about the influence of

---

[35] According to the report of the Special Advisor on corruption to the Head of State Joseph Kabila, Mr. LUZOLO BAMBI, the flow of State revenue is estimated annually at more than 15 billion US dollars, while the budget of the State hardly reaches 5 billion US dollars.
[36] LUTUTALA et al, op.cit.
[37] For this part, we refer to LUTUTALA et al,

music and religion in the life of "Kinois". Kinshasa is not only a city of rapid population growth, but also a place of profound cultural transformation. There is a truly human dynamism. Cultural life in Kinshasa is also marked by ethnic and religious affiliations. Music, theater groups (sketches), churches, the media (mainly radio and television), etc often convey the values resulting from these networks. Currently, it is mainly through music, theaters and religion that the vast majority of the population of this city tries to solve the problems relating to the socio-economic crisis (Raquin, 2004).

- Music is undoubtedly one of the great Congolese cultural riches. One cannot imagine, in Kinshasa, a funeral, a celebration of marriage, communion, graduation, major religious or political events, which are not embellished by music ... (Shomba, 2004, pp. 35-36). In the absence of jobs in the formal sector, "Kinois" have embarked on the informal sector where they demonstrate great ingenuity and creative imagination. Since the beginning of the 90s, several "Kinois" have converted into musicians, actors of theaters (actors in particular), and servants of God (evangelists, pastors, prophets, apostles ...) in the so-called Revival churches ...

  For lack of jobs, music, theatre and Revival churches are for the time being the areas where unemployed young people, including minors, take refuge. The musical groups use these young people as dancers, singers,...[38] This is a real economic and even sexual exploitation. Once engaged in these activities, many young people still in school drop out of school. As is the case with music, young "Kinois" are also

---

[38] www.congo2000.net/musiquecongo.html (2005)

very engaged in theatrical troupes where they are seriously exploited[39].

– With regard to Revival churches, according to their functioning, several Revival churches are real small and medium-sized enterprises or, in the words of Shomba (2004), "shops for many of their promoters" (Shomba, 2004, p.62). They have several activities (voluntary and/or remunerative), which employ unemployed young people to the point that their structures have often replaced a deficient state infrastructure[40]. They employ young people of all backgrounds and levels of Education, who perform various functions, sometimes unrelated to their level of education or basic training. Within the churches, young people include Deacons, evangelists, musicians, choristers, hospitality workers, spiritual intercessors. For churches that have other socio-economic activities: radio and/or television channels, schools, health centers ... young people occupy administrative and technical responsibilities[41]. Despite numerous moral or financial scandals in his Revival churches, their number continues to increase. In addition, faced with the concerns of the faithful to the many problems of daily survival, the pastors 'response to the faithful is the same: "NZAMBE AKOSALA", (that is, "God will act"). The Revival churches, which have become completely autonomous from the "mother" churches, these organizations bear several denominations. Some are "ministries", others are "assemblies", "tabernacles", "missions" or outright "churches". Revival churches in terms of their mode of operation, whatever their form, these neo-Protestant churches commonly known as "Revival churches"

---

[39] www.congo2000.net/musiquecongo.htm, op.cit.

[40] KAYEMBE, Institut Panos Paris et DFID, 2004, p. 80; L'Express du 23/03/200519

[41] https://dial.uclouvain.be/pr/boreal/en/object/boreal:4845/datastream/PDF_09/view

and whose main philosophy is the prosperity of followers, operate almost the same way. They are founded on the initiative of a spiritually "enlightened" person who would have a strong divine anointing; Prophet, Apostle, Bishop, elder, or in English bishop, archbishop... Some are educated (students, higher education teachers, civil servants, managers belonging to the generation of "disappointed" after independence) while others are illiterate and charlatans (Devey, 2004). They say they have a force that would allow them to operate and distribute miracles: healing from sometimes-incurable diseases such as AIDS, marriages to desperate singles, maternity to infertile women, work to the unemployed, facilitating travel abroad... (Kanyonga, 2003; L'express, 2005).

The faithful or followers are from all sides proselytes of Christianity and former Christians of Catholic churches or Protestant obedience (Evangelical or Pentecostal) and the reasons that justify their adherence are diverse.

Although the main reason mentioned is the new birth and the assurance of eternal life after death, it appears from Devey (2004) that these faithful are looking for solutions to material problems: money, health, work, love, children, travel, etc..., these solutions involve the search for new ways of being and living. Because of leadership or for reasons, which are often described as spiritual, that is, doctrinal, these churches divide regularly, which explains their very large number: 2,687 in 2003 (DRC, Ministry of Social Affairs, 2003). This number is actually underestimated, as this Ministry does not list many of them[42].

---

[42] LUTUTALA et al, op.cit.

VI. SOCIO-ECOLOGICAL ENVIRONMENT

The city faces significant ecological and environmental problems.

1. In the first place, the problem of energy. Indeed, despite the strong hydroelectric potential of the Inga I and II dams, the electricity grid is aging, poorly calibrated and not very extensive. Illegal hookups and daily incidents, both natural and human, cause repeated outages. The lack of energy available everywhere and cheap explains the use of other energy sources. Marc Pain (1984) shows that about 45 % of the population cooks with oil-based fuels, the vast majority of the rest with wood or charcoal from deforestation. Solutions are sought to manage fast-growing plantations (eucalyptus, Pines). In 2010, the consumption of charcoal is estimated at 500,000 tons and a large project, called "Makala ", is launched to better manage the wood-energy sector[43].

2. The second is water management. Households have direct access to drinking water of the order of 64%; 25% are supplied from neighbor's taps and 11% from wells or springs. The water loss rate in the distribution network is 20%. Drinking water is provided by the public company Regideso. However, the water treatment and delivery infrastructure is also outdated and limited, so unable to meet the growing demands of the city. Suspicion of water quality is the reason why a market for bottled water grows and filtration systems are installed in wealthy individuals. Without running water, entire neighborhoods use System D. Work is under way to solve the problem. There is no sewage treatment plant. Wastewater is

---

[43] https://fr.wikipedia.org/wiki/kinshasa

therefore discharged directly into rivers and the Congo River, implying latent pollution. The whole sewer only concerns the city center and some neighborhoods. The same applies to the discharge of runoff. Despite this, the current system is poorly maintained so almost useless. As a result, floods and sometimes epidemics regularly affect Kinshasa. The REGIDESO drinking water distribution network does not cover the entire city of Kinshasa. It is located in the business center, Municipality of Gombe, the ancient cities of Barumbu, Kinshasa as well as the Northern Districts of Bandalungwa and Kintambo, the planned cities of Kasa-Vubu, Kalamu, Matonge, Matete, Lemba, n'djili, Ngaliema, Ngiri-Ngiri, parts of Limete, Mama Mobutu City and Green City. The informal extension communes of Masina, Kisenso, Selembao, Bumbu, Makala, Kimbanseke, part of Mount Ngafula.

With a population of nearly 16 million in 2020, the stakes are indeed major for the city of Kinshasa. The drinking water supply rate is only 64% with a level of Service, which is not continuous in most of the 24 municipalities, and which is often disrupted especially during heavy rains and fluctuations in electricity supply; In addition, some confusion exists regarding the roles and responsibilities of different actors, with unsustainable cost management and renewal models. Water security in Kinshasa's urban areas is indeed a major challenge and most current urban water planning and management models have shown their limitations in terms of both financial profitability and technical performance as well as social equity and environmental sustainability. A change of approach, which must go beyond a single improvement in performance indicators, is needed to propose an alternative way of designing and thinking about urban water management. It is thus proposed to adopt a new approach: Integrated Urban Water Management (IWRM). This approach is not a prescriptive model, but a development process that invites cities to adjust certain planning and management practices in force, taking into account their own hydrological and environmental reality and the local socio-economic context. The above-mentioned project will also identify approaches and actions contributing to adaptation and resilience to climate change as well as to the mitigation of environmental impacts in order to ensure the integrated management of the city's urban waters on the one hand; and to ensure the drinking water supply of West Kinshasa according to an integrated approach. In summary, the province of Kinshasa suffers from significant delays in the energy, water and sanitation sector.

This situation is mainly the result of insufficient infrastructure, which is itself the result of limited investment in the sector in view of the evolution of the population whose number has increased by 7 times in forty years.

The City-province of Kinshasa will therefore have to make significant efforts in these areas, beginning in particular with the development of a blueprint for the development of the province.

3. The third is waste management. There is a waste treatment service but remains insignificant. Sorting does not exist. Fortunately, economic recycling takes place in the population. Thus, metals are reused, or resold by weight, and plastic containers are reused. Inert materials, such as cement, brick and earthenware, are pounded and resold as gravel. Wood is used as fuel. However, as the city produces a very large

amount of waste, there are still many untapped detritus, soft plastic in the lead. The common technique is to group them in piles and then burn them, or even bury them. As a result, invisible pollution of soil, air and water by soot, toxic gases and heavy metals is not to be ruled out.

Photo Gutu Kia Zimi

CHAPTER III

THE URBAN RESIDENTIAL SPACE OF KINSHASA

———————•❋•———————

We did not come to fear the future. We came here to shape it (2009)
I don't get too high, don't get too low
OBAMA (March 21, 2015

TITLE I: BIRTH OF ANTHROPOGENIC VEGETATION

As Francis Lelo Nzuzi (2017) points out, Kinshasa spreads indefinitely in all directions, but without adequate infrastructure. Its downtown is modernizing while its outskirts slum. The new neighborhoods under construction of the last decade in the capital have nothing to do with social housing. Abandoned, some "Kinois" manage alone to stay in spontaneous neighborhoods and outlying slums[44]. The Urban arboriculture of Kinshasa is also linked to the procedure of acquiring a plot depending on whether it is in an old district or in a new subdivision of a peripheral district in peri-urban area. By studying urban vegetation in residential plots of Kinshasa, our main goal is to count the tree species in the different plots.

---

[44] Francis LELO NZUZI, Les bidonvilles de Kinshasa, L'Harmattan, 2017, p.27

Photo GKZ

However, it would be incomplete to limit ourselves to this one aspect if we do not associate an analysis on this spatial environment where the tree is planted, and where it lives in association with man, in this ecosystem that we call the plot. The services rendered by trees in the city are numerous. They are all the more important in the city as the urban population increases.

However, some adverse effects, such as allergies, should be monitored and reduced. During this period of global warming and its consequences on climate change, several major metropolises have launched ambitious programmes of "reforestation or revegetalization" of cities. It is important to note that the space reserved for trees in the plots is strongly linked to the conditions of development of the plot, and this taking into account factors such as: density, its stand and especially physical and ecological conditions of the environment such as the appearance of the land, for example, flat land (case of Bandalungua, Gombe), Sandy (case of Ndjili, Nsele), rugged (my countryside, Ngaliema), marshy (case of Mombele), mountainous (case of Mont-ngafula, etc. We know that the organization of housing responds to a number of factors or parameters, such as population density, demographic pressure, commercial or economic activities..., which are variable in time and space. These factors largely influence urban arboriculture. Thus, the comparison of an old commune (Gombe, Matonge, Kinshasa, Barumbu, Lingwala, Kintambo...) and a new one (Ngaliema, Ndjili, Nsele, Mount Ngafula...) does not offer the same vegetation cover.

Photo GKZ

Very often, the individual who acquires or buys a plot in an old neighborhood, he proceeds according to his income to different modifications of the elements, which make up the plot. This modification or development of the plot will be dictated by the means of the new purchaser but also by the destination of the new use of the plot (trade, housing, etc.). It is increasingly observed in Kinshasa that the new buyer decides to destroy the old buildings in order to erect new, more modern and appropriate buildings. Currently, under demographic pressure, we observe more and more in the different neighborhoods and municipalities of Kinshasa, fully built plots leaving no space to plant a tree. It often happens that the new buyer proceeds to expand the old existing construction according to his taste and style.

This internal development may result in the removal of existing trees if they occupy the space reserved for the new construction. In the future, the owner will be able to plant other trees if he deems it necessary. It happens that the plot is completely destroyed in order to erect a new construction on it, which will not leave space for trees. Depending on time and space, this process is currently transforming the urban landscape of the different districts of the municipalities of the city of Kinshasa by destroying the vegetation cover in favor of new constructions and other developments. This is currently the case, in the different districts and communes of Kinshasa where we see new constructions being erected in floor often in single block or single building, which occupy the entire space of the plot. This new process of land development by the aforementioned constructions is changing the physiognomy of the city of Kinshasa but also destroying the vegetation cover of the city. Another process is that seen in the new housing estates of the outlying districts of the peri-urban communes of Maluku, Nsele, Mount Ngafula, Ndjili, Ngaliema,... and also in the districts of extension in peri-urban areas such as Mitendi, Mpasa, Mbudi, Lutendele, Kinsuka, Kimbondo, etc.spaces of virgin land are distributed and sold in parcels to new owners or buyers, who initially will work to clear the land. This clearing consists in stripping the land by clearing it of any original shrubby and grassy vegetation. This led to the near-total destruction of the original vegetation of the city of Kinshasa. The new plot is therefore ready to accommodate the new construction, which will be erected there. This pioneering work is littered with several obstacles and requires a lot of sacrifice and above all patience. Sometimes palabras arise for a conflict of land boundary or plot ownership. Very often it happens that the plot was sold to several people. Often, this is the beginning of a long conflict, which degenerates into a judicial confrontation and whose lucky winner can only be known after a harassing and expensive trial in court, similar to a real war of attrition. The photo below gives us an illustration of the birth of a neighborhood[45].

SOURCE: LEON DE SAINT MOULIN

At first, it is observed that the vegetation is completely destroyed, and then gradually the vegetation arises with the gradual occupation of the population. This situation of parcel conflict, which feeds the courts and tribunals, is a drama and even a fraud, which is often wanted and maintained by the agents of the administration of the cadaster and land titles service in charge of the new subdivisions. How to explain that several individuals find themselves in possession with the same official documents of the cadastral service granting them title to a single plot. The disorder of land titles is fuelling the market for issuing false land title documents to the great benefit of

---

[45] LEON DE SAINT MOULIN, (2016), Kinshasa, ma ville... Etat des lieux et perspectives. Dossier: L'Afrique centrale, La jaune et la rouge, Magazine N°565, Mai 2001, https://www. lajauneetlarouge.com/kinshasa-ma-ville-etat-des-lieux-et-perspectives/

civil servants, magistrates and lawyers in the country's courts and Tribunals. Nevertheless, the individual who has acquired the plot will bring the appropriate care including weeding, looscning before erecting the new construction, first timidly for those of the owners, who have modest financial means, or very quickly for those, who have significant financial means. At this stage, the development of the plot is organized little by little. Very often, to realize the ownership of the premises or the plot, we plant voluntarily or fortuitously a few trees without a spccific order. Most often, it is fruit trees, which are quickly planted and, which will grow after a few years. Some of these trees will survive; others will be cut to meet the need for the new development of the plot.

This often involves the construction of an annex for rent, or for a new house construction, a chicken coop, a septic tank, a kitchen or a shed, etc. This shows that the layout of the plot is not a static but dynamic process. So after a few years, with the development of the plots, the neighborhood takes shape. The names of the streets and avenues are fixed there, the various activities also spring up and are organized in the neighborhood. These are mainly commercial activities (shops or *"ligablo"*), the establishment of churches, schools, dispensaries, markets or *"wenze"*, etc. In the meantime, the trees that have been planted there are flowering and already bearing fruit. Over the years, the sparse vegetation at the beginning gradually becomes dense with the evolution of the neighborhood[46].

---

[46] This processus is illustrated by Marc Pain, Kinshasa, Ecologie et Organisation urbaine, Thèse de doctorat, Université de Toulouse-Mirail, 1979, p.350

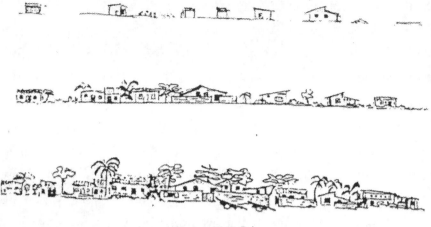

Source: Marc Pain

Thus arises an urban vegetation of anthropogenic origin from an ecoenvironmental cell that we call: the plot. Gradually, the neighborhood is taking shape and becoming more individual. The small huts or construction sheds built upon the acquisition of the plot are abandoned in favor of permanent and sustainable constructions. Either these new buildings made from sustainable materials will be rented out to a new tenant looking for a house to rent or they will allow new owners to settle there. These new occupants, owners of the new plots in the neighborhood, are often former tenants, tired of the humiliations and other harassments of the former owners of the plots. These new buyers discover the great pleasure of owning their own plot. In the meantime, the trees in the plots continue to grow, while the species of trees planted are diversifying and enriching. In the meantime, the neighborhood's vegetation becomes more and more dense and vigorous. This process affirms the anthropogenic origin of vegetation. While, the dense or scattered vegetation cover confirms the appearance of the district and its environment.

SECTION I: THE NEIGHBORHOOD: ITS BIRTH, EVOLUTION AND ORGANIZATION

Compared to the plot that we consider an environmental unit, the district constitutes an important macro-environmental unit by its plant cover, by its density of population and habitat, by its various infrastructures, by the establishment of socio-economic organizations. (markets or *"wenze"*, shop or *"ligablo"*[47], schools, dispensaries, churches, bars and dance clubs) and especially by the development of various informal activities. At the birth of the district, it developed around certain strategic points (bars, market or *"wenze"*,), various and other innumerable activities ranging from the small itinerant seller passing to the small "ligablo" shop in front of the plot until to structured socio-economic organizations. It is important to point out the determining role of the water supply and the supply of electricity in accelerating the process of birth and development of the neighborhood. These two infrastructures (Water and Electricity) allow the populations to settle quickly in the neighborhood.

Photo GKZ

---

[47] « Ligablo » is a small shop usually in front of the plot. *"Wenze"* is a small public market usually in different quarters.

One finds almost throughout the city of Kinshasa a series of elements of homogeneity and habits, which integrate the district into a larger and more complex inhabited area. It is obvious that a neighborhood with socio-economic infrastructure will experience faster development. With the housing crisis in the city of Kinshasa, the birth of the district and its development took place in a very short time. Every month and every year, the neighborhood changes its face. In Kinshasa, despite a very difficult socio-economic situation, constructions are growing like mushrooms. The first inhabitants in the new districts sometimes settle there in difficult conditions often without water and electricity, supplying themselves with water from wells. It will take years to be connected to water and electricity. Despite this pioneering life, often informal activities (small businesses) are organized without delay, first in the street or in front of the plot, then on a small lot, or part of a large avenue.

I. CHARACTERISTICS OF THE KINSHASA DISTRICTS

The city of Kinshasa has 24 administrative municipalities, themselves subdivided into 365 neighborhoods. From the point of view of location, we could distinguish two types of neighborhoods: old neighborhoods and new neighborhoods. Old quarters are often characterized by high floor space coefficients. They are made up of heterogeneous buildings or constructions where old houses remain. There are fewer houses under construction on the plots for lack of free space. On the other hand, new constructions, which are erected there, are the consequences of demolition plots taken back or bought back by new owners or buyers. This phenomenon is on the rise in the various districts of the city, especially in the old districts of the municipalities of Kinshasa, Barumbu, Gombe, Lingwala, and their extensions as Quarter GB, Nganda, Ma Campagne, etc ... where new constructions especially in height grow like mushrooms. While the new neighborhoods in the municipalities of the urban periphery such as Mont-Ngafula, Nsele, Masina, Kimbanseke, etc.), are remarkable for the number of new houses under construction and waiting huts or construction huts. There are small solid constructions with low floor space coefficients. This is because housing construction is left to individual initiative. Everyone is doing within his or her means and income. With this policy of self-construction, it is difficult to have Congolese cities with beautiful urbanized neighborhoods according to architectural, aesthetic and environmental standards like European or Western cities.

Photo Gutu Kia Zimi

Today, we distinguish:

–   The extended districts of Masina, Bumbu, Kisenso, Kimbanseke, Selembao, Makala, Ndijli and other Ngaba, contain a large and very precarious population. Overall, the physiognomy of Kinshasa's housing can be analyzed through its different neighborhoods. In addition to these extended neighborhoods, we also distinguish:

—   Residential neighborhoods: They are located in the municipalities of Lemba (Righini), Gombe, Limete and Ngaliema (Mbinza / Ma-Campagne and Mbinza / IPN).

These high-class neighborhoods benefit from an urbanization plan and are endowed with real infrastructure (asphalt roads, drainage of runoff, etc.). The population density is low and the informal economy is little but increasingly visible. Well-off, most residents get around using their vehicles. This is where you will find the beautiful villas, swimming pools, golf and tennis courts, numerous chic bars, hotels and restaurants.

—   The districts of the old cities: They are located in the communes of Kinshasa, Lingwala, Barumbu and Kintambo. Most of the old dwellings there have been turned into slums. The roads are degraded, the water pipes completely blocked and the pedestrian pavements still waiting to be improved. Sanitation is therefore a serious problem. Very dense and of middle class, the population develops many informal activities in these areas. With the extension of the Gombe business center, the plots of these neighborhoods are being bought out by mainly foreign traders (Lebanese, Indo-Pakistani, etc.), who set up shops and hotels there. This is the case of the "Kato market" in the town of Kinshasa on the outskirts of the large Kinshasa market.

Photo GKZ

—   The districts of the planned cities: They are found in the communes of Lemba, Matete, Ndijli (districts 1-7), Kalamu and Bandalungwa. They have infrastructure and amenities, but are dilapidated and unsuitable. The homes, originally designed for a couple with 2 children, now house an average of 7 or more, in plots that do not exceed 300 m2. Also of average level, the very many inhabitants are struggling with a non-existent or out of use greywater system.

—   Semi-rural districts: Located in the territory of the municipalities of Maluku, Nsele, Mont-Ngafula. Sparsely inhabited, these municipalities constitute the agricultural and industrial suburb (iron and steel industry of Maluku) of Kinshasa. As dormitories (Mpasa), they also host recreational activities (Kinkole, Nsele) and market gardening (Mont-Ngafula).

In addition, according to the Atlas of Kinshasa (1975), we distinguish the classification of neighborhoods below:

- Residential neighborhoods are those, which have hard-built roads (butimated) and spacious plots often greater than 1000 m_2. Wastewater and runoff water are evacuated through a generally functional piping system. Informal activities are low in the streets. Car and pedestrian accessibility is good and equipped. The infrastructures are present; they are in good condition, but underused. Private vehicles because of the low demand for public transport do most of the travel. In these neighborhoods, the density is low, at 20 inhabitants per hectare.

- The quarters of the old cities are very old quarters where the dwellings are generally dilapidated and slackened. The streets are partly blocked, the water pipes are blocked. The population density is very high (about 400 inhab. / Ha). Informal jobs are present. Walking, as a mode of transportation, is very important. The infrastructure is insufficient and degraded. The pedestrian roads are not developed. These neighborhoods suffer from serious sanitation problems. The plots are overcrowded; they contain an average of ten households.

- The districts of planned cities are cadastral, planned and provided with urban amenities. However, the pipes are old and undersized; those of gray water are almost non-existent. The population density is high, ie 350 inhabitants per hectare. Informal jobs are very important. Pedestrian mobility is very important. The plots do not exceed 300 m_2. The infrastructures are saturated and degraded.

- The eccentric and extended neighborhoods are essentially self-built. They are isolated, not registered and mostly inhabited by low-income social strata. Some of these districts are created on non-aedificandi sites: floodplains and erodible hills. Accessibility is haphazard and impractical in some places. Pedestrian mobility is important. Public infrastructure is almost non-existent. Public transport is unpredictable and pedestrian accessibility is difficult and undeveloped.

Photo GKZ

– Semi-rural areas are sparsely occupied. Informal jobs are low and depend on the age of the neighbourhood. These districts alone occupy more than 50% of the area of the city. They are almost empty and are more than 60 km from the city center. They perform both the functions of agricultural, industrial, vegetable and Recreation suburbs.

II. DENSITY OF HABITAT AND
POPULATION OF DISTRICTS

The density of the population is obtained by the ratio between the population and the area of the communes or districts. The INS study was able to determine the area of the various communes of Kinshasa and calculate the population density based on data from the last scientific census of 1984. In addition, Eleonore Wolff and all (2002), in another study, were able to determine with more accuracy the exact area of the different municipalities of Kinshasa, thanks to the SPOT satellite image. The identification of the built-up space by the satellite image made it possible, on the one hand, to determine the municipal boundaries in a geographic information system, and on the other hand, the built-up areas by municipalities according to the classification carried out by Flouriot. Then, the population densities were calculated relative to the built-up space. Finally, this calculation shows that the extension of the city of Kinshasa coexists with a phenomenon of densification and that this one absorbs nearly two thirds of the increase in the population between 1969 and 1995. According to these authors[48], it turns out that the density of all the municipalities of Kinshasa increases, but it reached values greater than 20,000 inhab./km² in 1995 for the small municipalities already largely built in 1969, that is to say the cities and south-western extensions of the typology of Flouriot. According to this typology, Flouriot categorized the municipalities of Kinshasa into six groups[49]:

- Ancient cities;
- New cities;
- Planned cities;
- Residential High standing;
- South-West extensions;
- East extensions

[48] ELEONORE WOLFF et VIRGINIE DELBART, Extension urbaine et densité de la population à Kinshasa. Contribution de la télédétection satellitaire, Belgeo, Revue Belge de Géographie, 2002, p. 45.
[49] FLOURIOT J., Atlas de Kinshasa, BEAU, Kinshasa, 1975

– The large peripheral rural municipalities and the municipalities with high residential standing (Gombe, Ngaliema, Limete) maintain much lower densities (less than 20,000 inhab./km²) even if their growth is strong. In the new suburbs of Kinshasa, constructions under construction and waiting represent more than half of the cases, and one in two plots is unoccupied or inhabited by a site guard.

– On the other hand, in the intermediate neighborhoods of communes such as Ngiri-Ngiri, Bumbu, Kalamu, Bandalungwa, Kasa-Vubu… so-called "new cities" and their extensions of cinderblock (cement) and stone block constructions are imposed. The size of the houses is relatively larger, small villas are erected everywhere, but their number decreases as one approaches the neighborhoods of the communes of the peri-urban area[50].

According to our study, the table below indicates that the population density in the various municipalities of Kinshasa is 1,076 inhabitants per km². However, the commune of Bumbu has the highest density, ie 96,289 inhabitants / km². The municipalities of Maluku and Nsele have the lowest density, respectively 65 inhabitants / km² (Maluku), and 409 inhabitants / km² (Nsele). Overall, the population density remains high in the intermediate communes of Ngaba (63,833 inhabitants / km²), Matete (84,268 inhabitants / km²), Makala (53,802 inhabitants / km²); but also in the old towns of Kintambo (62,160 inhabitants / km²) and Kinshasa (61,530 inhabitants / km²).

---

50 ELEONORE WOLFF et VIRGINIE DELBART, op.cit., p. 45

This upward trend is a corollary to the growth of the Kinshasa population and to demographic pressure, which is exerted in the so-called old and intermediate municipalities.

N°	Communes	SUP/Km2	%	Population*	%	Density	Plots	%	Quarters	%	Streets	%
1	BANDALUNGWA	6,82	0,07	316 002	2,9	46 335	8,404	1,4	8	2,2	233	1,6
2	BARUMBU	4,72	0,05	158 203	1,5	33 518	4,759	0,8	9	2,5	112	0,8
3	BUMBU	5,30	0,05	510 331	4,8	96 289	11,286	1,9	13	3,6	274	1,9
4	GOMBE	29,33	0,29	46 733	0,4	1593	2,994	0,5	10	2,7	200	1,4
5	KALAMU	6,64	0,07	357 847	3,3	53 892	11,801	2	18	4,9	409	2,8
6	KASA-VUBU	5,05	0,05	163 594	1,5	32 395	4,468	0,8	7	1,9	115	0,8
7	KIMBANSEKE	237,78	2,39	1 460 402	13,6	6 141	93,531	15,7	46	12,6	1,666	11,6
8	KINSHASA	2,87	0,03	176 591	1,6	61530	4,255	0,7	7	1,9	80	0,6
9	KINTAMBO	2,72	0,03	169 074	1,6	62 160	5,055	0,8	8	2,2	154	1,1
10	KISENSO	16,6	0,17	602 024	5,6	36 267	20,815	3,5	17	4,7	610	4,2
11	LEMBA	23,7	0,24	519 361	4,8	21914	18,628	3,1	15	4,1	440	3,1
12	LIMETE	67,6	0,68	502 549	4,7	7434	20,329	3,4	14	3,8	564	3,9
13	LINGWALA	2,88	0,03	122 049	1,1	42378	3,585	0,6	9	2,5	69	0,5
14	MAKALA	5,6	0,06	301 293	2,8	53802	12,947	2,2	18	4,9	242	1,7
15	MALUKU	7948,8	79,77	517 184	4,8	65	17,888	3	19	5,2	1,281	8,9
16	MASINA	69,93	0,7	1 051 048	9,8	15030	35,922	6	21	5,8	636	4,4
17	MATETE	4,88	0,05	411 229	3,8	84268	10,774	1,8	13	3,6	263	1,8
18	MONT NGAFULA	358,92	3,6	379831	3,5	1058	70,682	11,9	20	5,5	1784	12,4
19	NDJILI	11,4	0,11	538 497	5	47237	17,127	2,9	13	3,6	304	2,1
20	NGABA	4,00	0,04	255 331	2,4	63833	5,674	1	6	1,6	114	0,8
21	NGALIEMA	224,3	2,26	1 070 669	10	4773	97,698	16,4	21	5,8	2,211	15,4
22	NSIRI NSIRI	3,4	0,03	198 814	1,9	58475	5,499	0,9	8	2,2	105	0,7
23	NSELE	898,79	9,02	367 654	3,4	409	84,266	14,2	27	7,4	1987	13,8
24	SELEMBAO	23,18	0,23	530 414	4,9	22882	26,682	4,5	18	4,9	536	3,7
	TOTAL	9965,21	100	10 726 725	100	1076	595,069	100	365	100	14,389	100

SYNTHETIC TABLE OF THE POPULATION OF THE MUNICIPALITIES OF KINSHASA

Data based on 2012 population projection
SOURCE : LEON DE SAINT-MOULIN

Table n*1; Source: Gutu Kia Zimi (2020)

The table above gives us the indications of the population for the different districts of the municipalities of Kinshasa. As there has not been a rigorous demographic survey since 1984 at the level of the city of Kinshasa, the data on the population of Kinshasa are those of the projection of the 2012 population of Léon de Saint-Moulin. Although the data from the Housing department, available to the municipalities while being precious, because they are established by neighborhood, they nevertheless ignore a large part of the population. These are administrative statistics compiled by the Population and Housing

Service of the various municipalities of the city of Kinshasa. This is not census data. The last scientific population census dates from 1984, which is why their interpretation gives rise to some criticism when compared to the various demographic projections (Bienvenu Bolia Ikoli, 2014).

Nevertheless, on the basis of this table above:

- The municipalities of Kimbanseke with 1,460,402 inhabitants (13.6%), of Ngaliema with 1,070,669 (10%) and of Masima with 1,051,048 inhabitants (9.8%) are the most populous municipalities of the city of Kinshasa. While the commune of Gombe, seat of the institutions of the republic, and home to the majority of commercial and economic activities with 46,733 inhabitants (0.4%) is the least populated of the city of Kinshasa. Yet every day the commune of Gombe welcomes a very important flow of the population.
- The commune of Bumbu has the highest density (55,391 inhabitants / km²), while the lowest density is attributed to the commune of Maluku with 65 inhabitants / km²);
- The municipality of Maluku occupies the largest area (7,948.8 km²) and the municipality of Kintambo (2.72 km²) occupies the smallest area of the city;
- The municipality of Ngaliema has the largest number of plots, ie 97,698 (16.4%), followed by the municipality of Kimbanseke with 93,531 (15.7%). In addition, the municipality of Lingwala has only 3,585 plots (0.6%);
- The commune of Kimbanseke has the largest number of administrative districts, i.e. 46 (12.6%) and streets, i.e. 1.666 (11.6%), while the commune of Ngaba is the one with the least, i.e. 6 districts (1.6%) and 114 streets (0.8%).

Photo: Gutu Kia Zimi

SECTION II: THE PLOT, A FUNCTIONAL ENVIRONMENTAL UNIT

The basic living environment, before belonging to the neighborhood and the municipality, is that of the plot. The latter can be compared to a whole within which various elements intertwine: trees, houses, men, women, children, animals, etc. The various components are arranged in an order in an ecosystem functional so that each element can play its role. Specialized places are defined there and particular spaces are allocated to the members of this environmental unit. The plot is also a space in which we live and where we live there. This is why its interior design must meet all the conditions for a better development of the elements that compose it. Unfortunately, it is unfortunate to note that the development of plots in the various districts of the city of Kinshasa does not obey any urban planning rules, sometimes bordering on intolerance in matters of hygiene. We sometimes see in the plot of bins and latrines in the open, a shower made of some recovery materials, stagnant water, ...

Photo GKZ

The different moments of daily life that we spend in the plot, it happens outside of the house, due to certain physical constraints. Climatic conditions in the tropics with a strong burning heat, which require residents to stay outside dwellings for a long time. Since housing in Congolese cities in general and in Kinshasa in particular is an individual problem, the development of a plot is closely related to the income available to the owner of the plot. But on the other hand, the need to plant a tree in its plot does not require any financial means. It is a matter of conscience and culture, taste and common sense. The location of the plots in the districts of the urbanized communes of Bandalungwa, Matete, Lemba (Salongo), Kalamu (Matonge, Yolo), Mount Ngafula (Maman Mobutu, camp Badiadingi, etc...) does not often offer the possibility and freedom to the owner to plant a tree in the plot due to the narrow houses and free spaces, which surround the plots. The narrowness of the plots is also due to the phenomenon of fragmentation of the plots that we see at the moment following the population growth of the urban population. The fragmentation of the plots is often dictated by the survival needs of owners often of low income or very modest income. The latter are often unable to cope with the many financial and social needs such as: children's schooling, medical care, food, and the need to find the money to send a child to study abroad.

Photo: Gutu Kia Zimi

I. THE ORGANIZATION AND ARRANGEMENT OF THE PLOT

Generally speaking, the layout of the plot follows the following scheme:

-   A large house, sometimes small for the owner, very remarkable for its position, because usually it is built in the foreground, that is, in front of the plot;

- One or two other small houses called "annexes", which are offered for rent, often built behind the owner's large house;
- Common sanitary facilities (shower, toilet) for all inhabitants. Plots with individual sanitary facilities incorporated into the House are still in very small numbers in the dwellings, especially in the dwellings of the districts of the peripheral communes. In this regard, there is a very serious problem of sewage pipes in all the districts of the city of Kinshasa. This situation makes it very unhealthy to install private toilets in dwellings whose malfunction makes the house uncomfortable and unlivable with foul odors;
- A multifunctional free space, variable according to the area occupied by the various constructions or developments. All activities of the plot take place in this space or courtyard. The women cook; the children play, the adults rest and talk, or welcome their visitors. In most cases, it is often in this free space that we find trees that have been planted. However, there is no specific location for the trees. The latter are planted in front or behind the plot and sometimes between the spaces of the constructions. The use of the free space or the courtyard is sometimes a source of many disputes and other palabras between inhabitants of the plot; either a trash can of a housewife too filled in putrefaction brings too many flies and bad smells; or a child playing overturns a pot at the fire of a tenant, …

II. HABITAT AND SETTLEMENT STRATA IN THE PLOTS

Our survey focuses on shrubby vegetation but the population element is also the subject of our study. According to the density of habitat by neighborhood, Marc Pain (1979)[51] in his study distinguished four sets:

Group 1, which brings together the former cities where the number of buildings per hectare urbanized varies from 31-34; i.e. 31.4 (BARUMBU), 32.1 (KINSHASA); 34.4 (LINGWALA). On average, 17 inhabitants live in each plot or a density of 250-300 inhabitants per hectare.

Photo Gutu Kia Zimi

1. Group 2, more complex and less homogeneous, includes the new cities, the southern extensions and the older peripheral extensions (KASA - Vubu and NGIRI-NGIRI);
   - On average, 27 constructions per hectare (KASAVUBU and NGIRI-NGIRI); 22-23 constructions per hectare (Bumbu, MAKALA, NGABA), 22.5 constructions per hectare (NDJILI), 24.5 constructions per hectare (MASINA II), 22.6 constructions per hectare (KIMBANSEKE).

---

[51] MARC PAIN, op.cit, p.352

- Are also in this category, planned cites with an average of 24 dwellings per hectare, i.e. 26 dwellings per hectare (YOLO) and 23 dwellings per hectare (MATETE).
- The new cities have 14 inhabitants / plot, an average density of 187 people per hectare.
- The planned cities with 8.6-9.6 people per housing reach densities of the order of 200 inhabitants per hectare.

2. Group 3, which is more homogeneous, brings together some peripheral and recent extensions and has 17-20 constructions per hectare. These are the extensions of KINTAMBO-NGANDA, MOMBELE, KINSUKA, BINZA-NGALIEMA, KINGABWA. In these extensions, the plots are occupied by 7-9 people, which corresponds to a population density of 70-80 inhabitants per hectare.

3. Group 4, brings together the current urban fringe neighborhoods where there are 12-15 buildings per hectare with a population density of 70-80 inhabitants per hectare. In these urban fringes, 4-5 people occupy the plots. These residential areas are remarkable for their creation and realization; 3-5 constructions per hectare with a density of 20 inhabitants per hectare[52].

Based on the results of our survey, following the table below, we observe that:

- In zone A, 37.2% of plots live 6-10 people and 20.7% of plots with 11-15 people. In addition, 1.6% of plots with 31-35 people were observed and 2.2% of plots with 26-30 people.
- In zone B, 40.6 % of plots with 11-15 people and 21.3 % of plots with 6-10 people 3% of the plots were also observed with 31-35 people.

---

[52] GUTU KIA ZIMI, Naissance d'une arboriculture urbaine au Zaïre (CONGO), in DES FORETS ET DES HOMMES, Environnement Africain, ENDA, DAKAR, Vol IX, 1-2-3-4, 1993, pp.221-247

– In zone C, 40.7 % of plots with 11-15 people and 25.6% of plots with 6-10 people living there. Only 1.2 % of plots with 1-5 people and 25 plots (3%) with 31-35 people.

– In zone D, 28.9 % of the plots with 21-25 people living there. On the other hand, 0.1% is 2 plots with only 1-5 people and 16.1% of plots with 31-35 people.

– In zone E, 29.1% of plots with 21-25 people; 19.5% of plots with 16-20 people and 19.4% of plots with 21-25 people. Only 8 plots (0.5 %) with 1-5 people and 13.3% of plots with 31-35 people;

POPULATION TABLE BY PLOT

Number Inhabitants	ZONE A Number of Plots	%	ZONE B Number of Plots	%	ZONE C Number of Plots	%	ZONE D Number of Plots	%	ZONE E Number of Plots	%	TOTAL	%
1h-5h	451	18,7	9	2,3	10	1,2	2	0,1	8	0,5	480	6,6
6h-10h	898	37,2	85	21,3	213	25,6	58	2,7	95	6,1	1349	18,5
11h-15h	501	20,7	162	40,6	339	40,7	326	15,4	185	12	1513	20,7
16h-20h	350	14,5	57	14,3	150	18	354	16,8	301	19,5	1212	16,6
21h-25h	124	5,1	39	9,8	53	6,4	610	28,9	450	29,1	1276	17,5
26h-30h	53	2,2	35	8,8	43	5,2	421	19,9	300	19,4	852	11,7
31h-35h	39	1,6	12	3	25	3	340	16,1	206	13,3	622	8,5
TOTAL	2416	100	399	100	833	100	2111	100	1545	100	7304	100

Source : Gutu Kia Zimi

Table n*2; Source Gutu Kia Zimi (2020)

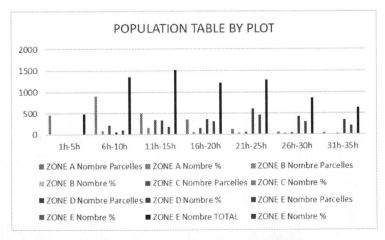

Chart n*1; Source: Gutu Kia Zimi (2020)

Overall, according to the results of our survey, it is observed in the municipalities of Kinshasa that it is in 20.7% of the plots with 11-15 people; 18.5% of the plots with 6-10 people; 17.5% plots with 21-25 people; 16.6% plots with 16-20 people; 11.7% of the plots with 26-30 people; 8.5% of the plots with 31-35 people and only 6.6% of 1-5 people, who live there.

Photo GKZ

III. NUMBER OF BUILDINGS AND HOUSING PER PLOT

Another study by the National Institute of statistics cited by Marc Pain (1979), reveals a clear cut between old and new cities as well as peripheral extensions. From the point of view of the number of constructions per plot, the most common situation is two constructions per plot in the old and new cities for 38% -43% of cases, while it is one construction per plot in the extension areas, 63.5% in the southern extension neighborhoods and 74.8% in the outlying neighborhoods. The study also notes that the plots occupied by three buildings represent approximately one in three (1 in 3) cases in the old cities while they represent only one in four (1 in 4) cases in the new cities. However, the case of one in three plots (1 in 3 plots) of new cities with two houses occurs only once in five (1 in 5 times). In the new cities, the number of dwellings per plot is 2.4 with an average of 7.1 rooms, while, this average is 1 dwelling in the recent extensions with two rooms[53].

---

[53] MARC PAIN, op.cit.

RATIO BETWEEN THE POPULATION AND THE PLOTS				
ZONE A	COMMUNES	POPULATION*	PLOTS	DENSITY
	GOMBE	46 733	75	623,1
	LIMETE	502 549	115	4370
	NGALIEMA	1 070 669	324	3304,b
TOTAL	3	1 619 951	514	3151,7
ZONE B	COMMUNES		PLOTS	
	KINSHASA	176 591	75	2354,5
	LINGWALA	122 049	61	2000,8
	BARUMBU	158 203	63	2511,2
	KINTAMBO	169 074	99	1707,8
TOTAL	4	625 917	298	2100,4
ZONE C	COMMUNES		PLOTS	
	LEMBA	519 361	72	7213,3
	MATETE	411 229	94	4374,8
	KALAMU	357 847	123	2909,3
	BANDALUGWA	316 002	97	3257,8
TOTAL	4	1 604 439	386	4156,6
ZONE D	COMMUNES		PLOTS	
	MASINA	1 051 048	91	11550
	KISENSO	602 024	73	8246,9
	SELEMBAO	530 414	110	4821,9
	MAKALA	301 293	95	3171,5
	N'DJILI	538 497	203	2652,7
	BUMBU	510 331	81	6300,4
	KIMBANSEKE	1 460 402	107	13648,6
	NGABA	255 331	105	2431,7
	NGIRI-NGIRI	198 814	109	1824
	KASA-VUBU	163 594	102	1603,9
TOTAL	10	5 611 748	1076	5215,4
ZONE E	COMMUNES		PLOTS	
	MALUKU	517 184	114	4536,7
	NSELE	367 654	90	4085
	MONT NGAFULA	379 831	311	1221,3
TOTAL	3	1 264 669	515	2455,7
TOTAL GENERAL	24	10 726 724	2789	3846,1
SOURCE : GUTU KIA ZIMI				

Table n*3; Source: Gutu Kia Zimi (2020)

IV. DENSITY OF TREES IN PLOTS

It is important to note that the evolution of neighborhoods towards a gradual densification of habitat and people is accompanied by the creation and development of a plant cover whose size and number varies with the age of the neighborhood. Normally, vegetation cover is denser in older neighborhoods, while it is poorly developed, sometimes dotted, in younger neighborhoods. It turns out according to the results of our survey; urban vegetation is very sparse in the old districts of the communes of Kinshasa. Rather, it is in degradation and endangered due to the aging of the trees on the one hand, and its destruction by new constructions on the other. Seen from the sky or from the top of its hills, the city of Kinshasa has the appearance of a small forest in its large part, but then, a "forest" of anthropogenic origin entirely made up in large part of fruit trees with an average of 4 trees per plot, that is 45-55 adult trees per hectare (Marc Pain, 1979).

Photo GKZ

This average is very variable depending on whether it is an old neighborhood, new cities or in peri-urban neighborhoods. Indeed, it is important to know, that the plots with the highest number of trees have fewer constructions and inhabitants. On the other hand, those with the fewest trees have a high human density and a high number of constructions. It does not matter, whether it is in old or new neighborhoods. However, the survey reveals that it is in the districts of the peripheral municipalities (Kimbanseke, Masina, Ndjili, Nsele, Mount Ngafula, Kingabwa, Kisenso..., where there is a high human density and a high densification of trees, unlike the old districts, which also show a high human density but with a low densification of trees. This is explained by the fact that the destruction of trees by new constructions is more important in the old districts of Kinshasa, Kintambo, Barumbu, Lingwala, Ngaliema, Limete, etc..., than in the new districts of the peripheral communes where the vegetation is still young and vigorous.

According to our study, the table below shows the density of trees by municipality according to the following distribution:

- AREA A (3.8 trees per plot);
- AREA B (4.4 trees per plot);
- AREA C (6.2 trees per plot;
- AREA D (5.8 trees per plot);
- AREA E (5.3 trees per plot).

TREES DENSITY PER PLOTS			
ZONE A	COMMUNES	NBR PLOTS	NBR TREES	DENSITY
	GOMBE	75	200	2.7
	LIMETE	115	418	3.6
	NGALIEMA	324	1329	4.1
TOTAL	3	514	1947	3.8
ZONE B	COMMUNES	NBR PLOTS	NBR TREES	
	KINSHASA	75	215	2.9
	LINGWALA	61	213	3.5
	BARUMBU	63	240	3.8
	KINTAMBO	99	632	6.4
TOTAL	4	298	1300	4.4
ZONE C	COMMUNES	NBR PLOTS	NBR TREES	
	LEMBA	72	545	7.6
	MATETE	94	446	4.7
	KALAMU	123	752	6.1
	BANDALUGWA	97	632	6.5
TOTAL	4	386	2375	6.2
ZONE D	COMMUNES	NBR PLOTS	NBR TREES	
	MASINA	91	616	6.8
	KISENSO	73	451	6.2
	SELEMBAO	110	702	6.4
	MAKALA	95	440	4.6
	N'DJILI	203	1013	5
	BUMBU	81	561	6.9
	KIMBANSEKE	107	649	6.1
	NGABA	105	630	6
	NGIRI-NGIRI	109	611	5.6
	KASA-VUBU	102	619	6.1
TOTAL	10	1076	6292	5.8
ZONE E	COMMUNES	NBR PLOTS	NBR TREES	
	MALUKU	114	798	7
	NSELE	90	746	8.3
	MONT NGAFULA	311	1191	3.8
TOTAL	3	515	2735	5.3
TOTAL GENERAL	24	2789	14649	5.3
	SOURCE : Gutu Kia Zimi			

Table n*4; Source: Gutu Kia Zimi (2020)

However, there is a density of 5.3 trees per plot in all municipalities. It can also be observed that it is in the districts of the communes of Study Area C and D that there is a high density of trees per plot, and relatively in the districts of the communes of zone E. This result (5.8

trees per plot) is relatively similar to the study by Marc Pain (1979), which reveals an average of 4 trees per plot, very variable average depending on whether it is an old neighborhood, new cities or peri-urban neighborhoods. However, an important factor may justify this increase in density. It is important to note that between 1979 and 2019, the districts of the peripheral municipalities experienced a very strong extension and the number of plots increased sharply.

Photo Gutu Kia Zimi

V: RELATIONSHIP BETWEEN POPULATION DENSITY AND NUMBER OF TREES

Population density is a measure of the number of individuals or inhabitants occupying a given area. It is most often expressed in individuals per unit area (e.g. inhabitants/km2). In practice, this can be calculated for a city, an agglomeration, a neighborhood, a country or the whole world. Currently the densest communes of Kinshasa are Bumbu, Kinshasa, Kintambo, Makala, Ngaba, Kalamu, Matete, Ngiri Ngiri.

N°	COMMUNES	X(Density)	Y(Trees)	X²	Y²	XY
	POPULATION DENSITY AND NUMBER OF TREES CORRELATION COEFFICIENT					
1	Gombe	1.593,4	513	2.538.923,6	263,169	817414,2
2	Limete	7.434,2	1820	55267329,6	3.312,400	13.530.244
3	Ngaliema	4.773,4	2510	22.785.347,6	6.300.100	11.981.234
4	Kinshasa	61,53	215	3.782,3	46,225	13.228,95
5	Lingwala	42.738,1	213	1826545191,6	45,369	9.103.215,3
6	Barumbu	33.517,6	240	1123429510	57,600	8.044.224
7	Kintambo	62.159,6	756	3863815872	571,536	46.992.657,6
8	Lemba	21.914	745	480223396	555,025	16.325.930
9	Matete	84.268,2	446	7101129531	198,916	37.583.617,2
10	Kalamu	53.892,6	752	2904412335	565,504	40.527.235,2
11	Bandalungwa	46.334,6	632	2146895157	399,424	29.283.467,2
12	Masina	15,03	1897	225	3.598,609	28.511,91
13	Kisenso	36.266,5	451	1315259022	203,401	16.356.191,5
14	Selembao	22.882,4	1002	523604229,8	1.004,004	22.928.164,8
15	Makala	53.802,3	809	2894687485	654,481	43.526.060,7
16	Ndjili	47.236,6	1013	2231296380	1.026,169	47.850.675,8
17	Bumbu	96.288,9	561	9271552263	314,721	54.018.072,9
18	Kimbanseke	6.141,8	2878	37721707,2	8.282,884	17.676.100,4
19	Ngaba	63.832,8	630	4074626356	396,900	40.214.664
20	Ngiri-Ngiri	58.474,7	611	3419290540	373,321	35.728.041,7
21	Kasa-Vubu	32.394,9	619	1049429546	383,161	20.052.443,1
22	Maluku	65,1	798	4238	636,804	51.949,8
23	Nsele	409,1	2487	167362,8	6.185,169	1.017.431,7
24	Mont Ngafula	1.058,3	2983	1119998,9	8.898,289	3.156.908,9
	TOTAL	98474,0	25581	42441204078,6	44273181	516.807.684,86

Table n*5; Source: Gutu Kia Zimi (2020)
R = 9.884.321.043, 6/20292821395.2 = 0.5

The correlation coefficient (r = 0.5) indicates a strong relationship between population density and the number of trees in Kinshasa plots. It turns out that in neighborhoods with less dense population, it is largely the abundance of trees that makes the environment more pleasant for humans. It is necessary to do everything so that it remains so, otherwise it would be completely futile to leave the Old City Centers for the outskirts[54].

---

[54] R.J. OLEMBO ET P. DE RHAM, Foresterie urbaine dans deux mondes différents, http://www.fao.org/3/s1930f04.htm

VI. ESTIMATED NUMBER OF TREES ACCORDING TO POPULATION DENSITY

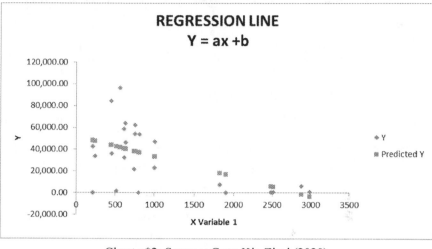

Chart n*2; Source: Gutu Kia Zimi (2020)
Y = Number of trees; X = Density of population
Y = ax + b
A = 0,01; B = 1026,1
Y = 0,01x + 1026,1

Estimating the number of trees by the regression line (Y = 0.01 x+1026.1) shows that the number of trees in residential plots in Kinshasa decreases with population density. Concretely, as the population density increases, the number of trees in the plots decreases.

SECTION III: THE STREET, AN ECOLOGICAL ENTITY

The street or avenue is the support on which the plot is identified. It is also a significant and equally important ecological entity. During the investigation, we made an unfortunate finding, which we did not count a single tree in the streets and avenues of the neighborhoods surveyed. This finding is not the same in some avenues of the residential areas of the municipality of Limete and La Gombe bordered by some trees. If this finding is real for the aforementioned residential neighborhoods, the finding is poor in the streets of other "African" neighborhoods where we can count timidly some trees on some major avenues such as Lumumba Boulevard in Limete. Since it is the private feeling, which motivates the owner, his concern is to plant a tree in his plot first. It is up to the public power, that is, the community, the municipality, and the neighborhood, owner of the street to plant trees in the streets and avenues for the benefit of its citizens and the beauty of the city. However, between the concerns to plant a tree in his plot and on the street, there is only one-step. It is a matter of conscience. According to urban development plans, there was no space for planting trees on the street. And yet, knowing the important role of vegetation in our life, it would contribute enormously to the beautification of our environment and to the improvement of our quality of life. For example, fight against noise, erosion, air pollution, etc. ... The lack of trees and green spaces is only one of the aspects of the often desolate situation of the environment in the different districts of the Urban communes of Kinshasa. It is sometimes understandable that high priority is not always given to planting trees in residential plots. Yet, each December 5, every year is the national Tree Day in DRCongo.

It is an opportunity for the public authorities of the country, to invite the population to plant a tree, as is the case in the Republic of Congo (Brazzaville), which has established a directive inviting every citizen to plant a tree on this day. Trees, due to their size, shape, color, seasonal changes and importance in the landscape are the most visible and therefore most valuable natural living element. Green is the most relaxing color for the eyes, presumably because humanity once evolved in an environment where Green predominated. Trees restore harmony to the urban environment and thus contribute powerfully to alleviate social tensions[55]. As Nathalie Long (2012) states, urban vegetation is also considered as a response to the social demand of urban populations[56]. The national reforestation Service of the Ministry of the environment will have to be aware of this problem especially in this period of fight against global warming. It is also prudent to note that the aging of trees in plots and streets of neighborhoods deserves attention from the public authorities and the population. It is a certain fact, that the old trees in the plots and those, which line the streets, pose a danger to the inhabitants as well as passers-by during the stormy rains.

Photo Gutu Kia Zimi

---

[55] R.J. OLEMBO ET P. DE RHAM, op.cit
[56] NATHALIE LONG ET BRICE TONINI (2012), « Les espaces verts urbains: étude exploratoire des pratiques et du ressenti des usagers », *VertigO - la revue électronique en sciences de l'environnement* [En ligne], Volume 12 Numéro 2 | septembre 2012, mis en ligne le 31 octobre 2012, consulté le 06 septembre 2020. URL: http://journals.openedition.org/vertigo/12931; DOI: https://doi.org/10.4000/vertigo.12931

There is an environmental Service in each municipality. Currently, there is legislation, which states that before cutting a tree, it will be necessary to obtain permission from the Environmental Service of the municipality in advance. This regulation is very positive for the conservation of urban vegetation. A shady street offers a peaceful setting for pedestrians as well as for motorists.

During our investigation in all neighborhoods of Kinshasa, we found the anti-hygienic and anti-environmental practice of emptying garbage bins of household and other garbage in the streets, so much so that the street becomes inaccessible to the passage of vehicles and even pedestrians.

Photo Gutu Kia Zimi

The consequence of this practice that the "Kinois" have instituted to transform the streets into dumps carries a great prejudice on the urban sanitation of the different districts of the city of Kinshasa. Not to mention, other consequences on the environment including the proliferation of flies and mosquitoes, causes of several diseases (Malaria, typhoid), release of foul odors, etc ... the solution to this problem would come from equipping the various districts of the city municipalities with public dumps. Currently, the "Kinois" remain unsolved in the face of this thorny problem of garbage that affects everyone. The problem is the responsibility of the public authority, which will have to invest in the management and recycling of garbage with an appropriate system of garbage collection. The consequences on housing mean that some streets in the neighborhoods are unlivable because they offer unacceptable and intolerable hygienic conditions. It is unfortunate that tenants, who refuse to live in these unhygienic conditions, despite some streets and avenues in Kinshasa's neighborhoods, which have beautiful buildings. This situation also has a very negative impact, which affects the socio-economic activities of the street and the neighborhood, especially for the tenants of bars, hotels, dancing club, shops and other *"Nganda"*.

As part of the aesthetics of the city of Kinshasa, trees could be planted on some large avenues, some public squares. We often forget that some trees are witnesses of time and history. Who has not heard of Stanley's baobab in Boma in the study of the history of Congo? Natural witnesses in this case some trees also materialize the history of some neighborhoods of Kinshasa.

Photo Gutu Kia Zimi
A plot with ornamental plants

Photo GKZ
A street in Kinshasa with palm trees "*Elaeis Guineensis*" as
an ornamental plant in the Commune of Ngaliema

Photo Gutu Kia Zimi
A small street in the Nganda quarter of Kintambo Commune

Photo Gutu Kia Zimi
An avenue in the Ma Campagne quarter of which
we can observe "ligablo" (a small shop)

Photo Gutu Kia Zimi

CHAPTER IV

URBAN ARBORICULTURE OF KINSHASA

---❀---

Our constitution is a remarkable, beautiful gift.
But it's really just a piece of parchment. It has no power on its own.
We, the people, give it power with our participation, and the choices we make.
OBAMA
January 10, 2017

The concept of urban vegetation refers to any vegetation present in the city, whether spontaneous or introduced by man. Urban arboriculture concerns only that of anthropogenic origin, that is, that is, which is deliberately planted and then maintained. As explained earlier, the survey was carried out in the residential plots of the different districts of the communes of Kinshasa. This study integrates space (plots), vegetation (trees), and community (population). Before going into the details of the results, we will begin by presenting a general overview of the study areas on the one hand, and the determination of the sample on the other. This will allow the reader to get an overall idea of the survey.

I. DETERMINATION OF STUDY AREAS

We have defined five study areas following the characteristics of the districts of the communes of the city of Kinshasa[57]

---

[57] Atlas de Kinshasa, 1975, Kinshasa, typologie des quartiers.

1. Zone A: residential areas. These are the districts of the municipalities of Gombe, Limete, Ngaliema.
2. Zone B: Kinshasa, Barumbu, Lingwala, Kintambo
3. Zone C: Lemba, Matete, Kalamu, Bandalungwa
4. Zone D: Kasa-Vubu, Ngiri-Ngiri, Bumbu, Makala, Ngaba, Selembao, Masina, Kisenso, Ndjili, Kimbanseke
5. Zone E: Mount Ngafula, Nsele, Maluku

II. DETERMINATION OF SAMPLE

The survey was carried out in 7.304 plots of the quarters of the communes explained above:

DISTRIBUTION OF PLOTS BY STUDY AREA		
Survey Area	Nbr of Plots	%
AREA A	2.416	33,1
AREA B	399	5,4
AREA C	833	11,5
AREA D	2.111	28,9
AREA E	1.545	21,2
TOTAL	7.304	100
SOURCE : GUTU KIA ZIMI		

Table n*6; Source: Gutu Kia Zimi (2020)

The city of Kinshasa has 24 municipalities, 14,389 streets or avenues, 365 neighborhoods with 595,069 plots. Our sample covers 7,304 plots, or 1.2% of all plots in the city of Kinshasa. Given the expansion of the city (urban growth), it should be noted that since 2014 to date, it is assumed that the number of plots has increased especially in the outlying municipalities. In the plots, we counted the following number of trees; a total of 25,581 trees (100%) counted as undermentioned (Table n*7):

Photo Gutu Kia Zimi

DISTRIBUTION OF TREES BY STUDY AREA		
STUDY AREA	NBR of TREES	%
AREA A	4.843	18,9
AREA B	1.424	5,5
AREA C	2.575	10
AREA D	10.471	41,2
AREA E	6.268	24,5
TOTAL	25581	100
SOURCE : GUTU KIA ZIMI		

Table n*7; Source: Gutu Kia Zimi (2020)

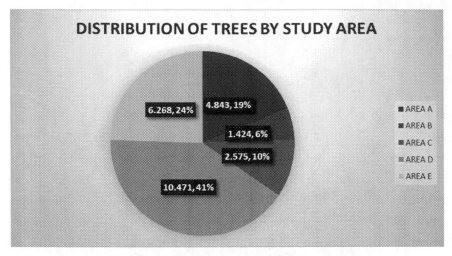

Chart n*3; Source: Gutu Kia Zimi

	AREA A				
	DISTRIBUTION OF TREES PER QUARTER				
	COMMUNE OF THE GOMBE				
QUARTERS	NBR OF PLOTS	%	NBR OF TREES	%	
	Surveyed		Counted		
Batetela	35	16,2	65	12,7	
Cliniques	16	7,4	47	9,2	
Commerce	42	19,4	77	15	
Croix Rouge	13	6	42	8,2	
Fleuve	11	5,1	38	7,4	
Gare	14	6,5	45	8,8	
Golf	19	8,8	50	9,7	
Haut Command.	33	15,3	53	10,3	
Lemera	15	6,9	47	9,2	
Revolution	18	8,3	49	9,6	
TOTAL	216	100	513	100	
	Source : Gutu Kia Zimi				

Table n*8; Source: Gutu Kia Zimi (2020)

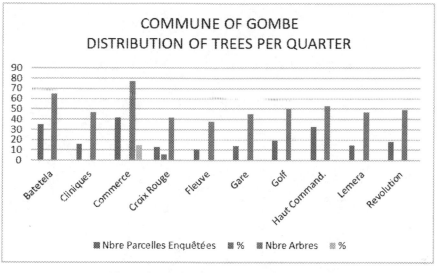

Chart n*4; Source: Gutu Kia Zimi (2020)

According to this table, in the commune of Gombe, the districts with more trees are respectively the Commerce (15%), "Batetela" (12.7%) and "Haut Commandement" (10.3%) districts. The "Fleuve" district is the least populated with trees (7.4%). This is also justified by the number of plots surveyed.

	AREA A			
	DISTRIBUTION OF TREES PER QUARTER			
	COMMUNE OF LIMETE			
QUARTERS	NBR OF PLOTS	%	NBR OF TREES	%
	Surveyed		Counted	
Agricole	50	7,1	130	7,1
Général Masidia	46	6,6	125	6,9
Industriel	50	7,1	130	7,1
Kingabwa	68	9,7	160	8,8
Mateba	46	6,6	125	6,9
Mayulu	48	6,9	126	6,9
Mbamu	48	6,9	126	6,9
Mfumu Mvula	49	7	128	7
Mombele	49	7	128	7
Mososo	50	7,1	130	7,1
Ndanu	48	6,9	126	6,9
Nzadi	48	6,9	126	6,9
Residentiel	50	7,1	130	7,1
Salongo	50	7,1	130	7,1
TOTAL	700	100	1820	100
	SOURCE : GUTU KIA ZIMI			

Table n*9; Source: Gutu Kia Zimi (2020)

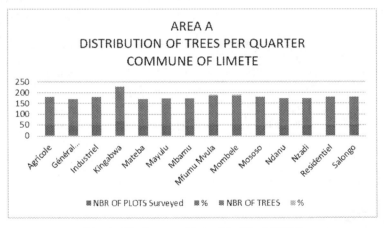

Chart n*5; Source: Gutu Kia Zimi (2020)

According to this table, the Kingabwa district is the most tree-populated (8.8%). Next come the Salongo, Residential, Mososo, Agricultural and Industrial districts with respectively (7.1%) trees, as well as the Mombele and Mfumu Mvula districts respectively with 7% trees.

84

AREA A				
DISTRIBUTION OF TREES PER QUARTER				
COMMUNE OF NGALIEMA				
QUARTERS	NBR OF PLOTS	%	NBR OF TREES	%
	Surveyed		Counted	
Anciens Comb.	70	4,7	116	4,6
Bangu	70	4,7	116	4,6
Basoko	70	4,7	116	4,6
Binza Pigeon	79	5,3	142	5,7
Bumba	72	4,8	119	4,7
Congo	71	4,7	118	4,7
Djelo Binza	71	4,7	118	4,7
Joli Parc	70	4,7	116	4,6
Kimpe	72	4,8	119	4,7
Kinkenda	71	4,7	118	4,7
Kinsuka Pêcheurs	79	5,3	143	5,7
Lonzo	70	4,7	116	4,6
Lubudi	70	4,7	116	4,6
Lukunga	70	4,7	116	4,6
Mama yemo	71	4,7	118	4,7
Manenga	71	4,7	118	4,7
Mfinda	71	4,7	118	4,7
Munganga	70	4,7	116	4,6
Musey	70	4,7	116	4,6
Ngomba Kikusa	72	4,8	119	4,7
Punda	70	4,7	116	4,6
TOTAL	1500	100	2510	100
SOURCE : GUTU KIA ZIMI				

Table n*10; Source: Gutu Kia Zimi (2020)

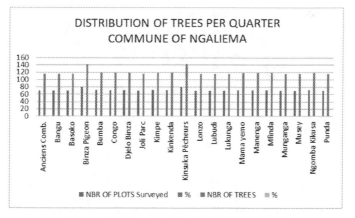

Chart n*5; Source: Gutu Kia Zimi (2020)

The Binza Pigeon and Kinsuka Pêcheurs neighborhoods have the most trees (5.7%). But overall, all neighborhoods in Ngaliema commune are populated with trees (4.6% -4.7%).

	AREA B			
	DISTRIBUTION OF TREES PER QUARTER			
	COMMUNE OF KINSHASA			
QUARTERS	NBR OF PLOTS	%	NBR OF TREES	%
	Surveyed		Counted	
Aketi	11	14,5	31	14,4
Boyoma	10	13,3	30	14
Djalo	10	13,3	30	14
Madimba	11	14,5	31	14,4
Mongala	11	14,5	31	14,4
Ngbaka	12	16	32	14,9
Pende	10	13,3	30	14
TOTAL	75	100	215	100
	SOURCE : GUTU KIA ZIMI			

Table n*11; Source: Gutu Kia Zimi (2020)

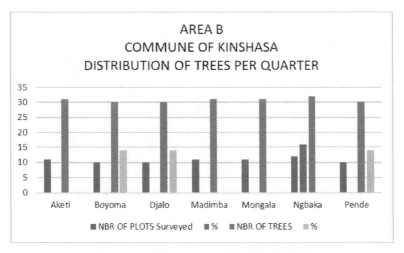

Chart n*6; Source: gutu Kia Zimi (2020)

Overall, in the neighborhoods of Kinshasa commune, a percentage of trees is observed, which varies between 14% -14.9%. However, there is a decrease in shrub vegetation in this town.

	AREA B			
	DISTRIBUTION OF TREES PER QUARTER			
	COMMUNE OF LINGWALA			
QUARTERS	NBR OF PLOTS Surveyed	%	NBR OF TREES Counted	%
30 Juin	6	9,8	23	10,8
Camp Lufungula	7	11,5	24	11,3
CNECI	7	11,5	24	11,3
La voix du peuple	6	9,8	23	10,8
Lokole	7	11,5	24	11,3
Ngunda Lokombe	7	11,5	24	11,3
Pakadjuma	6	9,8	23	10,8
Singa Mopepe	6	9,8	23	10,8
Wenze	9	14,8	25	11,7
TOTAL	61	100	213	100
	SOURCE : GUTU KIA ZIMI			

Table n*12; Source: Gutu Kia Zimi (2020)

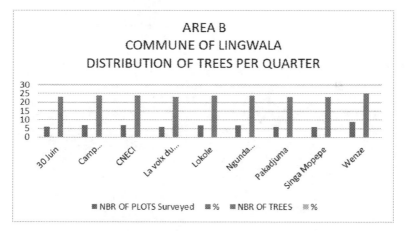

Chart n*7; Source: Gutu Kia Zimi (2020)

In all of the 61 plots surveyed in the districts of Lingwala commune, the percentage of trees varies between 10.8% -11.7%. It is among the municipalities where we observe a decreasing number of shrub vegetation.

	AREA B				
	DISTRIBUTION OF TREES PER QUARTER				
	COMMUNE OF BARUMBU				
QUARTERS	NBR OF PLOTS	%	NBR OF TREES	%	
	Surveyed		Counted		
Bitshaku Tshaku	8	12,7	29	12,1	
Funa I	8	12,7	29	12,1	
Funa II	6	9,5	25	10,4	
Kapinga Bapu	6	9,5	25	10,4	
Kasai	7	11,1	26	10,8	
Libulu	8	12,7	29	12,1	
Mozindo	7	11,1	26	10,8	
Ndolo	7	11,1	26	10,8	
Tshimanga	6	9,5	25	10,4	
TOTAL	63	100	240	100	
SOURCE : GUTU KIA ZIMI					

Table n*13; Source: Gutu Kia Zimi (2020)

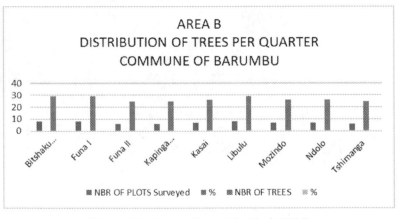

Chart n*8; Source: Gutu Kia Zimi (2020)

	AREA B			
	DISTRIBUTION OF TREES PER QUARTER			
	COMMUNE OF KINTAMBO			
QUARTERS	NBR OF PLOTS	%	NBR OF TREES	%
	Surveyed		Counted	
Itimbiri	24	12	93	12,3
Kilimani	25	12,5	94	12,4
Lisala	25	12,5	94	12,4
Lubudi Luka	24	12	93	12,3
Lubudi Nganda	24	12	93	12,3
Salongo	25	12,5	94	12,4
Tshinkela	25	12,5	94	12,4
Wenze	28	14	101	13,4
TOTAL	200	100	756	100
SOURCE : GUTU KIA ZIMI				

Table n*14; Source: Gutu Kia Zimi (2020)

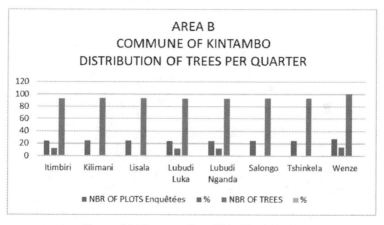

Chart n*9; Source: Gutu Kia Zimi (2020)

	AREA C				
	DISTRIBUTION OF TREES PER QUARTER				
	COMMUNE OF LEMBA				
QUARTERS	NBR OF PLOTS Surveyed	%	NBR of TREES Counted	%	
Camp Bumba	20	6,7	50	6,7	
Camp Kabila	20	6,7	50	6,7	
Commercial	20	6,7	50	6,7	
Echangeur	19	6,3	49	6,6	
Ecole	19	6,3	49	6,6	
Foire	20	6,7	50	6,7	
Gombele	18	6	48	6,4	
Kemi	18	6	48	6,4	
Kimpwanza	18	6	48	6,4	
Livulu	32	10,7	57	7,7	
Mandrandele	20	6,7	50	6,7	
Masano	20	6,7	50	6,7	
Mbanza Lemba	19	6,3	49	6,6	
Molo	19	6,3	49	6,6	
Salongo	18	6	48	6,4	
TOTAL	300	100	745	100	
	SOURCE : GUTU KIA ZIMI				

Table n*15; Source: Gutu Kia Zimi (2020)

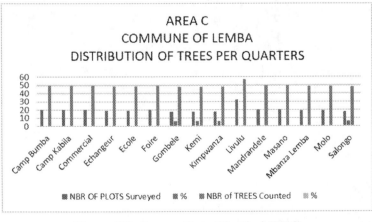

Chart n*10; Source: Gutu Kia Zimi (2020)

	AREA C				
	DISTRIBUTION OF TREES PER QUARTER				
	COMMUNE OF MATETE				
QUARTERS	NBR OF PLOTS	%	NBR OF TREES	%	
	Surveyed		Counted		
Dondo	6	6,4	33	7,4	
Loeka	6	6,4	33	7,4	
Lubefu	7	7,4	34	7,6	
Lumumba	7	7,4	34	7,6	
Lukunga	11	11,7	39	8,7	
Lunionzo	8	8,5	35	7,8	
Malemba	6	6,4	33	7,4	
Maziba	6	6,4	33	7,4	
Mbomb'Ipoku	8	8,5	35	7,8	
Sankuru	8	8,5	35	7,8	
Sumbuka	7	7,4	34	7,6	
Totaka	7	7,4	34	7,6	
Vivi	7	7,4	34	7,6	
TOTAL	94	100	446		
	SOURCE : GUTU KIA ZIMI				

Table n*16; Source: Gutu Kia Zimi (2020)

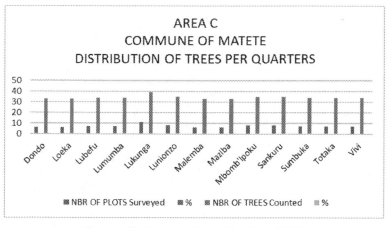

Chart n*11; Source: Gutu Kia Zimi (2020)

	AREA C			
	DISTRIBUTION OF TREES PER QUARTER			
	COMMUNE OF MATETE			
QUARTERS	NBR OF PLOTS	%	NBR OF TREES	%
	Surveyed		Counted	
Dondo	6	6,4	33	7,4
Loeka	6	6,4	33	7,4
Lubefu	7	7,4	34	7,6
Lumumba	7	7,4	34	7,6
Lukunga	11	11,7	39	8,7
Lunionzo	8	8,5	35	7,8
Malemba	6	6,4	33	7,4
Maziba	6	6,4	33	7,4
Mbomb'Ipoku	8	8,5	35	7,8
Sankuru	8	8,5	35	7,8
Sumbuka	7	7,4	34	7,6
Totaka	7	7,4	34	7,6
Vivi	7	7,4	34	7,6
TOTAL	94	100	446	
	SOURCE : GUTU KIA ZIMI			

Table n*17; Source: Gutu Kia Zimi (2020)

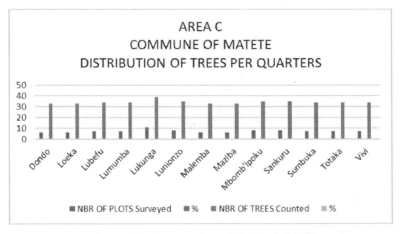

Chart n*12; Source: Gutu Kia Zimi (2020)

	AREA C			
QUARTERS	DISTRIBUTION OF TREES PER QUARTER			
	COMMUNE OF KALAMU			
	NBR OF PLOTS	%	NBR OF TREES	%
	Surveyed		Counted	
Imocongo	16	5,5	41	5,5
Kauka I	16	5,5	41	5,5
Kauka II	16	5,5	41	5,5
Kauka III	15	5,2	40	5,3
Kimbangu I	15	5,2	40	5,3
Kimbangu II	15	5,2	40	5,3
Kimbangu III	17	5,9	42	5,6
Matonge I	17	5,9	42	5,6
Matonge II	15	5,2	40	5,3
Matonge III	16	5,5	41	5,5
Pinzi	16	5,5	41	5,5
Yolo Nord I	17	5,9	42	5,6
Yolo Nord II	17	5,9	42	5,6
Yolo Nord III	16	5,5	41	5,5
Yolo Sud I	16	5,5	41	5,5
Yolo Sud II	15	5,2	40	5,3
Yolo Sud III	15	5,2	40	5,3
Yolo Sud IV	19	6,6	57	7,6
TOTAL	289	100	752	100
	SOURCE : GUTU KIA ZIMI			

Table n*18; Source: Gutu Kia Zimi (2020)

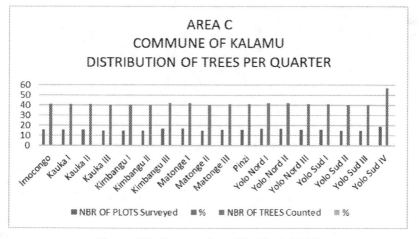

Chart n*13: Source: Gutu Kia Zimi (2020)

AREA C DISTRIBUTION OF TREES PER QUARTER COMMUNE OF BANDALUNGWA				
QUARTERS	NBR OF PLOTS Surveyed	%	NBR OF TREES Counted	%
Adoula	18	12	78	12,3
Bisengo	19	12,7	79	12,5
Camp Kokolo	21	14	83	13,1
Kasa-Vubu	18	12	78	12,3
Lingwala	19	12,7	79	12,5
Lubudi	19	12,7	79	12,5
Lumumba	18	12	78	12,3
Makelele	18	12	78	12,3
TOTAL	150	100	632	100
SOURCE : GUTU KIA ZIMI				

Table n*19: Source: Gutu Kia Zimi (2020)

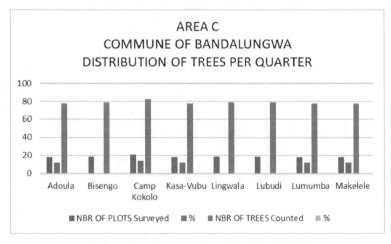

Chart n*14; Source: Gutu Kia Zimi (2020)

	AREA D			
	DISTRIBUTION OF TREES PER QUARTER			
	COMMUNE OF MASINA			
QUARTERS	NBR OF PLOTS Surveyed	%	NBR OF TREES Counted	%
Abattoir	19	4,6	89	4,7
Boba	19	4,6	89	4,7
Congo	20	4,9	90	4,7
Efoloko	20	4,9	90	4,7
Imbali	18	4,4	88	4,6
Kasai	18	4,4	88	4,6
Kimbangu	21	5,1	91	4,8
Kivu	21	5,1	91	4,8
Lokari	18	4,4	88	4,6
Lubambu	18	4,4	88	4,6
Mafuta Kizola	20	4,9	90	4,7
Mandiangu	20	4,9	90	4,7
Mapela	19	4,6	89	4,7
Matadi	19	4,6	89	4,7
Mfumu Nsuka	20	4,9	90	4,7
Nzuzi Wa Mbombo	20	4,9	90	4,7
Pelende	18	4,4	88	4,6
Sans fil	25	6,1	112	5,9
Television	19	4,6	89	4,7
Tshangu	19	4,6	89	4,7
Tshuenge	19	4,6	89	4,7
TOTAL	410	100	1897	100
	SOURCE : GUTU KIA ZIMI			

Table n*20; Source: Gutu Kia Zimi (2020)

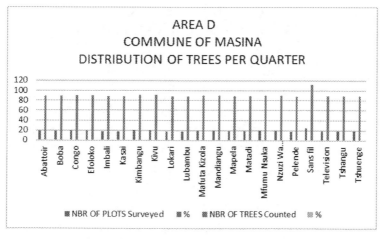

Chart n*15; Source: Gutu Kia Zimi (2020)

QUARTERS	AREA D DISTRIBUTION OF TREES PER QUARTIER COMMUNE OF KISENSO			
QUARTERS	NBR OF PLOTS Surveyed	%	NBR OF TREES Counted	%
17 Mai	9	8,7	37	8,2
Amba	6	5,8	26	5,8
Bikanga	7	6,8	27	6
Dingi Dingi	5	4,9	25	5,5
Kabila	5	4,9	25	5,5
Kitomesa	6	5,8	26	5,8
Kisenso Gare	7	6,8	27	6
Kumbu	7	6,8	27	6
Liberation	6	5,8	26	5,8
Mbuku	5	4,9	25	5,5
Mission	6	5,8	26	5,8
Mujinga	6	5,8	26	5,8
Ngomba	5	4,9	25	5,5
Nsola	5	4,9	25	5,5
Paix	6	5,8	26	5,8
Regideso	6	5,8	26	5,8
Revolution	6	5,8	26	5,8
TOTAL	103	100	451	100
Source : Gutu Kia Zimi				

Table n*21; Source: Gutu Kia Zimi (2020)

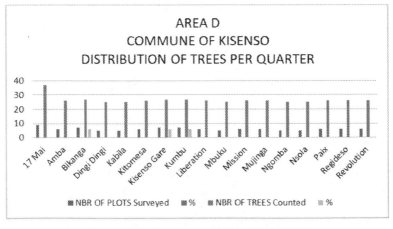

Chart n*16; Source: Gutu Kia Zimi (2020)

QUARTERS	AREA D DISTRIBUTION OF TREES PER QUARTER COMMUNE OF SELEMBAO			
	NBR OF PLOTS Surveyed	%	NBR OF TREES Counted	%
Radindingi	9	8,2	67	6,7
Cité Verte	8	7,3	62	6,2
Inga	3	2,7	50	5
Herady	4	3,6	52	5,2
Kalunga	4	3,6	52	5,2
Konde	7	6,4	56	5,6
Liberation	7	6,4	56	5,6
Lubudi	5	4,5	54	5,4
Madiata	5	4,5	54	5,4
Mbala	7	6,4	56	5,6
Molende	7	6,4	56	5,6
Muana turu	6	5,5	55	5,5
Ndobe	6	5,5	55	5,5
Ngafani	7	6,4	56	5,6
Nkingu	7	6,4	56	5,6
Nkombe	6	5,5	55	5,5
Nkulu	6	5,5	55	5,5
Pululu Mbambu	6	5,5	55	5,5
TOTAL	110	100	1002	100
Source : Gutu Kia Zimi				

Table n*22; Source: Gutu Kia Zimi (2020)

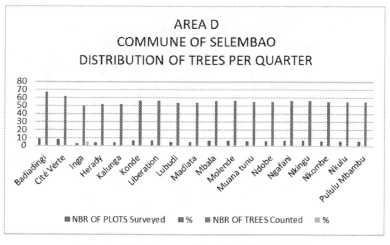

Chart n*17; Source: Gutu Kia Zimi (2020)

AREA D DISTRIBUTION OF TREES PER QUARTER COMMUNE OF MAKALA				
QUARTERS	NBR OF PLOTS Surveyed	%	NBR OF TREES Counted	%
Bahumbu	3	3,2	38	4,7
Bagata	6	6,3	45	5,6
Bolima	5	5,3	44	5,4
Kabila	7	7,4	56	6,9
Kisantu	7	7,4	56	6,9
Kwango	5	5,3	44	5,4
Lemba Village	6	6,3	45	5,6
Mabulu I	4	4,2	41	5,1
Mabulu II	4	4,2	41	5,1
Mawanga	5	5,3	44	5,4
Malala	5	5,3	44	5,4
M'fidi	6	6,3	45	5,6
Mikasi	5	5,3	44	5,4
Salongo	5	5,3	44	5,4
Selo	6	6,3	45	5,6
Tampa	6	6,3	45	5,6
Uele	5	5,3	44	5,4
Wamba	5	5,3	44	5,4
TOTAL	95	100	809	100

SOURCE : GUTU KIA ZIMI

Table n*23; Source: Gutu Kia Zimi (2020)

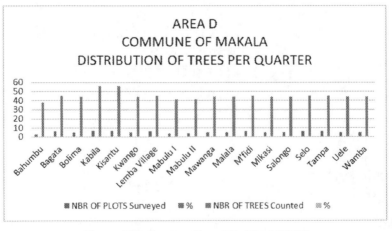

Chart n*18; Source: Gutu Kia Zimi (2020)

QUARTERS	AREA D			
DISTRIBUTION OF TREES PER QUARTER				
COMMUNE OF NDJILI				
QUARTERS	NBR OF PLOTS	%	NBR OF TREES	%
	Surveyed		Counted	
Q1 Makasi	33	9,3	92	9,1
Q2 Bilombe	24	6,8	73	7,2
Q3 Equateur	25	7	75	7,4
Q4 Katanga	29	8,2	79	7,8
Q5 Kivu	26	7,3	76	7,5
Q6 Kasai	27	7,6	77	7,6
Q7 Oriental	26	7,3	76	7,5
Q8 Ubangi	26	7,3	76	7,5
Q9 Mongala	29	8,2	79	7,8
Q10 Goma	28	7,9	78	7,7
Q11 Tshuapa	28	7,9	78	7,7
Q12 Bandundu	27	7,6	77	7,6
Q13 Inga	27	7,6	77	7,6
TOTAL	355	100	1013	100
SOURCE : GUTU KIA ZIMI				

Table n*24; Source: gutu Kia Zimi (2020)

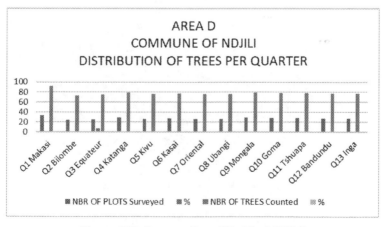

Chart n*19; Source: Gutu Kia Zimi (2020)

QUARTERS	AREA D				
	DISTRIBUTION OF TREES PER QUARTER				
	COMMUNE OF BUMBU				
QUARTERS	NBR OF PLOTS	%	NBR OF TREES	%	
	Surveyed		Counted		
Dipiya	9	8,9	44	7,8	
Kasai	10	9,9	53	9,4	
Kwango	8	7,9	43	7,6	
Lt Mbaki	9	8,9	44	7,8	
Lokoro	9	8,9	44	7,8	
Lukenie	8	7,9	43	7,6	
Maindombe	6	5,9	40	7,1	
Mbandaka	6	5,9	40	7,1	
Matadi	7	6,9	42	7,5	
Mfimi	7	6,9	42	7,5	
Mongala	8	7,9	43	7,6	
Ntomba	8	7,9	43	7,6	
Ubangi	6	5,9	40	7,1	
TOTAL	101	100	561	100	
	SOURCE : GUTU KIA ZIMI				

Table n*25; Source: Gutu Kia Zimi (2020)

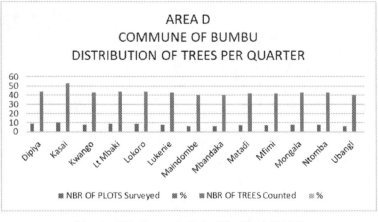

Chart n*20; Source: Gutu Kia Zimi (2020)

QUARTERS	NBR OF PLOTS Surveyed	%	NBR OF TREES Counted	%
AREA D				
DISTRIBUTION OF TREES PER QUARTER				
COMMUNE OF KIMBANSEKE				
Bahumbu	12	2,3	65	2,3
Bamluwu	10	1,9	60	2,1
Batumona	8	1,6	58	2
Bikuku	11	2,1	61	2,1
Biyela	10	1,9	60	2,1
Boma	13	2,5	66	2,3
Disasi	10	1,9	60	2,1
17 Mai	9	1,8	59	2,1
Esanga	10	1,9	60	2,1
Kabila	13	2,5	66	2,3
Kakudji	11	2,1	61	2,1
Kamba Mulumba	11	2,1	61	2,1
Kamboko	10	1,9	60	2,1
Kasa Vubu	12	2,3	65	2,3
Kayolo	12	2,3	65	2,3
Kikimi	10	1,9	60	2,1
Kimbunda	11	2,1	61	2,1
Kisangani	13	2,5	66	2,3
Kisantu	12	2,3	65	2,3
Kutu	11	2,1	61	2,1
Lueba	9	1,8	59	2,1
Mabinda	10	1,9	60	2,1
Malonda	12	2,3	65	2,3
Mangana	11	2,1	61	2,1
Maviokele	13	2,5	66	2,3
Mayengele	12	2,3	65	2,3
Mbemba mfundu	9	1,8	59	2,1
Mbuala	9	1,8	59	2,1
Mfumu nkento	15	2,9	71	2,5
Mikondo	15	2,9	71	2,5
Mokali	14	2,7	69	2,4
Mulie	12	2,3	65	2,3
Munkonda	10	1,9	60	2,1
Ngamazita	13	2,5	66	2,3
Ngamayama	10	1,9	60	2,1
Ngampani	13	2,5	66	2,3
Ngandu	10	1,9	60	2,1
Ngiesi	8	1,6	58	2
Nsanga	10	1,9	60	2,1
Nsumabua	11	2,1	61	2,1
Pandanzila	10	1,9	60	2,1
Pierre Fokom	11	2,1	61	2,1
Révolution	13	2,5	66	2,3
Sakombi	10	1,9	60	2,1
Salongo	12	2,3	65	2,3
Way way	12	2,3	65	2,3
TOTAL	514	100	2878	100
SOURCE : GUTU KIA ZIMI				

Table n*26; Source: Gutu Kia Zimi (2020)

	AREA D				
	DISTRIBUTION OF TREES PER QUARTER				
	COMMUNE OF NGABA				
QUARTERS	NBR OF PLOTS	%	NBR OF TREES	%	
	Surveyed		Counted		
Baobab	36	17	105	16,7	
Bulambemba	35	16,5	103	16,3	
Luyi	34	16	102	16,2	
Mateba	34	16	102	16,2	
Mukulwa	36	17	105	16,7	
Mpila	37	17,5	113	17,9	
TOTAL	212	100	630	100	
	SOURCE : GUTU KIA ZIMI				

Table n*27; Source: Gutu Kia Zimi (2020)

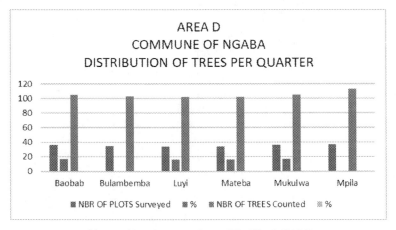

Chart n*21; Source: Gutu Kia Zimi (2020)

AREA D				
DISTRIBUTION OF TREES PER QUARTER				
COMMUNE OF NGIRI NGIRI				
QUARTERS	NBR OF PLOTS	%	NBR OF TREES	%
	Surveyed		Counted	
Assossa	14	12,8	76	12,4
Diangienda	14	12,8	76	12,4
Diomi	12	11	75	12,3
Elengesa	13	11,9	74	12,1
Khartoum	14	12,8	76	12,4
24 Novembre	14	12,8	76	12,4
Peti Peti	12	11	75	12,3
Saio	16	14,7	83	13,6
TOTAL	109	100	611	100
SOURCE : GUTU KIA ZIMI				

Table n*28; Source: Gutu Kia Zimi (2020)

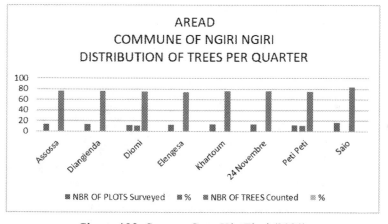

Chart n*22; Source: Gutu Kia Zimi (2020)

	AREA D				
	DISTRIBUTION OF TREES PER QUARTER				
	COMMUNE OF KASA VUBU				
QUARTERS	NBR OF PLOTS	%	NBR OF TREES	%	
	Surveyed		Counted		
Anc. Combattants	16	15,7	92	14,9	
Assossa	13	12,7	86	13,9	
Katanga	14	13,7	87	14,1	
Lodja	15	14,7	88	14,2	
Lubumbashi	15	14,7	88	14,2	
ONL	13	12,7	86	13,9	
Salongo	16	15,7	92	14,9	
TOTAL	102	100	619	100	
SOURCE : GUTU KIA ZIMI					

Table n*29; Source: Gutu Kia Zimi (2020)

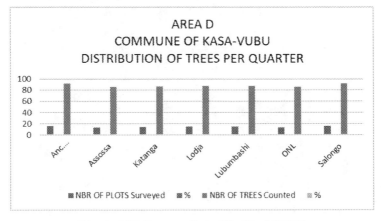

Chart n*23; Source: Gutu Kia Zimi (2020)

QUARTERS	AREA E DISTRIBUTION OF TREES PER QUARTER COMMUNE OF MALUKU			
	NBR OF PLOTS Surveyed	%	NBR OF TREES Counted	%
Bu	5	4,4	40	5
Dumi	7	6,1	42	5,3
Kikimi	6	5,3	41	5,1
Kimpoko	6	5,3	41	5,1
Kingakati	8	7	53	6,5
Kinguru	4	3,5	39	4,9
Kinzono	5	4,4	40	5
Maluku	5	4,4	40	5
Maindombe	7	6,1	42	5,3
Mangengenge	6	5,3	41	5,1
Mbankana	7	6,1	42	5,3
Menkao	6	5,3	41	5,1
Monaco	6	5,3	41	5,1
Mongata	6	5,3	41	5,1
Mwe	4	3,5	39	4,9
Ngana	8	7	52	6,5
Nguma	7	6,1	42	5,3
Yosso	5	4,4	40	5
You	6	5,3	41	5,1
TOTAL	114	100	798	100
SOURCE : GUTU KIA ZIMI				

Table n*30; Source: Gutu Kia Zimi (2020)

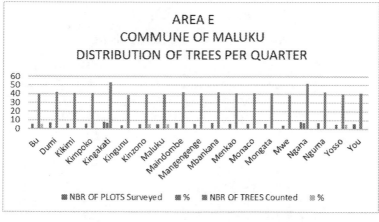

Chart n*24; Source: Gutu Kia Zimi (2020)

QUARTERS	AREA E DISTRIBUTION OF TREES PER QUARTER COMMUNE OF NSELE			
	NBR OF PLOTS Surveyed	%	NBR OF TREES Counted	%
Badara	13	4,2	94	3,8
Bahumbu I	11	3,6	92	3,7
Bahumbu II	12	3,9	93	3,7
Bibwa I	12	3,9	93	3,7
Bibwa II	13	4,2	94	3,8
Buma	10	3,2	90	3,6
Dingi Dingi	11	3,6	92	3,7
Kikimi	12	3,9	93	3,7
Domaine	13	4,2	94	3,8
Kindobo	12	3,9	93	3,7
Maba	14	4,5	98	3,9
Mangenge	7	2,3	85	3,4
Mibu	8	2,6	84	3,4
Mikala I	14	4,5	98	3,9
Mikala II	11	3,6	92	3,7
Mikondo	9	2,9	87	3,5
Mikonga I	13	4,2	94	3,8
Mikonga II	12	3,9	93	3,7
Mobanse	11	3,6	92	3,7
Mpasa I	10	3,2	90	3,6
Mpasa II	13	4,2	94	3,8
Munke	12	3,9	93	3,7
ngampama	11	3,6	92	3,7
Ngina	11	3,6	92	3,7
Pecheurs	10	3,2	90	3,6
sicotra	12	3,9	93	3,7
Tala ngai	11	3,6	92	3,7
TOTAL	308	100	2487	100
SOURCE : GUTU KIA ZIMI				

Table n*31; Source: Gutu Kia Zimi (2020)

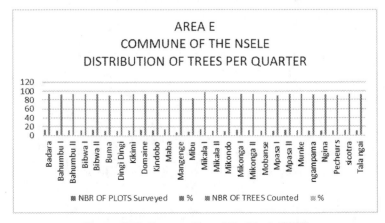

Chart n*25; Source: Gutu Kia Zimi (2020)

AREA E				
DISTRIBUTION OF TREES PER QUARTER				
COMMUNE OF MONT NGAFULA				
QUARTERS	NBR OF PLOTS Surveyed	%	NBR OF TREE Counted	%
CPA Mushie	52	4,6	61	2
Kimbondo	56	5	80	2,7
Kimbuala	59	5,3	95	3,2
Kimwenza	50	4,5	69	2,3
Kindele	41	3,7	47	1,6
Lutendele	72	6,4	337	11,3
Maman Mobutu	35	3,1	55	1,8
Maman Yemo	39	3,5	60	2
Masanga Mbila	49	4,4	68	2,3
Masumu	58	5,2	91	3,5
Matadi kibala	69	6,1	310	10,4
Matadi mayo	61	5,4	126	4,2
Mazamba	48	4,3	70	2,3
Mbuki	56	5	97	3,3
Mitendi	63	5,6	247	8,3
Musangu	73	6,5	404	13,5
Ndjili Kilambu	68	6,1	301	10,1
Ngansele	71	6,3	320	10,7
Plateau	56	5	80	2,7
Vunda Manenga	47	4,2	65	2,2
TOTAL	1123	100	2983	100
SOURCE : GUTU KIA ZIMI				

Table n*32; Source: Gutu Kia Zimi (2020)

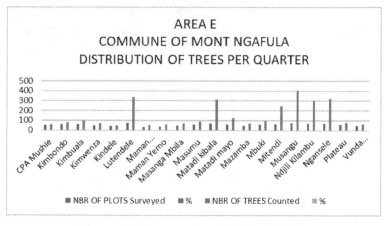

Chart n*26; Source: Gutu Kia Zimi (2020)

SYNTHETIC TABLE OF SURVEY RESULTS
DISTRIBUTION OF TREES BY STUDY AREA AND COMMUNES

Area A	Communes	POPULATION*	%	Nbr of Plots	%	Nbr of Trees	%
	Gombe	46 733	0.4	216	3	513	2
	Limete	502 549	4.7	700	9.6	1820	7.1
	Ngaliema	1 070 669	10	1500	20.5	2510	9.8
Total	3	1 619 951	15.1	2416	33.1	4843	18.9
Area B	Communes			Nbr of Plots		Nbr of Trees	
	Kinshasa	176 591	1.6	75	1	215	0.8
	Lingwala	122 049	1.1	61	0.8	213	0.8
	Barumbu	158 203	1.5	63	0.9	240	0.9
	Kintambo	169 074	1.6	200	2.7	756	3
Total	4	625 917	5.8	399	5.4	1424	5.5
Area C	Communes			Nbr of Plots		Nbr of Trees	
	Lemba	519 361	4.8	300	4.1	745	2.9
	Matete	411 229	3.8	94	1.3	446	1.7
	Kalamu	357 847	3.3	289	4	752	2.9
	Bandalungwa	316 002	2.9	150	2.1	632	2.5
Total	4	1 604 439	15	833	11.5	2575	10
Area D	Communes			Nbr of Plots		Nbr of Trees	
	Masina	1 051 048	9.8	410	5.6	1897	7.4
	Kisenso	602 024	5.6	103	1.4	451	1.8
	Selembao	530 414	4.9	110	1.5	1002	4
	Makala	301 293	2.8	95	1.3	809	3.2
	Ndjili	538 497	5	355	4.9	1013	4
	Bumbu	510 331	4.8	101	1.4	561	2.2
	Kimbanseke	1 460 402	13.6	514	7	2878	11.3
	Ngaba	255 331	2.4	212	2.9	630	2.5
	Ngiri-Ngiri	198 814	1.9	109	1.5	611	2.4
	Kasa-Vubu	163 594	1.5	102	1.4	619	2.4
Total	10	5 611 748	52.3	2111	28.9	10471	41.2
Area E	Communes			Nbr of Plots		Nbr of Trees	
	Maluku	517 184	4.8	114	1.6	798	3.1
	Nsele	367 654	3.4	308	4.2	2487	9.7
	Mont Ngafula	379 831	3.5	1123	15.4	2983	11.7
Total	3	1 264 669	11.8	1545	21.2	6268	24.5
Total General	24	10 726 724	100	7304	100	25581	100

*Population data are derived from the 2012 population projection of LEON DE SAINT MOULIN

SOURCE : Gutu Kia Zimi

Table n*33; Source: Gutu Kia Zimi (2020)

SYNTHETIC TABLE OF THE POPULATION OF THE MUNICIPALITIES OF KINSHASA

N°	Communes	SUP/Km₂	%	Population*	%	Density	Plots	%	Quarters	%	Streets	%
1	BANDALUNGWA	6,82	0,07	316 002	2,9	46 335	8.404	1,4	8	2,2	233	1,6
2	BARUMBU	4,72	0,05	158 203	1,5	33 518	4.759	0,8	9	2,5	112	0,8
3	BUMBU	5,30	0,05	510 331	4,8	96 289	11.286	1,9	13	3,6	274	1,9
4	GOMBE	29,33	0,29	46 733	0,4	1593	2.994	0,5	10	2,7	200	1,4
5	KALAMU	6,64	0,07	357 847	3,3	53 892	11.801	2	18	4,9	409	2,8
6	KASA-VUBU	5,05	0,05	163 594	1,5	32 395	4.468	0,8	7	1,9	115	0,8
7	KIMBANSEKE	237,78	2,39	1 460 402	13,6	6 141	93.531	15,7	46	12,6	1.666	11,6
8	KINSHASA	2,87	0,03	176 591	1,6	61 530	4.255	0,7	7	1,9	80	0,6
9	KINTAMBO	2,72	0,03	169 074	1,6	62 160	5.055	0,8	8	2,2	154	1,1
10	KISENSO	16,6	0,17	602 024	5,6	36 267	20.815	3,5	17	4,7	610	4,2
11	LEMBA	23,7	0,24	519 361	4,8	21914	18.628	3,1	15	4,1	440	3,1
12	LIMETE	67,6	0,68	502 549	4,7	7434	20.329	3,4	14	3,8	564	3,9
13	LINGWALA	2,88	0,03	122 049	1,1	42378	3.585	0,6	9	2,5	69	0,5
14	MAKALA	5,6	0,06	301293	2,8	53802	12.947	2,2	18	4,9	242	1,7
15	MALUKU	7948,8	79,77	517 184	4,8	65	17.888	3	19	5,2	1.281	8,9
16	MASINA	69,93	0,7	1 051 048	9,8	15030	35.922	6	21	5,8	636	4,4
17	MATETE	4,88	0,05	411 229	3,8	84268	10.774	1,8	13	3,6	263	1,8
18	MONT NGAFULA	358,92	3,6	379 831	3,5	1058	70.682	11,9	20	5,5	1.784	12,4
19	NDJILI	11,4	0,11	538 497	5	47237	17.127	2,9	13	3,6	304	2,1
20	NGABA	4,00	0,04	255 331	2,4	63833	5.674	1	6	1,6	114	0,8
21	NGALIEMA	224,3	2,26	1 070 669	10	4773	97.698	16,4	21	5,8	2.211	15,4
22	NGIRI NGIRI	3,4	0,03	198 814	1,9	58475	5.499	0,9	8	2,2	105	0,7
23	NSELE	898,79	9,02	367 654	3,4	409	84.266	14,2	27	7,4	1.987	13,8
24	SELEMBAO	23,18	0,23	530 414	4,9	22882	26.682	4,5	18	4,9	536	3,7
	TOTAL	9965,21	100	10 726 725	100	1076	595.069	100	365	100	14.389	100

*Data based on 2012 population projection of LEON DE SAINT MOULIN

Source : Gutu Kia Zimi

Table n*34; Source: Gutu Kia Zimi (2020)

N*	COMMUNES	X(Plots)	Y(Trees)	X²	Y²	XY
	ESTIMATE NUMBER OF TREES IN THE PLOTS					
	REGRESSION LINE : Y = ax+b					
1	Gombe	216	513	46,656	263,169	110808
2	Limete	700	1820	490,000	3,312,400	1274000
3	Ngaliema	1500	2510	2,250,000	6,300,100	3765000
4	Kinshasa	75	215	5,625	46,225	16125
5	Lingwala	61	213	3,721	45,369	12993
6	Barumbu	63	240	3,969	57,600	15120
7	Kintambo	200	756	40,000	571,536	151200
8	Lemba	300	745	90,000	555,025	223500
9	Matete	94	446	8,836	198,916	41924
10	Kalamu	289	752	83,521	565,504	217328
11	Bandalungwa	150	632	22,500	399,424	94800
12	Masina	410	1897	168,100	3,598,609	777770
13	Kisenso	103	451	10,609	203,401	46453
14	Selembao	110	1002	12,100	1,004,004	110220
15	Makala	95	809	9,025	654,481	76855
16	Ndjili	355	1013	126,025	1,026,169	359615
17	Bumbu	101	561	10,201	314,721	56661
18	Kimbanseke	514	2878	264,196	8,282,884	1479292
19	Ngaba	212	630	44,944	396,900	133560
20	Ngiri-Ngiri	109	611	11,881	373,321	66599
21	Kasa-Vubu	102	619	10,404	383,161	63138
22	Maluku	114	798	12,996	636,804	90972
23	Nsele	308	2487	94,864	6,185,169	765996
24	Mont Ngafula	1123	2983	1,261,129	8,898,289	3349909
	TOTAL	**7304**	**25581**	**430,581**	**44273181**	**3819514**
	Average	304.33333	1065.88			

Source : Gutu Kia Zimi

Correlation coefficient r = 0.6

Table n*35; Source: Gutu Kia Zimi (2020)

The correlation coefficient (r = 0.6) indicates a very strong relationship between the number of trees and the plots. This shows that the increasing or decreasing evolution of shrub vegetation in residential plots is a function of the conditions in the plots. It can be deduced that the number of trees is conditioned by the development of the plots. Some plots do not provide space for planting trees, and some plot owners are unwilling to plant trees in their plots.

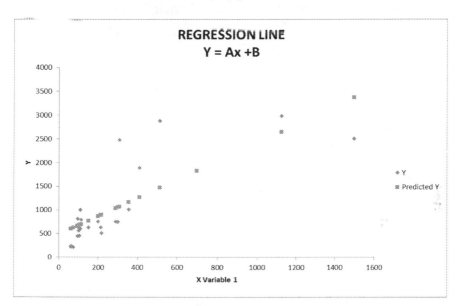

Chart n*28; Source: Gutu Kia Zimi (2020)

$$A = 2,2 \; ; b = 396,4$$
$$Y = 2,2x + 396,4$$

The estimate of shrub vegetation by the regression line ($Y = 2.2x + 396.4$) shows us overall a positive evolution of shrub vegetation in the residential plots of Kinshasa. However, this observation must be understood in a different way. Although overall, the trend is towards positive development, it will be necessary to give a selective interpretation, if it is on the one hand, in the plots of the districts of the old communes or in the plots of the peripheral districts, on the other go. In fact, the shrub vegetation is increasing in the plots of the outlying neighborhoods while it is decreasing and in severe decline in the plots of the neighborhoods of the former municipalities.

III. ANALYSIS OF THE SURVEY RESULTS

During the survey, we counted 25,581 trees, which represent 51 tree species in 7,304 plots. From the perspective of the sample of 7,304 plots, this represents an overall average of 25,581 trees per plot and an average of:

- 18.9% of trees for area A;
- 5.5% of trees for area B;
- 10.0% of trees for area C;
- 41.2% of trees for area D;
- 24.5% of trees for area E.

Photo GKZ

IV. DISTRIBUTION OF TREES BY SPECIES

According to our survey, the most common species of tree in the flora of the neighborhoods of the municipalities of Kinshasa is overall the mango tree (*Mangifera Indica*), the oil palm (*Elaeis guineensis*), the papaya tree (*Carica papaya*); avocado (*Persea Americana*), safout (*Dacryodes Edulis*), etc. Analysis of these results leads us to the following findings: it is a disparate flora with 51 species, dominated mainly by fruit trees. The predominance of mango trees is undoubtedly justified by its ecology, namely a climate with a rainfall of 1,000-1,200 mm during the rainy season and 50-60 mm during the dry season to induce flowering at a variable average temperature of 24- 27 * C in the rainy season and over 35 * C in the dry season. The mango tree, on the other hand, prefers a sandy clay soil with a PH close to 6. Kinshasa soil meets this requirement for both mango and palm trees, which also requires a soil with a clay content of 35 to develop. % -40% with a PH of 4-5. Another argument that we dare to put forward to justify the predominance of oil palms is undoubtedly the eating habits of the population.

In fact, the oil palm provides palm nuts, which are widely used in Congolese cuisine, especially in the preparation of "MOAMBE" or "MOSAKA". A study by Marc Pain (1979) in the communes of Kintambo and Gombe also revealed the predominance of palm trees (23.1%) in the commune of Kintambo, and 53.1% in the commune of Gombe; followed by avocado trees 18.2% and 16.98% respectively, mango trees 18.2% and 9.7%, and coconut trees (14.6% and 5.15%)[58]. The author also confirms that: "Fruit trees are indeed predominant in" African "neighborhoods: palm trees, coconut palms, mango trees and avocado trees are in the majority (75% in total), but we also meet many papaya trees, bananas, and safoutiers. Orange and lemon trees grow best on hills with sandy clay soil, while coconut, avocado and mango trees do well on sands of the plain. Palm trees are also more

---

[58] MARC PAIN, op. cit., p.23

beautiful in hills than on terraces where the trees can grow tall but produce little and dry out from a certain size ".

Photo GKZ

René de Maximy (1984) also provides us with the following explanation of the predominance of fruit trees in the urban vegetation of Kinshasa: "To avoid monotony in the development of neighborhoods, the colonizer favored the rapid growth of mainly fruit trees, also flamboyant ones. It has also and above all favored the plantations of coconut palms and Elaeis (palm trees). This last only tree protected by law, because it is a tree of industrial and domestic interest. The palm nut supplies all the palm oil used in local dishes. Therefore, the felling of a palm tree (Elaeis guineensis) was punishable by a fine "[59].

Mukania Bulembu (1986)[60] in another study carried out in the Petro-Congo district in the Commune of Masina, also reveals that the most cultivated plants in this district are fruit plants (36%)

[59] RENE DE MAXIMY, Kinshasa, Ville en suspens, Ed. Orstom, 1984, p.278
[60] MUKANIA BULEMBUE, L'élément végétal dans les parcelles résidentielles du Quartier Petro-Congo, Mémoire de 3*cycle Diplôme Spécial en Gestion de l'Environnement, UNIKIN/ Fac.Sciences, Document Inédit, 1986.

and vegetables (24%), even outside plots, it is these plants that are generally represented. The dominant trees in the flora of this district are: Mango tree (9.9%), Avocado trees (8.9%), Oil palm (6.7%), False Manioc (5.2%), Papaya (5, 2%), Sugar Cane (4.5%), Banana (3.5%), Cœur de Boeuf (2.3%), Guava (2.3%), Jam (2.3%), Lemon (2.2%), Coconut tree (1.7%), Safout tree (1.6%), Orange tree (0.2%), Cotton tree (0.1%), Mandarin tree (0.1%), Bamboo (0, 1%), Maracuja (0.04%), Badamier (0.04%), Red Apple (0.04%).

Photo GKZ

V. SURVEY OF NUMBER TREE SPECIES

The table below (Tree species survey) shows us the inventory of tree species counted in the residential plots in the districts of the municipalities surveyed. These are mainly tree species because we have deliberately excluded herbaceous and other species. It is important to point out that green spaces have disappeared in Kinshasa. These spaces were sold to wealthy national or foreign owners in complicity with the public authority to erect buildings for rental homes, businesses and others. If we are talking about the urban vegetation of Kinshasa, it is mainly the vegetation in the residential plots. This urban vegetation exists by the personal will of the owners of these plots, because there is no urban reforestation policy, which obliges the owners to plant trees in their plots. Paradoxical as it may seem, when it comes to cutting down a tree, the law requires the owner to obtain authorization from the environmental department of his municipality. Currently, the future of this urban vegetation is very worrying given the demographic pressure, which is exerted on the urban space of Kinshasa.

Photo GKZ

With the population growth, the owners of the plots prefer for lucrative reasons to build dwellings in the spaces formerly occupied by trees in their plots. There are also other constraints such as poverty, the size of households which continues to swell, the housing and housing crisis, etc. In addition, it is not enough only to plant the trees, they will also have to be maintained. There are diseases, which attack or destroy urban vegetation. Unfortunately, there is no service in Kinshasa for the spreading of insecticides or pesticides in the city to fight against pest species. We discovered during the investigation trees attacked or harboring multiple pests. These are sucking insects on the bark, leaf sucking insects, defoliators and leaf miners, galligens on leaves and stems, trunk and stalk borers (very common in trees in old quarters. communes of Kinshasa), bark beetles and spider mites. According to Steven D. Frank (2019), cities have dozens of species of range trees, each harboring multiple insect arthropod pests[61].

Photo GKZ

The table n*36 below shows us the inventory of tree species counted in the residential plots in the districts of the municipalities surveyed:

[61] STEVEN D. FRANK, A survey of key arthropod pests on common southeastern street trees, Arboriculture & urban forestry 45, Scientific Journal of the International Society of Arboriculture, Volume 45, N*5, September 2019, p.165, 2019

SURVEY OF TREE SPECIES COUNTED
Acacia Airiculifornis (Acacia)
Albizia lebbek benth (Albizia)
Adinsonia digitala (Baobab)
Acacia airiculifornis A.CUM. ex Benth. Acacia (Acacia)
Annona reticulata L. (Cœur de bœuf)
Artocarpus heterophyllus(Jaquier)
Artocarpus incisa Lf (Arbre à pain)
Averrhoa cararrbola L. (Caramolier) pakapaka
Buchholzia ITUCraptrylla Pax
Cassia siarrmea Lam (Cassier,conefier)
Carica papaya (Papayer)
Citrus aurantium (Oranger)
Citrus limon (L.) Burm (Citronier)
Citrus reticula Blanco (Mandarinier)
Citrus raxirra (Burm) Merr (Parrplenoussier)
Cupressus sp L. (Cyprès)
Cocos Nucifera (Cocotier)
Croton rubanga Muell. Arg (Croton rrubanga
Dacryodes edilis (G. Don) (Safautier)
Delonix regia (Flamboyant)
Diospyras heterotricha (B.L)
Dracaena nitens Welw.ex Bak.
Dracaena sp (Dragonier)
Elaeis guineensis Jacq (Palmier)
Eucalpyptus citriodara Hook
Eucalpyptus sp (Eucalyptus)
Eugenia ralaccensis (Pommier rouge)
Eugenia rosea D.C
Eugenia gambos L. (Pommier Rose)
Euphorbia tirucalli L. (Cactus)
Ficus sp (Figuier)
Flacourtia ramantchi L'Her (Prunier de Madagascar)
Garcinia rangastana L.(Mangoustanier)
Hura crepitans L
Jatropha circas L. (Pingnon dinde)
Lannea antiscorbutica
Lannea welwitschii (Hiern)
Leucena leucocephala (Lam) de Wit (Leucaena)
Mangifera Indica (Manguier)
Millettia laurentti De Wild (Wenge, Bois noir)
Millettia versicolor Welw.
Marinda lucica Benth (Maringa)
Musa Sinensis (Bananier)
Musanga cecropioides R.Br. (Parassolier)
Passiflora edilis (Maracuja)
Persea americana Mill (Avocatier)
Psidium guajava L. (Goyavier)
Ravenala madagascariensis (Arbre du voyageur)
Solarum
Spondias cytherea Sonn
Sterculia sp
Symphonia globulifera L. f.
Terminalia catappa L. (Badamier)
Vernonia amygdacina Del (Vernonie commune)
Zantedeschia ethiopica
TOTAL : 54 TREE SPECIES

Table n*36, Source: Gutu Kia Zimi (2020)

DISTRIBUTION OF TREE SPECIES PER COMMUNE								
STUDY AREA A								
TREE SPECIES	BOMBE	%	LIMETE	%	NGALIEMA	%	TOTAL	%
Acacia Auriculiformis (Acacia)	55	10,7	47	2,6	26	1	128	2,6
Albizia lebbek berth (Albizia)	37	7,2	21	1,2	24	1	82	1,7
Adansonia digitala (Baobab)	5	1			2	0,1	7	0,1
Annona reticulata L. (Cœur de bœuf)			12	0,7	21	0,8	33	0,7
Artrnrnrpux heterophyllus (Jacquier)			6	0,3	15	0,6	21	0,4
Artocarpus incisa Lf (Arbre à pain)	11	2,1	13	0,7	07	1,6	61	1,3
Averrhoa carambola L. (Carambolier) Pakapaka			21	1,2	31	1,2	52	1,1
Buchholzia macrophylia Pax			12	0,7	18	0,7	30	0,6
Cassia siammea Lam (Cassier, caréfier)			13	0,7	22	0,9	35	0,7
Carica papaya (Papayer)	12	2,3	138	7,6	149	5,9	299	6,2
Cocos Nucifera (Cocotier)	3	0,6	57	3,1	29	1,2	89	1,8
Citrus aurantium (Oranger)			15	0,8	12	0,5	27	0,6
Citrus limon (L.) Burm (Citronier)	2	0,4	14	0,8	11	0,4	27	0,6
Citrus reticula Bianco (Mandarinier)					5	0,2	5	0,1
Citrus maxima (Burm.) Merr (Pamplemoussier)			13	0,7	13	0,5	26	0,5
Cupressus sp L. (Cyprès)	2	0,4	3	0,2	21	0,8	26	0,5
Croton mubango Muell. Arg (Croton mubango)					16	0,6	16	0,3
Dacryodes edulis (G. Don) (Saf outier)			107	5,9	117	4,7	224	4,6
Delonix regia (Flamboyant)	36	7	56	3,1	14	0,6	106	2,2
Diospyros heterotricha (B.L)	6	1,2	15	0,8	16	0,6	37	0,8
Dracaena nitens Welw.ex Bak.	3	0,6	12	0,7	21	0,8	36	0,7
Dracaena sp (Dragonier)			17	0,9	26	1	43	0,9
Elaeis guineensis Jacq (Palmier)	26	5,1	215	11,8	312	12,4	553	11
Eucalpyptus sp (Eucalyptus)	2	0,4	16	0,9	16	0,6	34	0,7
Eugenia gambos L. (Pommier Rose)	12	2,3	2	0,1	42	1,7	56	1,2
Euphorbia tirucalli L. (Cactus)			3	0,2	3	0,1	6	0,1
Ficus sp (Figuier)			5	0,3	11	0,4	16	0,3
Flacourtia ramontchi L'Hér (Prunier de Madagascar)	1	0,2	29	1,6	26	1	56	1,2
Garcinia mangostana L.(Mangoustanier)	1	0,2					1	0
Hibiscus rosa sinensis	36	7	51	2,8	34	1,4	121	2,5
Hura crepitans L.	7	1,4	11	0,6	17	0,7	35	0,7
Jatropha curcas L. (Pingnon d'inde)	2	0,4	13	0,7	18	0,7	33	0,7
Lannea antiscorbutica	2	0,4	11	0,6	19	0,8	32	0,7
Lannea welwitschii (Hiern)	1	0,2	14	0,8	10	0,4	25	0,5
Leucaena leucocephala (Lam.) de Wit (Leucaena)	2	0,4	23	1,3	22	0,9	47	1
Mangifera Indica (Manguier)	27	5,3	298	16,4	402	16	727	15
Milletia laurentti De Wild (Wenge, Bois noir)	28	5,5	12		13		53	1,1
Milletia versicolor Welw.	6	1,2	14	0,8	32	1,3	52	1,1
Morinda lucida Benth (Moringa)	3	0,6	16	0,9	56	2,2	75	1,5
Musa Sinesis (Bananier)	2	0,4	96	5,3	109	4,3	207	4,3
Musanga cecropioides R.Br. (Parasolier)			24	1,3	34	1,4	58	1,2
Passiflora edulis (Maracuja)			22	1,2	51	2	73	1,5
Persea americana Mill (Avocatier)	4	0,8	167	9,2	198	7,9	369	7,6
Psidium guajava L. (Goyavier)					21	0,8	21	0,4
Ravensia madagascariensis (Arbre du voyageur)	25	4,9	23	1,3	66	2,6	114	2,4
Solanum	14	2,7	27	1,5	37	1,5	78	1,6
Spondias cytherea Sonn	18	3,5	14	0,8	43	1,7	75	1,5
Sterculia sp	15	2,9	23	1,3	38	1,5	76	1,6
Symphonia globulifera L. f.	21	4	17	0,9	39	1,6	77	1,6
Terminalia catappa L. (Badamier)	36	7	59	3,2	99	3,9	194	4
Vernonia amygdacina Del (Vernonie commune)	23	4,4	7	0,4	43	1,7	73	1,5
Zantedeschia ethiopica	27	5,3	16	0,9	53	2,1	96	2
Divers								
TOTAL	513	100	1820	100	2510	100	4843	

Source : Gutu Kia Zimi

Table n*37; Source: Gutu Kia Zimi (2020)

DISTRIBUTION OF TREE SPECIES PER COMMUNE
STUDY AREA B

TREE SPECIES	KIN	%	LIN	%	BAR	%	KINT	%	TOTAL	%
Acacia Auriculiformis (Acacia)	2	0.9	6	2.8					8	3.7
Albizia lebbek benth (Albizia)										
Adansonia digitala (Baobab)	1	0.5	4	1.9	1	0.4	9	1.2	15	4
Annona reticulata L. (Cœur de bœuf)					2	0.8	10	1.3	12	2.1
Artocarpus heterophyllus (Jacquier)					1	0.4	9	1.2	10	1.6
Artocarpus incisa Lf (Arbre à pain)	4	1.9					3	0.4	7	2.3
Averrhoa carambola L. (Carambolier) pakapaka	3	1.4			6	2.5			9	3.9
Buchholzia macrophylla Pax							9	1.2	9	1.2
Carica papaya (Papayer)	17	7.9	18	8.5	21	8.8	19	2.5	75	27.7
Cocos Nucifera (Cocotier)	3	1.4	2	0.9	16	6.7	9	1.2	30	10.2
Citrus Aurantium (Oranger)			1	0.5	9	3.8	6	0.8	16	5.1
Citrus limon (L.) Burm (Citronier)			3	1.4	7	2.9	7	0.9	17	5.2
Citrus reticula Blanco (Mandarinier)					2	0.8			2	0.8
Citrus maxima (Burm.) Merr (Pamplemoussier)					1	0.4	4	0.5	5	0.9
Dacryodes edulis (G. Don) (Safoutier)	1	0.5	2	0.9	8	3.3	17	2.2	28	6.9
Delonix regia (Flamboyant)	5	2.3	6	2.8	3	1.3	9	1.2	23	10.6
Elaeis guineensis Jacq (Palmier)	5	2.3	15	7	14	5.8	18	2.4	42	17.5
Eugenia malaccensis (Pommier rouge)	11	5.1	5	2.3	12	5			28	12.4
Euphorbia tirucalli L. (Cactus)							5	0.7	5	0.7
Flacourtia ramontchi L'Hér (Prunier de Madagascar)	7	3.3							7	3.3
Garcinia mangostana L.(Mangoustanier)							10	1.3	10	1.3
Hibiscus rosa sinensis	19	8.8	15	7	15	6.3	20	2.6	69	24.7
Lannea antiscorbutica	6	2.8			2	0.8			8	3.6
Leucena leucocephala (Lam.) de Wit (Leucaena)	2	0.9								0.9
Mangifera Indica (Manguier)	13	6	38	17.8	35	14.6	285	37.7	371	76.1
Millettia laurentti De Wild (Wenge, Bois noir)					2	0.8	28	3.7	30	4.5
Morinda lucida Benth (Moringa)	14	6.5	16	7.5	13	5.4	51	6.7	94	26.1
Musa Sinensis (Bananier)	7	3.3	5	2.3	9	3.8	45	6	66	15.4
Musanga cecropioides R.Br. (Parassolier)			1	0.5	1	0.4	5	0.7	7	1.6
Passiflora edulis (Maracuja)	3	1.4	7	3.3			25	3.3	35	8
Persea americana Mill (Avocatier)	9	4.2	6	2.8	23	9.6	120	15.9	159	32.5
Psidium guajava L. (Gayavier)					10	4.2	18	2.4	28	6.6
Ravenala madagascariensis (Arbre du voyageur)	11	5.1	15	7	8	3.3			34	15.4
Solanum	8	3.7	7	3.3	2	0.8			17	7.8
Spondias cytherea Sonn	7	3.3	4	1.9					11	5.2
Sterculia sp	9	4.2	9	4.2	2	0.8			20	9.2
Symphonia globulifera L. f.	7	3.3	3	1.4	1	0.4			11	5.1
Terminalia catappa L. (Badamier)	16	7.4	14	6.6	12	5	15	2	42	21
Vernonia amygdacina Del (Vernonie commune)	9	4.2							9	4.2
Zantedeschia ethiopica	16	7.4	11	5.2	2	0.8			29	13.4
TOTAL	215	100	213	100	240	100	756	100	1424	

Source : Gutu Kia Zimi

Table n*38; Source: Gutu Kia Zimi (2020)

DISTRIBUTION OF TREE SPECIES PER COMMUNE								
STUDY AREA C								
TREE SPECIES	LEM	%	MAT	%	KAL	%	BAN	%
Adansonia digitala (Baobab)	15	2	5	1,1	10	1,3	10	1,6
Annona reticulata L. (Cœur de bœuf)	8	1,1	6	1,3	6	0,8	7	1,1
Artocarpus heterophyllus (Jacquier)	5	0,7	4	0,9	1	0,1	3	0,5
Averrhoa carambola L. (Carambolier) pakapaka	7	0,9	12	2,7	14	1,9	14	2,2
Cassia siammea Lam (Cassier, canéfier)					2	0,3		
Carica papaya (Papayer)	27	3,6	29	6,5	17	2,3	24	3,8
Cocos Nucifera (Cocotier)	19	2,6	7	1,6	8	1,1	9	1,4
Citrus aurantium (Oranger)	14	1,9	8	1,8	6	0,8	12	1,9
Citrus limon (L.) Burm (Citronier)	17	2,3	11	2,5	9	1,2	9	1,4
Citrus reticula Blanco (Mandarinier)	10	1,3	8	1,8	6	0,8	7	1,1
Citrus maxima (Burm.) Merr (Pamplemoussier)	8	1,1					5	0,8
Dacryodes edulis (G. Don) (Safoutier)	22	3	26	5,8	10	1,3	22	3,5
Delonix regia (Flamboyant)	6	0,8			5	0,7	4	0,6
Elaeis guineensis Jacq (Palmier)	31	4,2	27	6,1	35	4,7	34	5,4
Eucalpyptus sp (Eucalyptus)	4	0,5						
Eugenia malaccensis (Pommier rouge)	6	0,8	12	2,7	3	0,4	2	0,3
Eugenia gambos L. (Pommier Rose)	5	0,7					3	0,5
Ficus sp (Figuier)			9	2				
Garcinia mangostana L.(Mangoustanier)	4	0,5	8	1,8			4	0,6
Hibiscus rosa sinensis	36	4,8			35	4,7	48	7,6
Mangifera Indica (Manguier)	252	33,8	134	30	281	37,4	201	31,8
Millettia laurentti De Wild (Wenge, Bois noir)	8	1,1	10	2,2			7	1,1
Millettia versicolor Welw.					58	7,7		
Morinda lucida Benth (Moringa)	50	6,7	45	10,1	23	3,1	39	6,2
Musa Sinensis (Bananier)	34	4,6	24	5,4	34	4,5	41	6,5
Musanga cecropioides R.Br. (Parassolier)	4	0,5			10	1,3		
Passiflora edulis (Maracuja)	11	1,5	7	1,6	30	4	10	1,6
Persea americana Mill (Avocatier)	114	15,3	46	10,3	135	18	100	15,8
Psidium guajava L. (Goyavier)	10	1,3	8	1,8	6	0,8	6	0,9
Spondias cytherea Sonn	8	1,1						
Terminalia catappa L. (Badamier)	10	1,3			8	1,1	11	1,7
TOTAL	745	100	446	100	752	100	632	100
Source : Gutu Kia Zimi								

Table n*39; Source: Gutu Kia Zimi (2020)

121

DISTRIBUTION OF TREE SPECIES PER COMMUNE STUDY AREA D																			
TREE SPECIES	MAS	%	KIS	%	SEL	%	MAK	%	NDJ	%	BUM	%	KIM	%	NSAE	%	NSI	%	KAS	%
Acacia Auriculiformis (Acacia)	15	0,8					1	0,1			2	0,4	2	0,1	2	0,3			3	0,5
Albizia lebbek berth (Albizia)	7	0,4					2	0,2	3	0,3			1	0					5	0,8
Adansonia digitda (Baobab)	3	0,2			2	0,2	3	0,4	3	0,3			3	0,1	2	0,3				
Annona reticulata L. (Cœur de bœuf)	25	1,3			18	1,8	4	0,5					2	0,1					13	2,1
Artocarpus heterophyllus (Jacquier)	32	1,7	9	2	2	0,2	11	1,4	13	1,2	13	2,3	5	0,2	7	1,1	3	0,5	9	1,5
Artocarpus incisa Lf (Arbre à pain)	19	1	4	0,9	10	1	10	1,2	13	1,3	9	1,6	40	1,4	10	1,6			9	1,5
Averrhoa carambola L. (Carambolier) pakapaka	27	1,4	5	1,1	13	1,3	17	2,1	19	1,9	10	1,8	52	1,8	14	2,2	1	0,2	11	1,8
Buchhlozia macrophylia Pax	39	2,1	19	4,2	29	2,9	35	4,3	34	3,4	10	1,8	16	0,6	5	0,8	5	0,8	8	1,3
Cassia siammea Lam (Cassier, acréfier)	18	0,9			9	0,9			10	1			13	0,5	7	1,1			3	0,5
Carica papaya (Papayer)	88	4,5	31	6,9	46	4,6	78	9,6	69	6,8	40	7,1	256	8,9	46	7,1	46	7,5	67	10,8
Cocos Nucifera (Cocotier)	80	4,2	11	2,4	18	1,8	45	5,6	42	4,1	22	3,9	83	2,9	34	5,4	95	15,5	13	2,1
Citrus Limonarum (Citronnier)	38	2	23	5,1	15	1,5	21	2,6	18	1,8	12	2,1	75	2,6	11	1,7	3	0,5	2	0,3
Citrus aurantium(Oranger)	25	1,3	6	1,3	14	1,4	20	2,5	16	1,6	11	2	53	1,8	13	2,1	16	2,6	2	0,3
Citrus reticula Bianco (Mandarinier)							3	0,4					3	0,1	2	0,3				
Citrus maxima (Burn.) Merr (Pamplemoussier)	19	1	8	1,8	14	1,4	10	1,2	17	1,7	3	0,5	56	1,9	10	1,6	2	0,3		
Cupressus sp L. (Cyprès)	13	0,7			5	0,5	9	1,1	14	1,4	1	0,2	35	1,2	7	1,1	1	0,2	3	0,5
Croton mubango Mueil. Arg (Croton mubango)	30	1,6	3	0,7									14	0,5					1	0,2
Dacryodes edulis (B. Dorj) (Safoutier)	90	4,7	7	1,6	65	6,5	30	3,7	61	6	52	9,3	89	3,1	38	6			4	0,6
Delonix regia (Flamboyant)	4	0,2									8	1,4	11	0,4	3	0,5				
Diospyros heterotricha (B.L.)	5	0,3			13	1,3					3	0,5	13	0,5						
Dracaena nitens Welw. ex Bak.	6	0,3									4	0,7	24	0,8	2	0,3				
Dracaena sp (Dragonier)	59	3,1	3	0,7	14	1,4			23	2,3	5	0,9	16	0,6	4	0,6			3	0,5
Elaeis guineensis Jacq (Palmier)	203	10,7	79	17,5	89	8,9	87	10,8	103	10,3	75	13,4	261	9,1	71	11,3	82	13,4	68	11
Eucalyptus sp (Eucalyptus)																				
Eugenia malaccensis (Pommier rouge)	65	3,4	35	7,8	80	5	25	3,1	57	5,6	26	4,6	87	3	20	0,3	23	3,8	9	1,5
Eugenia gambos L. (Pommier Rose)	16	0,8			4	0,4	8	1	2	0,2	4	0,7	19	0,7	5	0,8	2	0,3		
Euphorbia tirucalii L. (Cactus)	9	0,5			3	0,3			12	1,2			14	0,5			3	0,5		
Ficus sp (Figuier)	5	0,3			8	0,5	2	0,2			6	1,1			2	0,3			1	0,2
Flacourtia ramontchi L'Her (Prunier de Madagascar)	40	2,1			5	0,5	3	0,4	17	1,7	11	2	21	0,7	7	1,1				
Garcinia margostana L.(Mangoustanier)							1	0,1					2	0,1						
Hibiscus rosa sinensis	23	1,2			13	1,3	10	1,2	10	1	6	1,1	43	1,5					11	1,8
Hura crepitans L.	38	2	10	0,2	12	1,2	11	1,4	31	3,1	15	2,7	81	2,8	11	1,7	51	8,3	8	1,3
Jatropha curcas L. (Pignon d'inde)	30	1,6			6	0,6							21	0,7	3	0,5			18	2,9
Lannes antisorbutica	31	1,6			4	0,4							13	0,5						
Mangifera Indica (Manguier)	397	20,9	87	19,3	123	12,3	222	27,4	262	25,9	90	16	631	21,9	107	17	185	30,1	118	19,1
Milliettia laurentti De Wild (Wenge, Bois noir)	1	0			2	0,2	3	0,4			1	0,2	2	0,1			2	0,3		
Maringa lucida Berth (Moringa)	3	0,2	4	0,9	60	6			29	2,9			64	2,2	18	2,9			8	1,3
Musa Sinensis (Bananier)	60	3,2	24	5,3	32	3,2	29	3,6	42	4,1	29	5,2	173	6	27	4,3	54	8,8	14	2,3
Musanga cecropioides R.Br. (Parassolier)	24	1,1	11	2,4	27	2,7							23	0,8	2	0,3			1	0,2
Passiflora edulis (Maracuja)	40	2,1	9	2	39	3,9	8	1	9	0,3	7	1,2	45	1,6	14	2,2	2	0,3	12	1,9
Persea americana Mill (Avocatier)	49	2,6	18	4	40	4	27	3,3	25	2,5	21	3,7	279	9,7	15	2,4	35	5,7	53	8,6
Psidium guajava L. (Goyavier)	10	0,5			12	1,2							11	0,4	15	2,4				
Ravenala madagascariensis (Arbre du voyageur)	41	2,2	3	0,7	26	2,6					9	1,6	26	0,9	11	1,7			19	3,1
Solanum	29	1,5	4	0,9	19	1,9	6	0,7	5	0,5	9	1,6	38	1,3	13	2,1			21	3,4
Spondias cytherea Sonn	15	0,8			21	2,1							13	0,5	12	1,9			24	3,9
Sterculia sp	10	0,5			27	2,7					2	0,4	27	0,9					25	4
Symphonia globulifera L. f.	11	0,6			23	2,3							33	1,1	13	2,1			18	2,9
Terminalia cattappa L. (Badamier)	60	3,2	26	5,8	37	3,7	39	4,8	48	4,7	32	0,1	31	1,1	22	3,5	31	5,1	41	6,6
Vernonia amygdacina Del (Vernonie commune)	7	0,4			15	1,5							27	0,9	14	2,2				
Zanfedeschia ethiopica	41	2,2	12	2,7	21	2,1			7	0,7	13	2,3	31	1,1	13	2,1			2	0,3
Divers																				
TOTAL	1897	100	451	100	1002	100	809	100	1013	100	561	100	2878	100	630	100	611	100	639	100

Source : Gutu Kia Zimi

Table n*40; Source: Gutu Kia Zimi (2020)

DISTRIBUTION OF TREE SPECIES PER COMMUNE STUDY AREA E						
TREE SPECIES	MAL	%	NSE	%	MGF	%
Adansonia digitala (Baobab)					18	0,6
Annona reticulata L. (Cœur de bœuf)	21	2,6	17	0,7	14	0,5
Artocarpus heterophyllus (Jacquier)	11	1,4	36	1,4	8	0,3
Artocarpus incisa Lf (Arbre à pain)					15	0,5
Averrhoa carambola L. (Carambolier) pakapaka	22	2,8	72	2,9	10	0,3
Carica papaya (Papayer)	121	15,2	349	14	426	14,3
Cocos Nucifera (Cocotier)	42	5,3	126	5,1	240	8
Citrus aurantium (Oranger)	10	1,3	13	0,5	13	0,4
Citrus limon (L.) Burm (Citronier)	8	1	24	1	23	0,8
Citrus reticula Blanco (Mandarinier)	9	1,1	16	0,6	12	0,4
Citrus maxima (Burm.) Merr (Pamplemoussier)	5	0,6	10	0,4	14	0,5
Cupressus sp L. (Cyprès)			4	0,2		
Dacryodes edulis (G. Don) (Safoutier)	25	3,1	47	1,9	38	1,3
Delonix regia (Flamboyant)					9	0,3
Diospyros heterotricha (B.L)					4	0,2
Dracaena sp (Dragonier)					4	0,2
Elaeis guineensis Jacq (Palmier)	82	10,3	487	19,6	491	16,5
Eucalpyptus citriodora Hook					3	0,1
Eucalpyptus sp (Eucalyptus)			3	0,1	11	0,4
Eugenia malaccensis (Pommier rouge)	2	0,3	4	0,2	16	0,5
Eugenia gambos L. (Pommier Rose)			15	0,6	19	0,6
Garcinia mangostana L.(Mangoustanier)	13	1,6	13	0,5	11	0,4
Hibiscus rosa sinensis	26	3,3	84	3,4	71	2,4
Hura crepitans L					3	0,1
Mangifera Indica (Manguier)	241	30,2	576	23,2	724	24,2
Musa Sinensis (Bananier)	23	2,9	86	3,5	78	2,6
Millettia laurentti De Wild (Wenge, Bois noir)					6	0,2
Morinda lucida Benth (Moringa)	41	5,1	100	4	110	3,7
Musanga cecropioides R.Br. (Parassolier)					5	0,2
Passiflora edulis (Maracuja)	1	0,1	16	0,6	11	0,4
Persea americana Mill (Avocatier)	80	10	367	14,8	548	18,4
Psidium guajava L. (Goyavier)	6	0,8	9	0,4	9	0,3
Ravenala madagascariensis (Arbre du voyageur)					2	0,1
Solanum					2	0,1
Terminalia catappa L. (Badamier)	9	1,1	13	0,5	9	0,3
Vermonia amygdacina Del (Vernonie commune)					6	0,2
Divers						
TOTAL	798		2487		2983	

Source : Gutu Kia Zimi

Table n*41; Source: Gutu Kia Zimi (2020)

123

VI. VARIOUS STUDIES ON URBAN VEGETATION IN KINSHASA

1. Another study carried out by Jacques Paulus s.j, within the framework of the "Jardins et Elevages des Parcelles" (JEEP) project focused on different districts of Kinshasa. This study focused on a sample of 1,897 plots divided into six sites as follows[62]:

Site 1: Municipality of Kisenso (Mbuku district)
and Municipality of Lemba (Mbanza /
Lemba district)   : 402 plots
Site 2: Municipality of Kalamu   : 400 plots
Site 3: Municipality of Kinshasa   : 400 plots
Site 4: Municipality of Ndjili (District 11 and 12)   : 225 plots
Site 5: Municipality of Masina (District 3)   : 225 plots
Site 6: Municipality of Masina (Quartier Sans Fil   : 245 plots
and Lundula)

Analysis of the results of this study reveals a count of 268 cultivated or maintained plant species, which are distributed as follows: 59 species of trees; 74 species of shrubs and 135 species of grasses. However, these species include: 83 species intended for food; 60 species for medicinal use and 11 species, which are used for both food and medicine.

We also observe in the results of this survey that the flora of these districts is predominant in decreasing order by species of fruit trees such as mango, avocado and palm for the plots of the Mbanza-Lemba and Mbuku districts (site 1), Kalamu (site 2), Quartier 3 Masina (Site 5), and Quartiers 11 and 12 Ndjili (Site 4).

---

[62] PAULUS JACQUES s.j., Rapport d'enquête Projet JEEP, UNIKIN, Fac.Sciences, Document Inédit, 1988.

According to this study, Badamier appeared in second position in the flora of the districts of Kinshasa commune and third in those of districts 1 of the commune of Masina, and "SANS FIL" and "LUNDULA" districts of the commune of Masina.

We know that this tree is mainly planted for its shade than for its fruits. This explains the habits of the population to live outside than in the house, which is especially favored by the hot tropical climate.

2. Another study of the JEEP project, carried out in 1989 in the Kindele districts in the commune of Mont Ngafula, and Kingabwa in the commune of Limete, the following results were observed:

In Kingabwa, 318 plots were surveyed and 107 plant species were identified, the predominance of mango in 42% of the plots surveyed, oil palm in 30% of the plots, false cassava in 23% of the plots and finally the mango tree. papaya 11% in the plots visited.

3. Gutu Kia Zimi[63] in another study carried out in 443 plots of the Assossa district in the municipality of Kasa- Vubu counted 41 species of trees. The most common species of which in the flora of this district is the mango tree (*Mangifera indica*) or 36.8%, oil palm (*Elaeis guineensis*) 12.96%, badamier (*Terminalia catappa*) 9.8%, and avocado (*Persea americana*) 9.7%. On the other hand, in the 443 plots visited, there are: 66 plots (14.8%) with 0 trees; 80 plots (40.6%) with 1 tree; 114 plots (25.7%) with 2 trees; 50 plots (11.2%) with 3 trees; 20 plots (4.5%) with 4 trees; 10 plots (2.2%) with 5 trees; 2 plots (0.4%) with 6 trees; 1 plot (0.2%) with 9 trees.

---

[63] GUTU KIA ZIMI (1993), Naissance d'une arboriculture urbaine au Zaïre (Congo), in DES FORETS ET DES HOMMES, Environnement Africain N*33-34-35-36, Vol. IX, 1-2-3-4, ENDA, Dakar, 1993, pp.221-247.

4. A survey carried out on 201 plots of the municipality of Limete[64] made it possible to inventory 19 species of cultivated vegetables and 764 plants of 18 species of fruit plants, planted or maintained in this area. *Mangifera indica* is the most planted tree species and *Ipomoae batatas* is the most frequently cultivated vegetable species. Promoted and supervised, this urban agriculture can shape the physiognomy of the city's ecosystems with vegetation capable of purifying the air, regulating the climate, restoring soil fertility and providing households with vegetables and fruits.

5. Another study by Sambieni, Kouagou Raoul and all (2018)[65] describes the diversity and abundance of domestic tree vegetation in the urban vegetation of Kinshasa. According to this study, the urban area has a specific richness of 29 species against 43 in the peri-urban area. The values of the other calculated indices turn out to be high in the two zones of the urban-rural gradient. However, they are still relatively lower in the peri-urban area. We can thus say that there is a relatively strong specific diversity in the two zones. Nevertheless, that the distribution in proportion of species is more heterogeneous in peri-urban areas than in urban areas. Moreover, we observe that the specific wealth of peri-urban municipalities taken in isolation is generally greater than that of urban municipalities. According to this study: "the index values indicate that the urban commune of Ndjili is the most diversified, followed by the peri-urban commune of Makala. In addition, regardless of the urban or peri-urban area, we observe

---

[64] L. Lukoki s.j et all, Inventaire des espèces végétales mises en culture dans les parcelles en milieu urbain. Cas de la commune de Limete - Kinshasa - R. D. Congo, Revue TROPICULTURA, 2002, 20, 2, 89-95.

[65] SAMBIENI et al (2018), La végétation arborée domestique dans le paysage urbain et périurbain de la ville de Kinshasa, République Démocratique du Congo, in Tropicultura (2018), 36(3), p.478-498, also in Afrique SCIENCE 14(2) (2018) p.197 - 208; ISSN 1813-548X, (http://www.afriquescience.info).

that the frequent and dominant species are in reduced number, with the mango tree (*Mangifera indica*) in the lead. Regarding the abundance of domestic tree vegetation, the study tells us that the proportion of plots with at least one tree or shrub obtained for the peri-urban area is much higher than that of the urban area, i.e. respectively 53.3% against 29.3%. Likewise, the proportions recorded for peri-urban municipalities varying between 36.8% and 66.4% are higher than those for urban municipalities varying between 24.6% and 35.7%. In addition, concerning the average number of trees or shrubs per plot, the peri-urban area stands out with an average of 3 to 4 trees per plot, i.e. a difference of 1 to 2 trees more compared to the average observed in the urban area (2 to 3 trees). Peri-urban communes, with the exception of Makala commune, have the highest values (3 to 4 trees) compared to urban communes (2 to 3 trees). The value associated with the peri-urban commune of Makala (3 trees) turns out to be rather similar to those of the urban communes of Matete and Ndjili. The peri-urban area and most of the municipalities that make it up are clearly characterized by a greater abundance of "domestic tree vegetation" (VAD) compared to the urban one and the associated municipalities[66].

"*Crassoceohalum sarcobasis*" is found among the Kasaians. "*Psophocarpus scandens*" is mainly present in the plots of former nationals of villages bordering the plantations of the company P.L.C. (Plantation Lever in Congo). Trees fulfill various ecological and environmental functions and are used in particular for human or animal consumption, for trade and for aesthetics. They also play a psychological, medicinal or other function. However, why

---

[66] MBEMBA F. & REMACLE J., (1992), Inventaire et composition des aliments du Kwango-Kwilu au Zaïre. Presses Universitaires de Namur, Belgique, pp. 37-40.

the preference of owners to plant one species rather than another? To this question, few studies have been conducted in the city of Kinshasa on the reactions of different species or provenances to given conditions in the urban environment of Kinshasa. However, surveys of existing trees in cities can provide a great deal of information and give clues as to the advisability of planting a certain species in a designated urban setting (Jim, 1990a). The main shortcoming of these surveys is that they only assess species that have already been adopted (Miller R.W. 1988)[67]. According to Jim (1990b: 28), the lack of knowledge about the ability of species to adapt to urban conditions means "the tendency to accept 'easy' species is inexorably anchored. The lack of effective local research in arboriculture traps implementers in a closed circuit conservatism". In Kinshasa, the dominant species is the mango tree (*Mangifera indica*). Even though local people help choose which trees to plant in their plots, experience teaches us that they only cultivate valuable trees on land over which they exercise certain control. For example, when focusing on fruit production, they will be found to prefer hardy landraces to grafted varieties, less disease resistant and more nutrient demanding, in home gardens[68]. However, in Kinshasa on the choice of tree species, there are clearly defined differences between predominantly African and European residential neighborhoods. For example, in the "rich or affluent neighborhoods" where the African population dominates such as "Ma Campagne", "Quarter GB"…, there is a high percentage of indigenous or local ornamental species, while in the "westernized neighborhoods in high income" in the commune of Gombe, there are a large number of exotic ornamental trees.

---

[67] MILLER R.W. (1988) "Urban Forestry. Planning and Managing Urban Greenspaces".

[68] fao.org/3/T1680F/T1680F07.htm.

Reason why, one imagines that in the streets of these residential districts of Gombe, the trees should not bear fruit to avoid that the district is subsequently invaded by "kids", which does not also exclude adults in search of fruit.... In the poorest districts of Kinshasa such as "Camp Luka", "Quartier Congo", "Pakadjuma" ..., fruit trees occupy a preponderant place in the combinations of species, and only rare alignment and ornamental trees appear in some residential plots. Currently, the owners whose reasons are given below generally determine the choice of species planted in the residential plots of Kinshasa. Some considerations can be considered below, which should theoretically influence the decision-making in the choice of species to plant in residential plots.

- What function will the trees have to perform?
- Who will make the decision to plant the trees and who will use them?
- Where will the trees be planted?
- What kind of future management will be required?
- What species or species are available to plant and their origins?[69]

Among the reasons given, they are the following:

REASONS

1. Edible fruits
2. Medicinal leaves or bark
3. Edible nuts

---

[69] US immigration regulations prohibit passengers from bringing seeds of exotic plants and other fruits to US soil into the US. This is to avoid the risk of introducing dangerous species to the American flora

4. Manufacture of brooms
5. Shading
6. Ornament
7. Closure
8. Lumber
9. Palm wine
10. Toothbrush
11. Yellowing of the lips

Species such as *Elaeis guineensis* have been cited for various reasons such as: edible nuts, broom making, palm wine. While *Coco nucifera* has also been cited for edible nuts and the manufacture of brooms. We have grouped the various reasons mentioned by the inhabitants of the plots into six essential functions, including:

1. FOOD FUNCTION

According to the results of our survey, it turns out that the flora of the urban vegetation of Kinshasa is predominant in general, by the fruit or edible tree species, some of which are part of the eating habits of the population, in particular, the oil palm. Usually, people plant a tree in memory of a good fruit that they have eaten or a variety of tree whose species or variety they would like to keep or perpetuate. So it is during the picking, when the fruits reach maturity, they send a few quantities to family members, relatives and friends. This is especially the case with mango, safout, avocado, etc. Our study counted 54 species of trees in the residential plots. Among the species with edible fruits identified, we can cite the dominant species below listed in the flora of the urban vegetation of Kinshasa:

1. *Annona Reticulata L.*

2. *Annona Squamosa L.*

3. *Citrus Limon*

4. *Coco Nucifera*

5. *Dacryodes edulis*

6. *Elaeis guineensis*

7. *Mangifera indica*

8. *Persea Americana*

9. *Psidium Guajava*

10. *Spondias Cytherea*

There is no need to reiterate here the important role of fruits in our diet. Almost all fruits contain vitamins B1 (Thiamine), vitamin B2 (Riboflavin), vitamin B3 (Ascorbic Acid), Mineral salts (Iron, Calcium, Phosphorus), Energy materials and calories. Currently, fruits are a dietary supplement in the diet of the Kinshasa population.

2. COMMERCIAL FUNCTION

Initially, the original idea of the population is to plant a fruit tree in order to provide it with fruit for its domestic and family consumption. Therefore, the individual will plant one or two trees of the preferred fruit of their choice. But, it happens that with the low income of the population, the inhabitants pick the fruits to sell them, that is to say that the production of the tree exceeds the domestic consumption of the family and it is considered useful that the surplus is sold for avoid losses such as rot and waste. It is often rare that individuals initially intended to plant the tree for commercial purposes. In this hypothesis, they would reserve a large area for planting trees in the plot as is the practice for vegetable plants. Nevertheless, the sale of the fruits brings a substantial income to the population. As an example, we have observed the following prices for the fruits below which are very common for sale in the various markets of Kinshasa.

FRUIT	OBSERVED PRICE ($)
1 bunch of palm nuts	: 0.50 - 1.00
1 bunch of 5 mangoes	: 0.50 - 1.00
1 bunch of 5 oranges	: 1.00 - 1.50
1 coconut	: 2.00 - 2.50
1 pile of 5 safous	: 1.00 - 1.50
1 avocado	: 1.00 - 1.50

It is worth mentioning the case of the oil palm. This tree species is of various economic interest. It is used in the manufacture of palm oil, brooms; its twigs are used for adornment during festivals or mourning. It is also used as a building material. Another no less important use of this tree is the production of palm wine in both rural and urban areas. If we refer to the industrial use of oil palm, we note the manufacture of soap, margarine, vegetable oils and other miscellaneous industrial products.

3. ECOLOGICAL FUNCTION

It is known that trees often help stabilize the soil and are an effective means of erosion control. Certain species such as bamboo identified in the outlying districts of Kinshasa are much appreciated in the fight against erosion.

4. AESTHETIC FUNCTION

During the investigation, several times the owners replied that the tree in the plot serves as an ornament. It is often found that some locals prefer to plant an ornamental tree species in the plot to the detriment of a fruit species. This tendency is much noticed in the plots of the residential districts of Limete, Gombe, occupied mainly by a population of foreign origin especially European. This shows a cultural difference between the indigenous African and European population.

5. PSYCHOLOGICAL FUNCTION

It is essential if not essential for humans to live in perfect psychic and mental balance. Therefore, he needs a calm and serene environment provided by nature. By transporting the delights of nature to its plot, it only contributes to the perfect development of the individual. This is how the presence of trees in the plot offers peace, quiet and relaxation. Referring to the African way of life in general, more specifically that of the tropics, life on the plot is designed for the outdoors. All activities in the plot take place outside. The house is there only to sleep there. This is how the development of the plot, which is part of the dwelling, is organized into two parts. The built part, which serves as a resting place, where we sleep and shelter from the elements, on the one hand, and the unbuilt part where we live there during the day. To make this part of the habitat pleasant and attractive, the owner is considering planting trees there, which will not only give him fruit, but also shade. It is not surprising to find in the results of our survey that *Terminalia Catappa* (Badamier) occupies an important place in the vegetation of the flora of Kinshasa. This tree is very planted in the plots especially for its shade.

6. MEDICINAL FUNCTION

In the practice of traditional medicine, even in urban areas, the use of certain medicinal tree species is very common. Although they live in the city, some residents have not forgotten the virtue of certain species of medicinal plants, which they decide to plant in their plot.

It should be noted that the use and trade of medicinal plants in the Kinshasa population is very widespread. We counted during our investigation, medicinal plants such as *Morinda Lucida* (Nsiki), a plant well known for the treatment of amoeba, intestinal worms, stomach aches; as well as *Vernonia Amygdalina* (Nzete ya bololo, Malulu). Regarding the important role of traditional medicine in the Congolese population, MATA MA TSHAKALA wrote: "It is not for the Congolese people and their elite responsible for medical services to blindly espouse imported techniques and ideologies, which support them. We have realized our authenticity and the Congolese people are determined to use their own resources. He is aware of the great importance of seeking the values of his ancestors, in order to appreciate those, which are able to contribute to the harmonious development of his health "[70]. In addition, Doctor Jérôme Munyangi[71] denounces the silent carnage of Africans by China and India by fake drugs and vaccines, which are responsible for 500,000 to 1 million deaths in Africa. Developing the African pharmacopoeia is one of the solutions to put an end to this carnage on the one hand and developing medicinal plants, which have already demonstrated therapeutic virtues will also be the real solution in the fight against this silent carnage on the African continent, on the other hand. The use of medicinal plants varies according to the habits and regional or tribal origin of the population. Sometimes, it is the bark, the leaves, or the roots, which are used in the form of infusion, purge or even chewing.

---

[70] BILA EGONDA, Ecosystème urbain de Mbandaka: Les arbres du quartier Mbandaka II, Mémoire fin Licence Biologie, ISP/Mbandaka, Document inédit, 1989.
[71] Dr JEROME MUNYANGI, Congolese doctor and researcher on the fight against malaria.

Some uses of medicinal plants identified in the flora of the neighborhoods of Kinshasa:

TREES	PART USED	DISEASE TO BE TREATED
1. *Alstonia Congensis*	Bark (dust)	Tooth Decay
2. *Cecropia Leucocoma*	Bark (dust)	Bronchitis (Children)
3. *Citrus Aurantium*	Flowers	Insomnia
4. *Dacryodes Edulis*	Bark (dust)	Measles
5. *Mangifera Indica*	Bark	Post-maternity pains
6. *Psidium Guajava*	Young leaves	Diarrhea
7. *Persea Americana*	Young leaves	Anemia
8. *Rauwolfia Vomitoria*	Roots	Kill Lice
9. *Trema Guineensis*	Leaves	Cough (Children)
10. *Vernonia Amygdalina*	Leaves	Measles

7. LEGAL FUNCTION

The tree also plays a legal role. In Africa, the palaver tree[72] is a traditional gathering place, in the shade of which people express themselves on life in society, village problems, politics, etc. It is also a place where children come to listen to stories told by a village elder. By extension, the expression can designate the place of a village where there was a palaver tree, generally a baobab, a *Kambala*, etc. Some important decisions, which result from a final case, are materialized or better yet are recorded by a scar that is carved on the trunk of the tree, so that not everyone ignores it. This allows everyone involved to remember the meaning of this scar as a witness for the present and the future. In a plot surveyed in the Kimbangu district, Kalamu commune, we encountered a *safoutier* carved with two scars. The first scar relates to a family reconciliation case, which pitted family members against each other. The second relates to an

---

[72] The palaver is a custom of meeting, and creation or maintenance of social bond. It appears as a real social institution in which all or part of the community of a village participates. This custom also makes it possible to settle a dispute without the protagonists being harmed.

inheritance case, which pitted a family member against those close to him.

8. PROTECTION FUNCTION

Certain species of trees are planted in the plot to act as protection against lightning. This is the case with *Euphorbia tirucalli* (Cactus). According to some beliefs, certain species of trees are planted in the plot to scare away evil spirits, thus preventing wizards from entering the plot. In addition, others to scare away the snakes. This is the case with Mandrake. In addition, other species are found in the plots in an attempt to attract birds.

VII. INTERPRETATION OF THE SURVEY RESULTS

It appears that the number of trees decreases rapidly with the years in the districts of the former municipalities. Nevertheless, the major reason for this decrease in the number of trees is that when creating a new neighborhood, the owners of the plots find it beneficial to plant trees in the plot. However, as the neighborhood grows and ages, the spaces in the plots are rather occupied by constructions. Then the habitat stabilizes and the owners of the plots no longer find any interest in planting new trees. However, the regression of urban vegetation in Kinshasa is attributable to factors:

- On the one hand, socio-demographic including demographic growth and all its corollaries, namely, housing crisis, population density in the plots, etc.
- On the other hand, socio-economic including in particular the interest of the owners of the plots in more lucrative and

more profitable developments and constructions, namely, the development of bars, shops, dispensaries, garages, schools, mechanical workshops and various instead of trees.

In a fast growing city like Kinshasa with an estimated urban population of over sixteen million, real estate trading is a better investment. The demand for housing in Kinshasa is always greater than the supply. This is how the owners of the plots are showing more interest in building houses in the areas formerly occupied by trees. This situation is amplified by the housing and habitat crisis in the city of Kinshasa. Indeed, after a last action of development of its space in 1950, Kinshasa did not know any more a new policy on the habitat and will thus let develop a policy of the self-construction. This policy has negative consequences on the ability of these inhabitants to find decent housing within their means. From what precedes, the poor and the less well-off are therefore forced to rent their housing for lack of a concrete housing policy. Studies show, already at the end of the 1970s, the start of an announced housing crisis. Based on the same idea, the "Caisse Nationale d'Epargne et des Crédits Immobiliers" (CNECI, 1979) estimated a cumulative deficit of around 162,577 housing units between 1979 and 1985 (Kanene, 2001). Statistics today estimate 44% of tenants (Mukoko, cited by Lelo Nzuzi) in Kinshasa and others also estimate such as Kanene (op.cit) puts forward the figure of 34.7%, when we consider the distribution of the population according to the land use of housing in the city. The "MICS 2"[73] survey assesses at 43.6% of tenants, 2.7% of housed by employers, 12.3% of housed by a relative, friend or under housed and 1.2% others out of the 562,969 housing units in Kinshasa (Kanene. M, 2001). In view of the above, it is becoming more and more difficult

---

[73] Multiple Indicator Cluster Survey, UNICEF (MICS), 1995 et 2001

to find a rental house in the center of the city. Taking advantage of this situation, some lessors whose houses benefit from the location rent are subject to speculation issues taking advantage of the favors of the law of the market, that is to say of the law of supply and demand request. They raise rental prices while joining forces with agents who benefit from the percentages resulting from the rental guarantee. If today housing seems to be difficult to acquire, it is necessary to count on the unfortunate contribution of these "commission agents" who speculate and make this trade which, moreover, very lucrative, make access to housing a real journey through fighter. Because of this unscrupulous speculation, there is a galloping increase in demand for construction towards the periphery. Far from suspecting the consequences, the poorest will squat where they can, either in public buildings, or in unfinished houses, or in dilapidated warehouses. If finding a house to rent Kinshasa is a real headache, then what about the exorbitant prices that this implies and the criteria for selecting tenants by lessors which are purely subjective. Suffering from strong rental speculations, those who can and with the necessary capital find themselves in the need to change category to acquire plots of land in the outskirts of the city either in the outskirts or in non-aedificandi areas to no longer have to pay the rent. Today the city of Kinshasa knows a strong attraction on behalf of the surrounding populations and those coming from the interior of the country and all want either to buy or to rent a housing. Following all these requests, the price of housing in the city only increases and faces strong speculation in the cities from the first and second ring. Although the criteria for determining prices depend on the distance from the city center; which is no longer required.

It is therefore important to draw up an inventory of existing locations in the three crowns in order to give a correct image of housing in the city. Pushed back to the urban outskirts to acquire a piece of land, the former tenants prefer to settle down and start a new life of owner in the new districts of the city. Others, on the other hand, that is to say the most deprived, do not prefer to move too far from the center to live in the slums on unsuitable land, floodable valleys and non-aedificandi areas. In the hope of finding enough to live in the city center, the inhabitants of these slums admit that the price of land is too expensive because of speculation. They will no longer be able to benefit from the opportunities the city provides. Given the proximity to the city center and the reduced cost of transport, many of the latter prefer to stay in shantytowns because land speculation denies them formal access to land. It is in the center that the competition for land seekers is fiercest because the land supply is very limited. This is what is at the origin of land speculation on these lands reserved for purposes other than housing. The most desirable locations are the agricultural sites closest to the center or the most immediate to the city. The most accessible spaces are coveted in the first place because they are well located and because of the centrality, it provides. This sets up a strong land speculation, and the force of the law of the market decides new buyers of these lands in a word the highest bidder, he wins the piece of land hoping to take advantage of the amenities offered by the centrality. A mafia system is set up where the urban authorities illegally sell land with a specific destination such as: farmland, football field, market ... In other words, they sell tickets public, sidewalks to make drinking places commonly called "*Nganda*". The phenomenon is intensifying at an insane rate. Despite the disciplinary measures against the recalcitrant to the circulars issued by the urban authority (Gabriel KASHIMBA KAYEMBE, 2007). This housing and habitat crisis is an important factor in the decline of urban vegetation as shown in the tables below, which shows the evolution of urban vegetation in Kinshasa following the year of plantation.

A. STATISTICAL ANALYSIS OF THE RESULTS

Statistical analysis of the results will allow us to determine:

1. The future evolution of the vegetation by the regression line, respectively at the global level of shrub vegetation in the residential plots of the city of Kinshasa and also at the level of each municipality to know by the correlation coefficient, if it there is a relation
   - between the number of trees and the year the trees were planted;
   - between the density of the population and the number of trees;
   - the number of trees and the number of plots;

2. The statistical analysis of the results by the regression line at the level of each municipality will allow us to determine the future evolution of the shrub vegetation in the residential plots in each municipality. We can compare this result by taking into account other factors such as changes in the population of the municipality, population density, demographic pressure, etc.

VIII. CORRELATION BETWEEN YEARS OF TREE PLANTING AND NUMBER OF TREES

YEAR	X (Years)	Y (Trees)	XY	X²	Y²
1954	1	82	82	1	6561
1955	2	7	4	4	4
1956	3	8	24	9	64
1957	4	18	72	16	324
1958	5	15	75	25	225
1959	6	22	128	36	441
1960	7	48	336	49	2304
1961	8	86	688	64	7396
1962	9	88	792	81	7744
1963	10	125	1250	100	15625
1964	11	109	1199	121	11881
1965	12	209	2508	144	43681
1966	13	307	3991	169	94249
1967	14	311	4354	196	96721
1968	15	491	7365	225	241081
1969	16	502	8032	256	252004
1970	17	471	8007	289	221841
1971	18	522	9180	324	260100
1972	19	491	9329	361	241081
1973	20	566	11320	400	320356
1974	21	609	12789	441	370881
1975	22	557	12254	484	310249
1976	23	490	11270	529	240100
1977	24	544	13056	576	295936
1978	25	544	13600	625	295936
1979	26	645	16770	676	416025
1980	27	543	14661	729	294849
1981	28	615	17220	784	378225
1982	29	599	17371	841	358801
1983	30	735	22050	900	540225
1984	31	619	19189	961	383161
1985	32	674	21568	1024	454276
1986	33	667	22011	1089	444889
1987	34	591	20094	1156	349281
1988	35	630	22050	1225	396900
1989	36	543	19548	1296	294849
1990	37	490	18130	1369	240100
1991	38	520	19760	1444	270400
1992	39	519	20241	1521	269361
1993	40	461	18440	1600	212521
1994	41	524	21484	1681	274576
1995	42	377	15834	1764	142129
1996	43	463	19125	1849	198025
1997	44	341	15004	1936	116281
1998	45	331	14895	2025	109561
1999	46	305	14030	2116	93025
2000	47	377	17719	2209	142129
2001	48	375	18000	2304	140625
2002	49	379	18571	2401	143641
2003	50	407	20350	2500	165649
2004	51	359	18309	2601	128761
2005	52	385	20020	2704	148225
2006	53	307	16271	2809	94249
2007	54	388	20952	2916	150544
2008	55	413	22605	3025	168921
2009	56	436	24416	3136	190096
2010	57	343	19665	3249	119025
2011	58	362	20996	3364	131044
2012	59	417	24603	3481	173889
2013	60	493	29580	3600	243049
2014	61	487	29707	3721	237169
2015	62	467	28954	3844	218089
2016	63	464	29232	3969	215296
2017	64	476	30464	4096	226576
TOTAL	2080	25662	929151	89440	1257384
AVERAGE	32.5	399.7			

Correlation coefficient R = 0.43

Table n*42; Source: Gutu Kia Zimi (2020)

Following the result, there is a week correlation (r = 0.43) between the number of trees compared to the number of years.

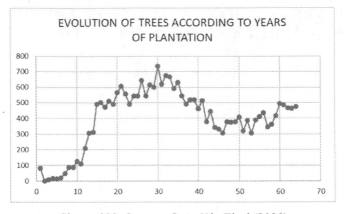

Chart n*29; Source: Gutu Kia Zimi (2020)

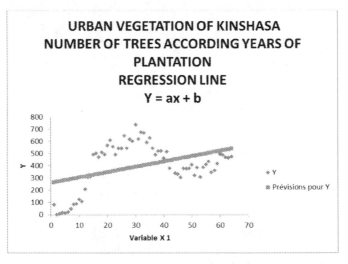

Chart n*30; Source: Gutu Kia Zimi (2020)
Correlation Coefficient R = 0.4

Overall or globally, the regression line indicates a positive evolution of urban vegetation. Nevertheless, this evolution is different from one commune to another, as we will see below by examining the case of each commune or municipality. As explained above, this overall change is selective depending on whether it is the shrub vegetation in the districts of the former municipalities on the one hand, or in the neighborhoods of peri-urban municipalities on the other hand. Indeed, the vegetation is regressive in the districts of the old communes of Kinshasa. In addition, it is increasing in the neighborhoods of peripheral municipalities.

IX. NUMBER OF TREES AND YEARS OF TREE PLANTING PER STUDY AREA

	AREA A				
	COMMUNE OF THE GOMBE				
	YEARS OF TREE PLANTING				
N*	YEARS	NBR OF TREES	N*	YEARS	NBR OF TREES
1	1954	1	33	1986	32
2	1955	0	34	1987	22
3	1956	0	35	1988	26
4	1957	1	36	1989	14
5	1958	0	37	1990	2
6	1959	1	38	1991	3
7	1960	2	39	1992	2
8	1961	2	40	1993	11
9	1962	1	41	1994	3
10	1963	32	42	1995	0
11	1964	0	43	1996	0
12	1965	14	44	1997	2
13	1966	21	45	1998	2
14	1967	0	46	1999	1
15	1968	14	47	2000	0
16	1969	19	48	2001	1
17	1970	10	49	2002	3
18	1971	11	50	2003	0
19	1972	0	51	2004	2
20	1973	16	52	2005	1
21	1974	11	53	2006	0
22	1975	35	54	2007	0
23	1976	20	55	2008	0
24	1977	15	56	2009	2
25	1978	13	57	2010	1
26	1979	24	58	2011	3
27	1980	27	59	2012	2
28	1981	28	60	2013	1
29	1982	17	61	2014	0
30	1983	18	62	2015	0
31	1984	0	63	2016	1
32	1985	23	64	2017	1
				TOTAL	513

Table n*43; Source: Gutu Kia Zimi (2020)

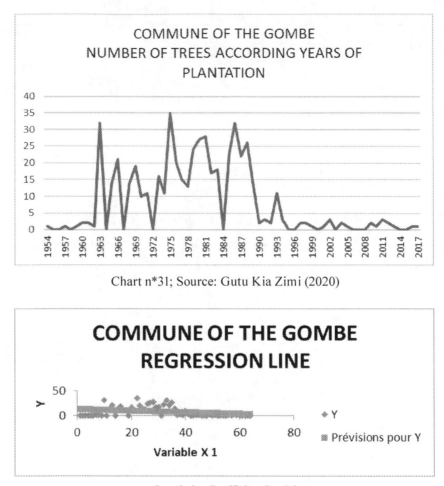

Chart n*31; Source: Gutu Kia Zimi (2020)

Correlation Coefficient R = 0.3
Chart n*32; Source: Gutu Kia Zimi (2020)

The correlation coefficient (R = 0.3) indicates a weak correlation between the number of the trees and the year of the plantation. In addition, the regression line indicates a negative evolution (decreasing) of the urban vegetation in this commune of the Gombe.

N*	YEARS	NBR OF TREES	N*	YEARS	NBR OF TREES
	AREA A COMMUNE OF LIMETE YEARS OF TREE PLANTING				
1	1954	0	33	1986	83
2	1955	0	34	1987	56
3	1956	0	35	1988	44
4	1957	1	36	1989	85
5	1958	2	37	1990	16
6	1959	3	38	1991	58
7	1960	1	39	1992	16
8	1961	15	40	1993	48
9	1962	11	41	1994	15
10	1963	2	42	1995	5
11	1964	0	43	1996	32
12	1965	12	44	1997	19
13	1966	21	45	1998	14
14	1967	17	46	1999	3
15	1968	26	47	2000	32
16	1969	45	48	2001	14
17	1970	25	49	2002	13
18	1971	0	50	2003	33
19	1972	48	51	2004	12
20	1973	23	52	2005	33
21	1974	87	53	2006	6
22	1975	37	54	2007	10
23	1976	27	55	2008	29
24	1977	38	56	2009	18
25	1978	22	57	2010	27
26	1979	71	58	2011	33
27	1980	42	59	2012	22
28	1981	93	60	2013	25
29	1982	78	61	2014	13
30	1983	85	62	2015	12
31	1984	69	63	2016	13
32	1985	64	64	2017	16
			TOTAL		1820

Table n*44; Source: Gutu Kia Zimi (2020)

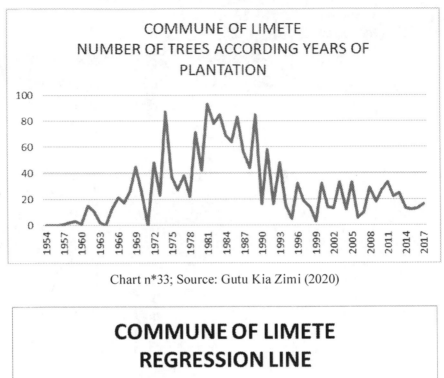

Chart n*33; Source: Gutu Kia Zimi (2020)

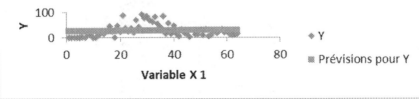

Correlation Coefficient R = 0.1
Chart n*34; Source: Gutu Kia Zimi (2020)

The correlation coefficient (R = 0.1) indicates a weak correlation between the number of trees and the year of plantation. In addition, the regression line indicates a negative evolution or decreasing of the vegetation as you can read on the graph.

	AREA A COMMUNE OF NGALIEMA YEARS OF PLANTING TREES				
N*	YEARS	NBR OF TREES	N*	YEARS	NBR OF TREES
1	1954	0	33	1986	25
2	1955	0	34	1987	27
3	1956	1	35	1988	45
4	1957	2	36	1989	21
5	1958	3	37	1990	43
6	1959	4	38	1991	35
7	1960	4	39	1992	27
8	1961	8	40	1993	18
9	1962	7	41	1994	30
10	1963	3	42	1995	22
11	1964	7	43	1996	34
12	1965	32	44	1997	20
13	1966	44	45	1998	23
14	1967	20	46	1999	29
15	1968	38	47	2000	34
16	1969	60	48	2001	38
17	1970	32	49	2002	42
18	1971	39	50	2003	36
19	1972	58	51	2004	35
20	1973	47	52	2005	58
21	1974	41	53	2006	50
22	1975	57	54	2007	81
23	1976	48	55	2008	72
24	1977	51	56	2009	55
25	1978	53	57	2010	67
26	1979	95	58	2011	51
27	1980	50	59	2012	49
28	1981	56	60	2013	83
29	1982	48	61	2014	72
30	1983	37	62	2015	97
31	1984	48	63	2016	69
32	1985	53	64	2017	76
			TOTAL		2510

Table n*45; Source: Gutu Kia Zimi (2020)

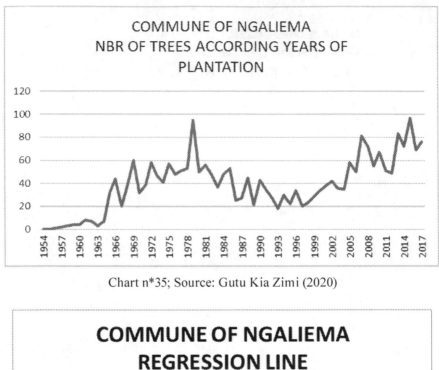

Chart n*35; Source: Gutu Kia Zimi (2020)

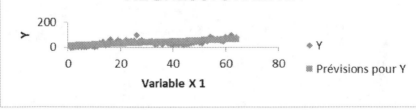

Correlation Coefficient R = 0.6
Chart n*36; Source: Gutu Kia Zimi (2020)

The correlation coefficient (R= 0.6) indicates a strong correlation between the number of trees and the year of the plantation of the trees. In addition, the regression line is showing a positive evolution or growth of the urban vegetation in this commune of Ngaliema.

N°	YEARS	NBR OF TREES	N°	YEARS	NBR OF TREES
AREA B					
COMMUNE OF KINSHASA					
YEARS OF PLANTING TREES					
1	1954	0	33	1986	7
2	1955	1	34	1987	6
3	1956	1	35	1988	8
4	1957	3	36	1989	5
5	1958	2	37	1990	8
6	1959	0	38	1991	2
7	1960	2	39	1992	4
8	1961	3	40	1993	9
9	1962	2	41	1994	4
10	1963	3	42	1995	2
11	1964	1	43	1996	9
12	1965	4	44	1997	7
13	1966	4	45	1998	5
14	1967	5	46	1999	4
15	1968	6	47	2000	1
16	1969	3	48	2001	1
17	1970	5	49	2002	1
18	1971	9	50	2003	1
19	1972	5	51	2004	1
20	1973	4	52	2005	1
21	1974	7	53	2006	0
22	1975	3	54	2007	0
23	1976	6	55	2008	0
24	1977	4	56	2009	0
25	1978	5	57	2010	0
26	1979	4	58	2011	0
27	1980	6	59	2012	0
28	1981	2	60	2013	0
29	1982	10	61	2014	0
30	1983	4	62	2015	0
31	1984	6	63	2016	0
32	1985	9	64	2017	0
				TOTAL	**215**

Table n*46; Source: Gutu Kia Zimi (2020)

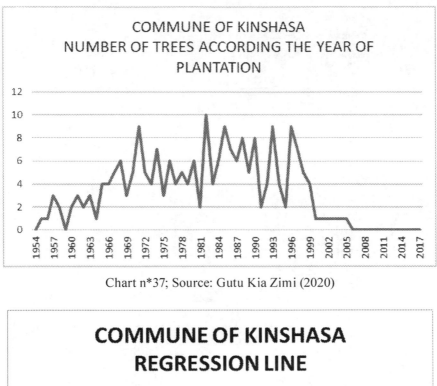

Chart n*37; Source: Gutu Kia Zimi (2020)

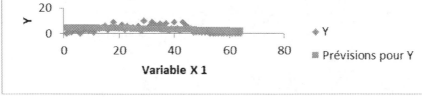

Correlation Coefficient R = 0.3
Chart n*38; Source: Gutu Kia Zimi (2020)

The correlation coefficient is showing a weak correlation between the number of the trees and the year of plantation. The regression line indicates a negative evolution (decrease) of the urban vegetation in this commune of Kinshasa.

N*	YEARS	NBR OF TREES	N*	YEARS	NBR OF TREES
	AREA B				
	COMMUNE OF LINGWALA				
	YEARS OF PLANTING TREES				
1	1954	9	33	1986	2
2	1955	9	34	1987	2
3	1956	9	35	1988	2
4	1957	9	36	1989	1
5	1958	9	37	1990	1
6	1959	8	38	1991	1
7	1960	8	39	1992	1
8	1961	8	40	1993	1
9	1962	8	41	1994	0
10	1963	8	42	1995	0
11	1964	7	43	1996	0
12	1965	7	44	1997	0
13	1966	7	45	1998	0
14	1967	7	46	1999	0
15	1968	7	47	2000	0
16	1969	6	48	2001	0
17	1970	6	49	2002	0
18	1971	6	50	2003	0
19	1972	6	51	2004	0
20	1973	6	52	2005	0
21	1974	6	53	2006	0
22	1975	5	54	2007	0
23	1976	5	55	2008	0
24	1977	5	56	2009	0
25	1978	5	57	2010	0
26	1979	4	58	2011	0
27	1980	4	59	2012	0
28	1981	4	60	2013	0
29	1982	4	61	2014	0
30	1983	4	62	2015	0
31	1984	3	63	2016	0
32	1985	3	64	2017	0
			TOTAL		213

Table n*47; Source: Gutu Kia Zimi (2020)

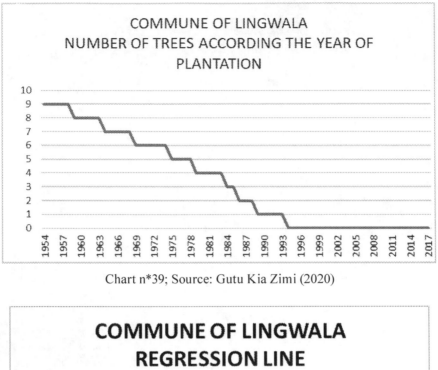

Chart n*39; Source: Gutu Kia Zimi (2020)

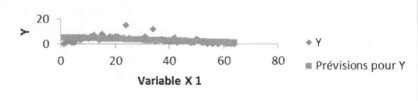

Correlation Coefficient R = 0.4
Chart n*40; Source: Gutu Kia Zimi (2020)

The correlation coefficient indicates a weak correlation between the number of the trees and the year of plantation. The regression line indicates also a negative evolution or decrease of the urban vegetation in the commune of Lingwala.

N*	YEARS	NBR OF TREES	N*	YEARS	NBR OF TREES
	AREA B				
	COMMUNE OF BARUMBU				
	YEARS OF PLANTING TREES				
1	1954	0	33	1986	4
2	1955	0	34	1987	3
3	1956	1	35	1988	3
4	1957	0	36	1989	3
5	1958	1	37	1990	5
6	1959	2	38	1991	3
7	1960	8	39	1992	1
8	1961	6	40	1993	2
9	1962	5	41	1994	2
10	1963	4	42	1995	2
11	1964	6	43	1996	2
12	1965	12	44	1997	2
13	1966	15	45	1998	2
14	1967	10	46	1999	1
15	1968	9	47	2000	1
16	1969	6	48	2001	1
17	1970	4	49	2002	1
18	1971	5	50	2003	1
19	1972	6	51	2004	1
20	1973	5	52	2005	1
21	1974	3	53	2006	0
22	1975	11	54	2007	1
23	1976	5	55	2008	1
24	1977	7	56	2009	0
25	1978	9	57	2010	0
26	1979	6	58	2011	0
27	1980	4	59	2012	2
28	1981	5	60	2013	0
29	1982	4	61	2014	1
30	1983	12	62	2015	0
31	1984	12	63	2016	0
32	1985	11	64	2017	0
			TOTAL		240

Table n*48; Source: Gutu Kia Zimi (2020)

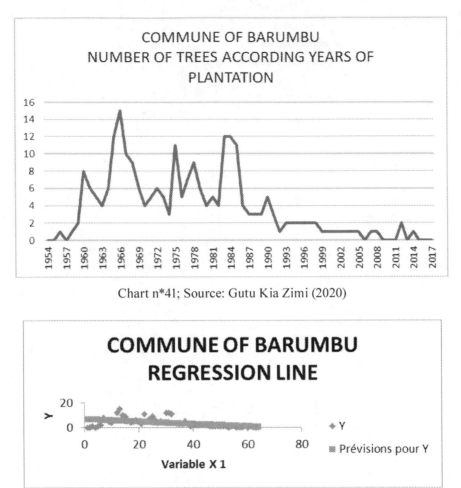

Chart n*41; Source: Gutu Kia Zimi (2020)

Correlation Coefficient R = 0.4
Chart n*42; Source: Gutu Kia Zimi (2020)

The correlation coefficient (R = 0.4) indicates a weak relation between the number of trees and the year of plantation. The regression line indicates a negative evolution (decrease) of the urban vegetation in the commune of Barumbu.

N*	YEARS	NBR OF TREES	N*	YEARS	NBR OF TREES
	AREA B				
	COMMUNE OF KINTAMBO				
	YEARS OF PLANTING				
1	1954	0	33	1986	37
2	1955	0	34	1987	11
3	1956	1	35	1988	27
4	1957	4	36	1989	11
5	1958	1	37	1990	22
6	1959	1	38	1991	16
7	1960	10	39	1992	9
8	1961	12	40	1993	7
9	1962	17	41	1994	11
10	1963	43	42	1995	9
11	1964	15	43	1996	13
12	1965	13	44	1997	16
13	1966	16	45	1998	18
14	1967	11	46	1999	15
15	1968	17	47	2000	7
16	1969	12	48	2001	9
17	1970	13	49	2002	6
18	1971	17	50	2003	17
19	1972	13	51	2004	6
20	1973	16	52	2005	7
21	1974	15	53	2006	6
22	1975	12	54	2007	13
23	1976	19	55	2008	6
24	1977	13	56	2009	4
25	1978	31	57	2010	5
26	1979	13	58	2011	3
27	1980	38	59	2012	3
28	1981	12	60	2013	2
29	1982	9	61	2014	3
30	1983	15	62	2015	1
31	1984	14	63	2016	1
32	1985	11	64	2017	1
			TOTAL		756

Table n*49; Source: Gutu Kia Zimi (2020)

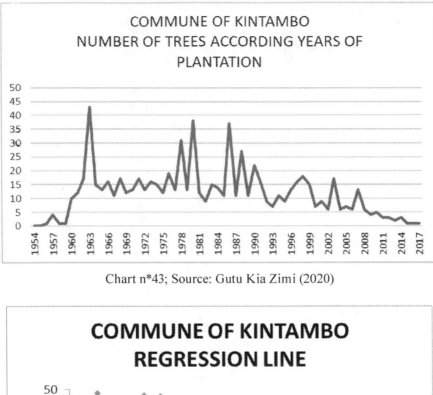

Chart n*43; Source: Gutu Kia Zimi (2020)

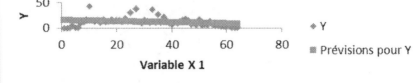

Correlation Coefficient R = 0.2
Chart n*44; Source: Gutu Kia Zimi (2020)

The correlation coefficient (R = 0.2) indicates a weak correlation between the number of trees and the year of plantation. In addition, the regression line indicates a decrease of urban vegetation in the commune of Kintambo.

		AREA C COMMUNE OF LEMBA YEARS OF PLANTING TREES			
N*	YEARS	NBR OF TREES	N*	YEARS	NBR OF TREES
1	1954	0	33	1986	23
2	1955	0	34	1987	28
3	1956	0	35	1988	26
4	1957	0	36	1989	12
5	1958	0	37	1990	22
6	1959	1	38	1991	18
7	1960	2	39	1992	11
8	1961	5	40	1993	11
9	1962	8	41	1994	17
10	1963	5	42	1995	10
11	1964	3	43	1996	18
12	1965	7	44	1997	12
13	1966	6	45	1998	10
14	1967	3	46	1999	9
15	1968	8	47	2000	13
16	1969	11	48	2001	9
17	1970	16	49	2002	5
18	1971	19	50	2003	12
19	1972	13	51	2004	7
20	1973	17	52	2005	11
21	1974	11	53	2006	12
22	1975	15	54	2007	8
23	1976	22	55	2008	16
24	1977	17	56	2009	13
25	1978	13	57	2010	0
26	1979	16	58	2011	15
27	1980	14	59	2012	13
28	1981	26	60	2013	8
29	1982	16	61	2014	13
30	1983	25	62	2015	2
31	1984	21	63	2016	7
32	1985	29	64	2017	5
				TOTAL	745

Table n*50; Source: Gutu Kia Zimi (2020)

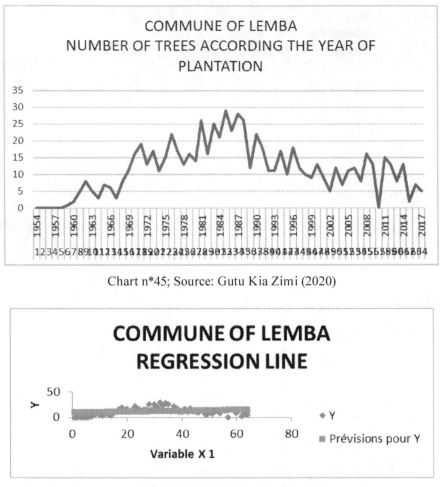

Chart n*45; Source: Gutu Kia Zimi (2020)

Correlation Coefficient R = 0.2
Chart n*46; Source: Gutu Kia Zimi (2020)

The correlation coefficient (R = 0.2) indicates a weak correlation between the number of trees and the year of plantation. In addition, the regression line indicates a decrease of urban vegetation in the commune of Lemba.

N*	ANNEE	NBR OF TREES	N*	YEARS	NBR OF TREES
	AREA C				
	COMMUNE OF MATETE				
	YEARS OF TREE PLANTING				
1	1954	0	33	1986	14
2	1955	0	34	1987	15
3	1956	0	35	1988	13
4	1957	0	36	1989	17
5	1958	0	37	1990	16
6	1959	1	38	1991	13
7	1960	9	39	1992	8
8	1961	8	40	1993	5
9	1962	3	41	1994	17
10	1963	12	42	1995	5
11	1964	11	43	1996	6
12	1965	9	44	1997	4
13	1966	10	45	1998	3
14	1967	5	46	1999	4
15	1968	7	47	2000	2
16	1969	10	48	2001	3
17	1970	19	49	2002	1
18	1971	11	50	2003	3
19	1972	8	51	2004	2
20	1973	9	52	2005	2
21	1974	10	53	2006	1
22	1975	15	54	2007	1
23	1976	5	55	2008	2
24	1977	8	56	2009	1
25	1978	9	57	2010	3
26	1979	10	58	2011	6
27	1980	8	59	2012	2
28	1981	13	60	2013	1
29	1982	16	61	2014	2
30	1983	8	62	2015	3
31	1984	15	63	2016	1
32	1985	19	64	2017	2
				TOTAL	446

Table n*51; Source: Gutu Kia Zimi (2020)

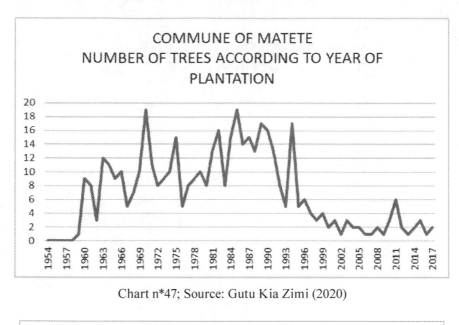

Chart n*47; Source: Gutu Kia Zimi (2020)

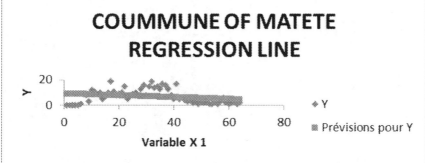

Correlation Coefficient R = 0.2
Chart n*48; Source: Gutu Kia Zimi (2020)
The correlation coefficient (R = 0.2) indicates a weak correlation between
the number of trees and the year of plantation. In addition, the regression line
indicates a decrease of urban vegetation in the commune of Matete.

	AREA C COMMUNE OF KALAMU YEARS OF TREE PLANTING				
N*	YEARS	NBR OF TREES	N*	YEARS	NBR OF TREES
1	1954	0	33	1986	14
2	1955	0	34	1987	16
3	1956	0	35	1988	12
4	1957	1	36	1989	11
5	1958	2	37	1990	19
6	1959	1	38	1991	20
7	1960	1	39	1992	14
8	1961	1	40	1993	21
9	1962	1	41	1994	13
10	1963	0	42	1995	14
11	1964	31	43	1996	15
12	1965	19	44	1997	15
13	1966	29	45	1998	10
14	1967	17	46	1999	9
15	1968	26	47	2000	19
16	1969	21	48	2001	19
17	1970	16	49	2002	17
18	1971	13	50	2003	16
19	1972	17	51	2004	14
20	1973	16	52	2005	13
21	1974	21	53	2006	8
22	1975	15	54	2007	9
23	1976	23	55	2008	11
24	1977	15	56	2009	3
25	1978	14	57	2010	1
26	1979	20	58	2011	2
27	1980	11	59	2012	3
28	1981	15	60	2013	4
29	1982	14	61	2014	1
30	1983	16	62	2015	1
31	1984	13	63	2016	2
32	1985	17	64	2017	0
			TOTAL		752

Table n*52; Source: Gutu Kia Zimi (2020)

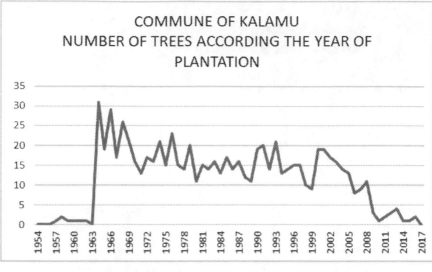

Chart n*49; Source: Gutu Kia Zimi (2020)

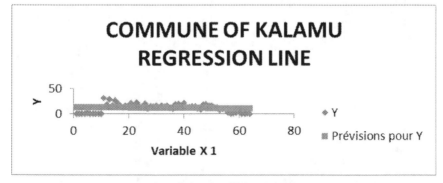

Correlation Coefficient R = 0.1

Chart n*50; Source: Gutu Kia Zimi (2020)

The correlation coefficient (R = 0.1) indicates a weak correlation between the number of trees and the year of plantation. In addition, the regression line indicates a decrease of urban vegetation in the commune of Kalamu.

N*	YEARS	NBR OF TREES	N*	YEARS	NBR OF TREES
	AREA C				
	COMMUNE OF BANDALUNGWA				
	YEARS OF TREE PLANTING				
1	1954	0	33	1986	10
2	1955	0	34	1987	17
3	1956	0	35	1988	22
4	1957	0	36	1989	16
5	1958	1	37	1990	18
6	1959	2	38	1991	8
7	1960	3	39	1992	7
8	1961	18	40	1993	17
9	1962	19	41	1994	9
10	1963	13	42	1995	6
11	1964	11	43	1996	16
12	1965	18	44	1997	6
13	1966	21	45	1998	14
14	1967	18	46	1999	12
15	1968	19	47	2000	13
16	1969	14	48	2001	12
17	1970	12	49	2002	3
18	1971	17	50	2003	12
19	1972	16	51	2004	5
20	1973	15	52	2005	11
21	1974	15	53	2006	4
22	1975	13	54	2007	10
23	1976	16	55	2008	3
24	1977	14	56	2009	0
25	1978	13	57	2010	1
26	1979	13	58	2011	3
27	1980	12	59	2012	1
28	1981	10	60	2013	1
29	1982	11	61	2014	0
30	1983	19	62	2015	1
31	1984	11	63	2016	1
32	1985	9	64	2017	0
			TOTAL		**632**

Table n*53; Source: Gutu Kia Zimi (2020)

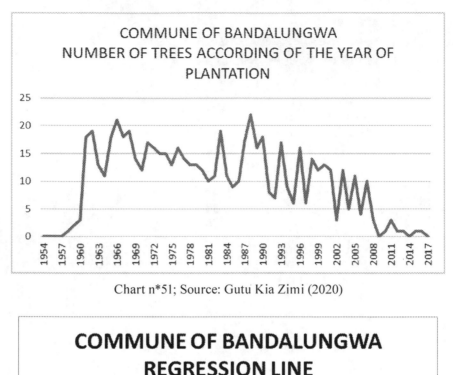

Chart n*51; Source: Gutu Kia Zimi (2020)

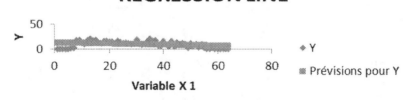

Correlation Coefficient R = 0.3
Chart n*52; Source: Gutu Kia Zimi (2020)
The correlation coefficient (R = 0.1) indicates a weak correlation between
the number of trees and the year of plantation. In addition, the regression line
indicates a decrease of urban vegetation in the commune of Bandalungwa.

N*	YEARS	NBR OF TREES	N*	YEARS	NBR OF TREES
	AREA D				
	COMMUNE OF MASINA				
	YEARS OF TREE PLANTING				
1	1960	0	30	1989	84
2	1961	0	31	1990	77
3	1962	0	32	1991	32
4	1963	0	33	1992	41
5	1964	7	34	1993	11
6	1965	11	35	1994	24
7	1966	32	36	1995	32
8	1967	27	37	1996	61
9	1968	13	38	1997	23
10	1969	18	39	1998	21
11	1970	16	40	1999	18
12	1971	17	41	2000	73
13	1972	19	42	2001	62
14	1973	23	43	2002	46
15	1974	28	44	2003	38
16	1975	31	45	2004	52
17	1976	13	46	2005	31
18	1977	41	47	2006	22
19	1978	32	48	2007	35
20	1979	49	49	2008	26
21	1980	16	50	2009	42
22	1981	13	51	2010	35
23	1982	61	52	2011	23
24	1983	71	53	2012	18
25	1984	57	54	2013	69
26	1985	19	55	2014	61
27	1986	34	56	2015	37
28	1987	29	57	2016	27
29	1988	73	58	2017	26
				TOTAL	1897

Table n*54; Source: Gutu Kia Zimi (2020)

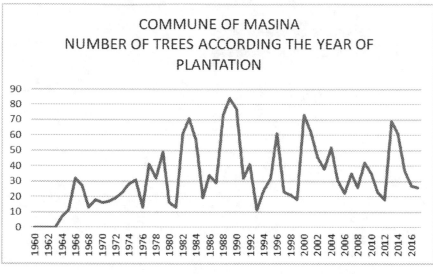

Graph n*53; Source: Gutu Kia Zimi (2020)

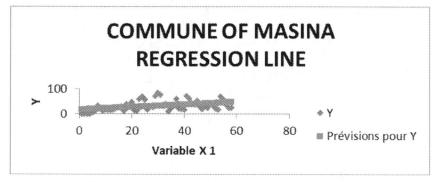

Correlation Coefficient R = 0.4

Graph n*54; Source: Gutu Kia Zimi (2020)

The correlation coefficient (R = 0.4) indicates a weak correlation between the number of trees and the year of plantation. In addition, the regression line indicates a growth of urban vegetation in the commune of Masina.

		AREA D			
		COMMUNE OF KISENSO			
		YEARS OF TREE PLANTING			
N*	YEARS	NBR OF TREES	N*	YEARS	NBR OF TREES
1	1960	0	30	1989	12
2	1961	0	31	1990	1
3	1962	0	32	1991	3
4	1963	0	33	1992	8
5	1964	0	34	1993	9
6	1965	3	35	1994	5
7	1966	1	36	1995	1
8	1967	2	37	1996	8
9	1968	16	38	1997	11
10	1969	13	39	1998	13
11	1970	17	40	1999	15
12	1971	23	41	2000	10
13	1972	9	42	2001	6
14	1973	3	43	2002	7
15	1974	11	44	2003	9
16	1975	8	45	2004	2
17	1976	13	46	2005	8
18	1977	3	47	2006	5
19	1978	8	48	2007	3
20	1979	7	49	2008	5
21	1980	12	50	2009	6
22	1981	3	51	2010	5
23	1982	6	52	2011	27
24	1983	8	53	2012	13
25	1984	21	54	2013	5
26	1985	2	55	2014	10
27	1986	8	56	2015	13
28	1987	6	57	2016	9
29	1988	7	58	2017	12
				TOTAL	451

Table n*55; Source: Gutu Kia Zimi (2020)

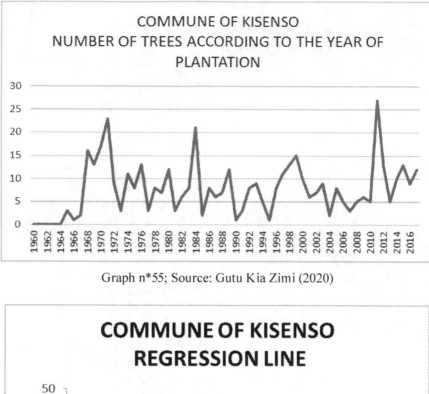

Graph n*55; Source: Gutu Kia Zimi (2020)

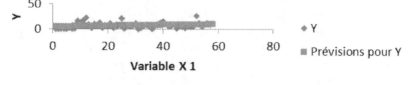

Correlation Coefficient R = 0.2
Graph n*56; Source: Gutu Kia Zimi (2020)
The correlation coefficient (R = 0.2) indicates a weak correlation between the number of trees and the year of plantation. In addition, the regression line indicates a growth of urban vegetation in the commune of Kisenso.

		AREA D			
		COMMUNE OF SELEMBAO			
		YEARS OF TREE PLANTING			
N*	YEARS	NBR OF TREES	N*	YEARS	NBR OF TREES
1	1960	0	30	1989	12
2	1961	0	31	1990	17
3	1962	0	32	1991	16
4	1963	0	33	1992	13
5	1964	0	34	1993	17
6	1965	0	35	1994	19
7	1966	0	36	1995	16
8	1967	0	37	1996	38
9	1968	15	38	1997	21
10	1969	12	39	1998	28
11	1970	19	40	1999	13
12	1971	7	41	2000	29
13	1972	3	42	2001	13
14	1973	14	43	2002	19
15	1974	18	44	2003	31
16	1975	42	45	2004	18
17	1976	37	46	2005	14
18	1977	42	47	2006	24
19	1978	36	48	2007	23
20	1979	38	49	2008	17
21	1980	17	50	2009	14
22	1981	19	51	2010	20
23	1982	12	52	2011	14
24	1983	13	53	2012	19
25	1984	17	54	2013	16
26	1985	19	55	2014	17
27	1986	18	56	2015	16
28	1987	21	57	2016	38
29	1988	19	58	2017	12
				TOTAL	1002

Table n*56; Source: Gutu Kia Zimi (2020)

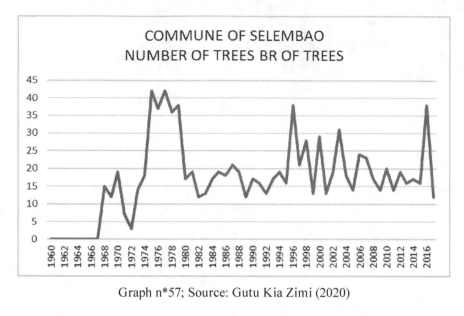

Graph n*57; Source: Gutu Kia Zimi (2020)

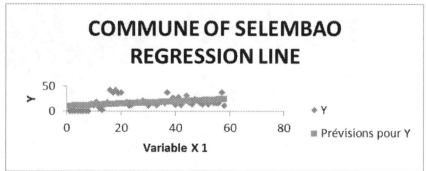

Correlation Coefficient R = 0.4

Graph n*58; Gutu Kia Zimi (2020)

The correlation coefficient (R = 0.4) indicates a weak correlation between the number of trees and the year of plantation. In addition, the regression line indicates a growth of urban vegetation in the commune of Selembao.

	AREA D COMMUNE OF MAKALA YEARS OF TREE PLANTIND				
N*	YEARS	NBR OF TREES	N*	YEARS	NBR OF TREES
1	1960	0	30	1989	15
2	1961	0	31	1990	5
3	1962	0	32	1991	23
4	1963	1	33	1992	10
5	1964	0	34	1993	13
6	1965	3	35	1994	36
7	1966	15	36	1995	43
8	1967	23	37	1996	51
9	1968	19	38	1997	17
10	1969	17	39	1998	6
11	1970	9	40	1999	2
12	1971	11	41	2000	26
13	1972	7	42	2001	12
14	1973	12	43	2002	38
15	1974	22	44	2003	46
16	1975	13	45	2004	4
17	1976	1	46	2005	21
18	1977	17	47	2006	3
19	1978	9	48	2007	7
20	1979	11	49	2008	5
21	1980	9	50	2009	9
22	1981	14	51	2010	7
23	1982	12	52	2011	6
24	1983	23	53	2012	12
25	1984	9	54	2013	16
26	1985	18	55	2014	8
27	1986	13	56	2015	6
28	1987	25	57	2016	13
29	1988	28	58	2017	8
				TOTAL	809

Table n*57; Source: Gutu Kia Zimi (2020)

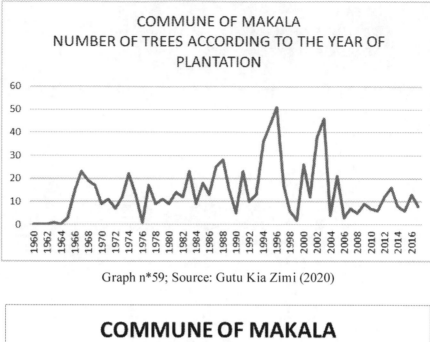

Graph n*59; Source: Gutu Kia Zimi (2020)

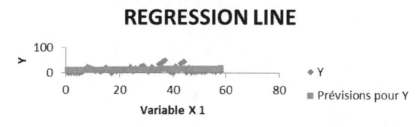

Correlation Coefficient R = 0.2

Graph n*60; Source: Gutu Kia Zimi (2020)

The correlation coefficient (R = 0.2) indicates a weak correlation between the number of trees and the year of plantation. In addition, the regression line indicates a decrease of urban vegetation in the commune of Makala.

	AREA D				
	COMMUNE OF NDJILI				
	YEARS OF TREE PLANTING				
N*	YEARS	NBR OF TREES	N*	YEARS	NBR OF TREES
1	1960	0	30	1989	14
2	1961	0	31	1990	12
3	1962	0	32	1991	16
4	1963	0	33	1992	23
5	1964	0	34	1993	16
6	1965	4	35	1994	15
7	1966	24	36	1995	34
8	1967	41	37	1996	13
9	1968	33	38	1997	12
10	1969	18	39	1998	4
11	1970	28	40	1999	29
12	1971	12	41	2000	7
13	1972	33	42	2001	17
14	1973	32	43	2002	24
15	1974	35	44	2003	12
16	1975	17	45	2004	7
17	1976	25	46	2005	10
18	1977	22	47	2006	13
19	1978	16	48	2007	8
20	1979	27	49	2008	6
21	1980	26	50	2009	15
22	1981	35	51	2010	4
23	1982	29	52	2011	2
24	1983	37	53	2012	11
25	1984	43	54	2013	14
26	1985	22	55	2014	9
27	1986	23	56	2015	12
28	1987	21	57	2016	15
29	1988	18	58	2017	18
				TOTAL	1013

Table n*58; Source: Gutu Kia Zimi (2020)

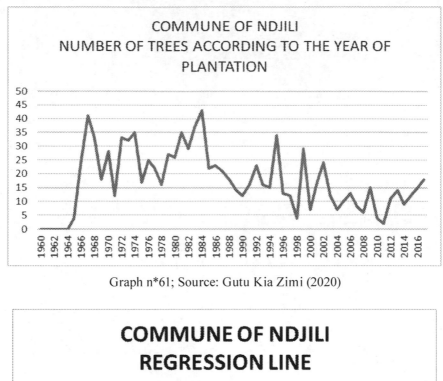

Graph n*61; Source: Gutu Kia Zimi (2020)

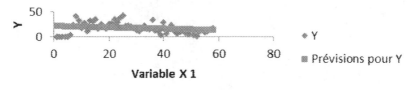

Correlation Coefficient R = 2

Graph n*62; Source: Gutu Kia Zimi (2020)

The correlation coefficient (R = 0.2) indicates a weak correlation between the number of trees and the year of plantation. In addition, the regression line indicates a decrease of urban vegetation in the commune of Ndjili.

	AREA D				
	COMMUNE OF BUMBU				
	YEARS OF TREE PLANTING				
N*	YEARS	NBR OF TREES	N*	YEARS	NBR OF TREES
1	1960	0	30	1989	15
2	1961	0	31	1990	6
3	1962	0	32	1991	32
4	1963	0	33	1992	15
5	1964	0	34	1993	8
6	1965	1	35	1994	15
7	1966	8	36	1995	5
8	1967	11	37	1996	7
9	1968	3	38	1997	9
10	1969	9	39	1998	13
11	1970	23	40	1999	7
12	1971	7	41	2000	10
13	1972	8	42	2001	11
14	1973	2	43	2002	6
15	1974	6	44	2003	15
16	1975	11	45	2004	2
17	1976	8	46	2005	17
18	1977	3	47	2006	2
19	1978	18	48	2007	13
20	1979	7	49	2008	3
21	1980	24	50	2009	15
22	1981	17	51	2010	6
23	1982	19	52	2011	8
24	1983	20	53	2012	21
25	1984	13	54	2013	12
26	1985	11	55	2014	9
27	1986	11	56	2015	8
28	1987	5	57	2016	5
29	1988	8	58	2017	13
				TOTAL	561

Table n*59; Source: Gutu Kia Zimi (2020)

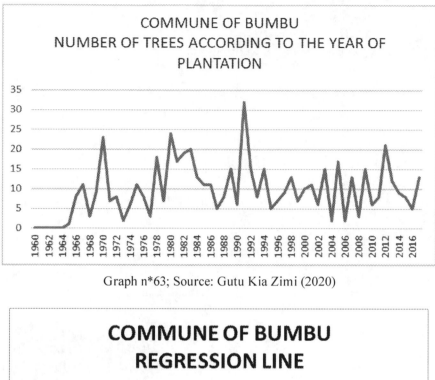

Graph n*63; Source: Gutu Kia Zimi (2020)

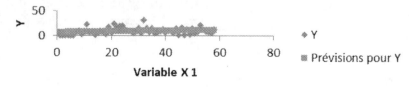

Correlation Coefficient R = 0.2

Graph n*64; Source: Gutu Kia Zimi (2020)

The correlation coefficient (R = 0.2) indicates a weak correlation between the number of trees and the year of plantation. In addition, the regression line indicates a growth of urban vegetation in the commune of Bumbu.

	AREA D COMMUNE OF KIMBANSEKE YEARS OF TREE PLANTING				
N*	YEARS	NBR OF TREES	N*	YEARS	NBR OF TREES
1	1960	0	30	1989	22
2	1961	0	31	1990	62
3	1962	0	32	1991	47
4	1963	0	33	1992	131
5	1964	0	34	1993	52
6	1965	0	35	1994	114
7	1966	3	36	1995	43
8	1967	15	37	1996	27
9	1968	89	38	1997	27
10	1969	96	39	1998	36
11	1970	77	40	1999	21
12	1971	133	41	2000	18
13	1972	101	42	2001	21
14	1973	122	43	2002	16
15	1974	103	44	2003	17
16	1975	51	45	2004	13
17	1976	67	46	2005	29
18	1977	44	47	2006	17
19	1978	38	48	2007	19
20	1979	67	49	2008	22
21	1980	53	50	2009	18
22	1981	60	51	2010	31
23	1982	35	52	2011	25
24	1983	143	53	2012	28
25	1984	49	54	2013	48
26	1985	111	55	2014	59
27	1986	124	56	2015	67
28	1987	66	57	2016	69
29	1988	59	58	2017	73
				TOTAL	2878

Table n* 60; Source: Gutu Kia Zimi (2020)

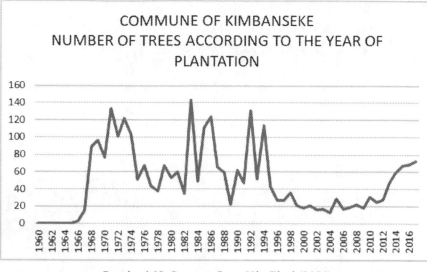

Graph n*65; Source: Gutu Kia Zimi (2020)

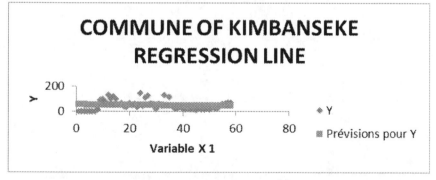

Correlation Coefficient R = 0.1

Graph n*66; Source: Gutu Kia Zimi (2020)

The correlation coefficient (R = 0.1) indicates a weak correlation between the number of trees and the year of plantation. In addition, the regression line indicates a growth of urban vegetation in the commune of Kimbanseke.

N*	YEARS	NBR OF TREES	N*	YEARS	NBR OF TREES
	AREA D				
	COMMUNE OF NGABA				
	YEARS OF TREE PLANTING				
1	1960	0	30	1989	18
2	1961	0	31	1990	12
3	1962	0	32	1991	6
4	1963	0	33	1992	8
5	1964	0	34	1993	14
6	1965	0	35	1994	7
7	1966	2	36	1995	3
8	1967	3	37	1996	2
9	1968	19	38	1997	8
10	1969	7	39	1998	7
11	1970	28	40	1999	6
12	1971	29	41	2000	2
13	1972	11	42	2001	8
14	1973	36	43	2002	6
15	1974	33	44	2003	2
16	1975	32	45	2004	4
17	1976	16	46	2005	13
18	1977	26	47	2006	9
19	1978	21	48	2007	11
20	1979	12	49	2008	1
21	1980	21	50	2009	11
22	1981	16	51	2010	3
23	1982	19	52	2011	7
24	1983	17	53	2012	6
25	1984	24	54	2013	3
26	1985	21	55	2014	6
27	1986	15	56	2015	4
28	1987	16	57	2016	1
29	1988	15	58	2017	3
			TOTAL		630

Table n*61; Source: Gutu Kia Zimi (2020)

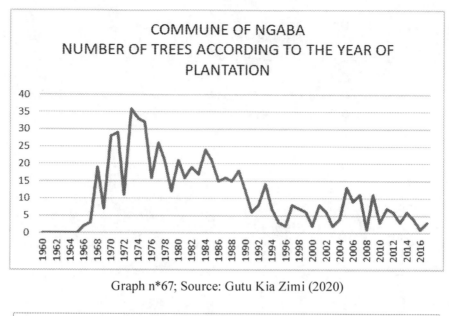

Graph n*67; Source: Gutu Kia Zimi (2020)

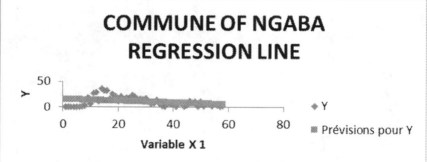

Correlation Coefficient R = 0.3
Graph n*68; Source: Gutu Kia Zimi (2020)
The correlation coefficient (R = 0.3) indicates a weak correlation between
the number of trees and the year of plantation. In addition, the regression line
indicates a decrease of urban vegetation in the commune of Ngaba.

N*	YEARS	NBR OF TREES	N*	YEARS	NBR OF TREES
	AREA D				
	COMMUNE OF NGIRI NGIRI				
	YEARS OF TREE PLANTING				
1	1954	0	33	1986	31
2	1955	0	34	1987	17
3	1956	0	35	1988	10
4	1957	3	36	1989	13
5	1958	1	37	1990	9
6	1959	1	38	1991	8
7	1960	0	39	1992	9
8	1961	0	40	1993	8
9	1962	3	41	1994	9
10	1963	2	42	1995	7
11	1964	4	43	1996	3
12	1965	21	44	1997	6
13	1966	12	45	1998	3
14	1967	5	46	1999	6
15	1968	24	47	2000	2
16	1969	19	48	2001	1
17	1970	20	49	2002	2
18	1971	30	50	2003	3
19	1972	33	51	2004	7
20	1973	28	52	2005	2
21	1974	27	53	2006	1
22	1975	11	54	2007	1
23	1976	10	55	2008	3
24	1977	37	56	2009	1
25	1978	36	57	2010	2
26	1979	16	58	2011	0
27	1980	22	59	2012	0
28	1981	14	60	2013	1
29	1982	18	61	2014	0
30	1983	10	62	2015	0
31	1984	16	63	2016	0
32	1985	23	64	2017	0
				TOTAL	611

Table n*62; Source: Gutu Kia Zimi (2020)

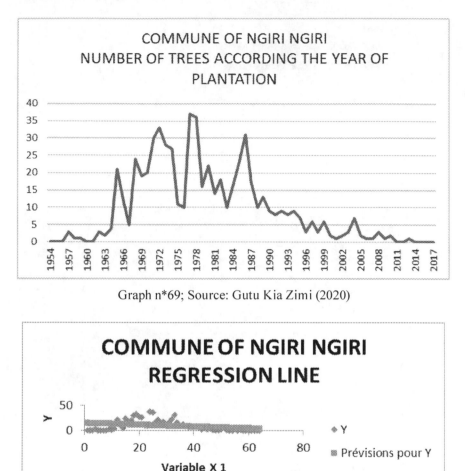

Graph n*69; Source: Gutu Kia Zimi (2020)

Correlation Coefficient R = 0.3
Graph n*70; Source: Gutu Kia Zimi (2020)
The correlation coefficient (R = 0.3) indicates a weak correlation between the number of trees and the year of plantation. In addition, the regression line indicates a decrease of urban vegetation in the commune of Ngiri Ngiri.

N"	YEARS	NBR. OF TREES	N*	YEARS	NBR OF TREES
AREA D					
COMMUNE OF KASA VUBU					
YEARS OF TREE PLANTING					
1	1954	1	33	1986	11
2	1955	0	34	1987	23
3	1956	1	35	1988	17
4	1957	2	36	1989	22
5	1958	1	37	1990	18
6	1959	0	38	1991	19
7	1960	1	39	1992	13
8	1961	2	40	1993	14
9	1962	3	41	1994	12
10	1963	0	42	1995	11
11	1964	4	43	1996	10
12	1965	15	44	1997	9
13	1966	13	45	1998	2
14	1967	12	46	1999	7
15	1968	8	47	2000	8
16	1969	11	48	2001	4
17	1970	15	49	2002	6
18	1971	12	50	2003	8
19	1972	10	51	2004	5
20	1973	23	52	2005	6
21	1974	19	53	2006	9
22	1975	27	54	2007	7
23	1976	16	55	2008	1
24	1977	25	56	2009	1
25	1978	33	57	2010	2
26	1979	14	58	2011	0
27	1980	13	59	2012	0
28	1981	21	60	2013	0
29	1982	20	61	2014	0
30	1983	17	62	2015	0
31	1984	16	63	2016	0
32	1985	19	64	2017	0
				TOTAL	**619**

Table n*63; Source: Gutu Kia Zimi (2020)

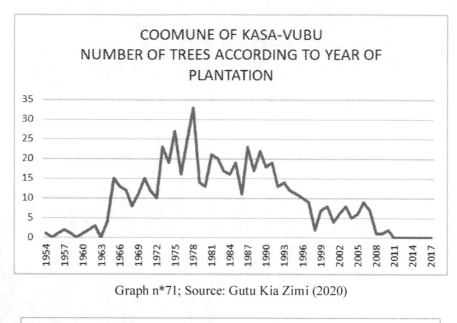

Graph n*71; Source: Gutu Kia Zimi (2020)

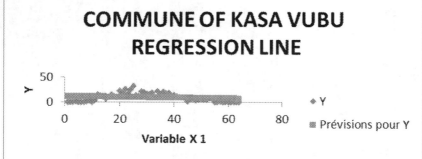

Correlation Coefficient R = 0.2
Graph n*72; Source: Gutu Kia Zimi (2020)
The correlation coefficient (R = 0.3) indicates a weak correlation between
the number of trees and the year of plantation. In addition, the regression line
indicates a decrease of urban vegetation in the commune of Kasa-Vubu.

N*	YEARS	NBR OF TREES	YEARS	NBR OF TREES	
AREA E					
COMMUNE DE MALUKU					
YEARS OF TREE PLANTING					
1	1960	0	30	1989	19
2	1961	0	31	1990	18
3	1962	0	32	1991	19
4	1963	0	33	1992	17
5	1964	0	34	1993	21
6	1965	0	35	1994	19
7	1966	0	36	1995	12
8	1967	2	37	1996	13
9	1968	13	38	1997	16
10	1969	8	39	1998	13
11	1970	5	40	1999	12
12	1971	7	41	2000	17
13	1972	2	42	2001	28
14	1973	12	43	2002	12
15	1974	9	44	2003	15
16	1975	7	45	2004	27
17	1976	8	46	2005	11
18	1977	11	47	2006	14
19	1978	13	48	2007	13
20	1979	21	49	2008	15
21	1980	15	50	2009	20
22	1981	29	51	2010	12
23	1982	21	52	2011	24
24	1983	23	53	2012	13
25	1984	28	54	2013	18
26	1985	21	55	2014	27
27	1986	11	56	2015	15
28	1987	19	57	2016	16
29	1988	12	58	2017	25
			TOTAL		**798**

Table n*64; Source: Gutu Kia Zimi (2020)

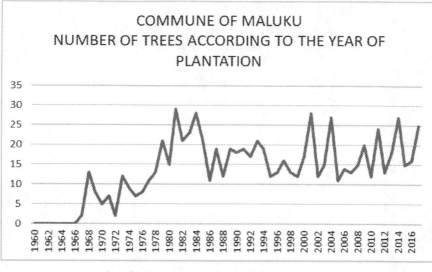

Graph n*73; Source: Gutu Kia Zimi (2020)

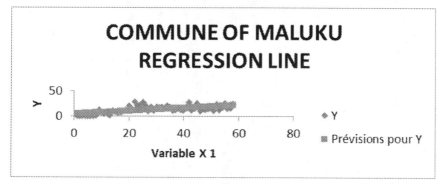

Correlation Coefficient R = 0.6

Graph n*74; Source: Gutu Kia Zimi (2020)

The correlation coefficient (R = 0.6) indicates a strong correlation between the number of trees and the year of plantation. In addition, the regression line indicates a growth of urban vegetation in the commune of Maluku.

	AREA E COMMUNE DE LA NSELE YEARS OF TREE PLANTING				
N*	YEARS	NBR OF TREES	N*	YEARS	NBR OF TREES
1	1960	0	30	1989	49
2	1961	0	31	1990	42
3	1962	0	32	1991	69
4	1963	0	33	1992	72
5	1964	0	34	1993	88
6	1965	0	35	1994	69
7	1966	2	36	1995	37
8	1967	3	37	1996	29
9	1968	13	38	1997	36
10	1969	19	39	1998	40
11	1970	21	40	1999	39
12	1971	29	41	2000	28
13	1972	25	42	2001	32
14	1973	37	43	2002	37
15	1974	24	44	2003	34
16	1975	30	45	2004	33
17	1976	23	46	2005	39
18	1977	27	47	2006	51
19	1978	31	48	2007	62
20	1979	41	49	2008	76
21	1980	38	50	2009	98
22	1981	35	51	2010	53
23	1982	45	52	2011	48
24	1983	39	53	2012	99
25	1984	65	54	2013	85
26	1985	66	55	2014	87
27	1986	56	56	2015	88
28	1987	57	57	2016	89
29	1988	61	58	2017	91
				TOTAL	2487

Table n*65; Source: Gutu Kia Zimi (2020)

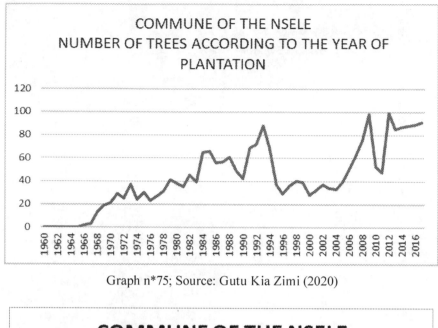

Graph n*75; Source: Gutu Kia Zimi (2020)

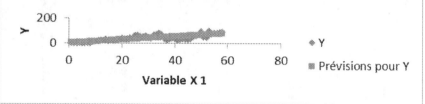

Correlation Coefficient R = 0.8

Graph n*76; Source: Gutu Kia Zimi (2020)

The correlation coefficient (R = 0.8) indicates a strong correlation between the number of trees and the year of plantation. In addition, the regression line indicates a growth of urban vegetation in the commune of Nsele.

	AREA E				
	COMMUNE OF MONT NGAFULA				
	YEARS OF PLANTING TREES				
N*	YEARS	NBR OF TREES	N*	YEARS	NBR OF TREES
1	1960	2	30	1989	61
2	1961	2	31	1990	36
3	1962	3	32	1991	52
4	1963	1	33	1992	57
5	1964	3	34	1993	38
6	1965	4	35	1994	37
7	1966	3	36	1995	53
8	1967	58	37	1996	37
9	1968	48	38	1997	40
10	1969	46	39	1998	42
11	1970	37	40	1999	46
12	1971	46	41	2000	41
13	1972	41	42	2001	52
14	1973	48	43	2002	58
15	1974	47	44	2003	42
16	1975	59	45	2004	57
17	1976	57	46	2005	45
18	1977	49	47	2006	49
19	1978	66	48	2007	53
20	1979	59	49	2008	89
21	1980	61	50	2009	90
22	1981	73	51	2010	59
23	1982	75	52	2011	62
24	1983	71	53	2012	79
25	1984	46	54	2013	80
26	1985	74	55	2014	89
27	1986	60	56	2015	84
28	1987	73	57	2016	87
29	1988	62	58	2017	94
			TOTAL		2983

Table n*66; Source: Gutu Kia Zimi (2020)

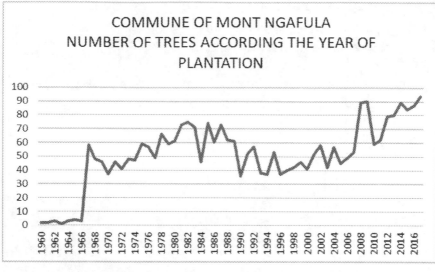

Graph n*77; Source: Gutu Kia Zimi (2020)

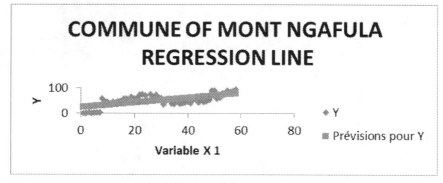

Correlation Coefficient R = 0.7

Graph n*78; Source: Gutu Kia Zimi (2020)

The correlation coefficient (R = 0.7) indicates a strong correlation between the number of trees and the year of plantation. In addition, the regression line indicates a growth of urban vegetation in the commune of Mont Ngafula.

In conclusion, Statistical analysis of the results leads us to the following observation:

1. Shrub vegetation in residential plots is on the rise in the neighborhoods of the peripheral municipalities of Nsele,

Maluku, Mont Ngafula, Kimbanseke, Ngaliema, Masina, Kimbanseke

2. On the other hand, vegetation is in decline in the districts of the former communes of Kinshasa, Barumbu, Gombe, Lingwala, Kalamu, Kintambo and of the other so-called new communes of KasaVubu, Bumbu, Bandalungwa, Selembao, Ndjili, Ngaba, NgiriNgiri, Makala, Matete, Lemba, Kisenso, Limete.

3. The estimate of shrub vegetation in residential plots by the regression line indicates that vegetation is growing in some municipalities such as Maluku, Nsele, Mont Ngafula, while it is decreasing in other municipalities.

4. In most communes there is a weak correlation between the years of tree planting and the number of trees in residential plots, except in the communes of Ngaliema, Maluku, Nsele, Mont Ngafula, Barumbu where there is a strong correlation.

5. Urban vegetation in residential plots decreases as population density increases.

CHAPTER V

URBAN GROWTH AND DEMOGRAPHIC GROWTH

——— ❈ ———

TITLE I: IMPACT OF URBAN AND DEMOGRAPHIC GROWTH ON THE URBAN VEGETATION OF KINSHASA

We will examine the impact of demographic (high density) and urban (urban sprawl) growth on urban vegetation. The population of Kinshasa increases slowly at first, going from 5,000 inhabitants in 1889 to 23,000 in 1923, but grows rapidly from 1940. After 1950, the population doubles approximately every five years and, at the end of the years 2000, reached 10 million inhabitants, a large part of whom live in areas of spontaneous settlement. Population growth is mainly due to internal migration and the expansion of government, but also to the retreat of the city limits. Kinshasa's population is young. More than half of Kinshasa are under 22, and only a small part are over 50[74].

---

[74] JAMES OLADIPO ADEJUWON, Dennis D. CORDELL, Janet MACGAFFEY, Wyatt MACGAFFEY, « KINSHASA », *Encyclopædia Universalis* [en ligne], consulté le 6 juillet 2020. URL: http://www.universalis.fr/encyclopedie/kinshasa/

Photo GKZ

The rural exodus sharply accelerated after independence. It is explained, on the one hand, by political unrest and the economic decline of rural areas devoid of any basic equipment and any possibility of development and, on the other hand, by the attractions of the city. While it traditionally welcomed immigrants from West Africa and neighboring countries of Central Africa, after independence, most of the new arrivals came from all over the country, particularly from the neighboring regions of Bandundu in east and Kongo Central to the south. Like most African cities, which are currently the main focus of global urbanization, Kinshasa provides a convincing example of the urgency to re-examine the logic of the exploitation of spaces and resources. Indeed, the lack of planning of this city since independence has led to its peri-urbanization characterized by a growing demography and the dispersed and spontaneous occupation of different geomorphological zones, suitable or not for construction.

This has resulted in environmental and landscape imbalance

due to environmental risks and damage such as erosion, flooding, pollution and others. It is therefore clear that the challenge of urban and peri-urban development in Kinshasa is linked to improving the environmental quality of habitats.

Photo GKZ

To do this, it is now recognized that it is necessary to calibrate and adapt management practices to the conditions of natural and human resources. This has resulted in environmental and landscape imbalance due to environmental risks and damage such as erosion, flooding, pollution and others. It is therefore clear that the challenge of urban and peri-urban development in Kinshasa is linked to improving the environmental quality of habitats. To do this, it is now recognized that it is necessary to calibrate and adapt management practices to the conditions of natural and human resources. In this perspective, this study is based also on the central hypothesis that the adaptation of the existing green system to the biophysical, socio-economic and cultural context, through the landscape approach. It is consisting in taking into account the quality of the environments and their appropriation by the inhabitants, opens up new perspectives to restore the balances disturbed by the spatial transformations underway in the urban and peri-urban context of Kinshasa. The urban and peri-urban landscape of Kinshasa is undergoing major spatial transformations to the detriment of the plant cover. However, it should be noted that in the urban and peri-urban fabric, there are still residual green spaces and plant development practices in the inhabited plots that could support environmental requalification. The application of the landscape approach allowed us to understand how to develop and / or define possibilities for action.

These are based on the dynamics of local plants to re-establish new interactions between natural resources and peri-urban agglomerations[75]. The urban expansion of the city of Kinshasa has also contributed to the destruction of the forest and the vegetation cover around the city. The conversion of land and agricultural land into urban space as a result of urban growth reduces the areas permeable to water, disrupts the natural flow and drainage patterns and causes serious flooding problems in many communes of the city. The municipalities of Kisenso, Mont-Ngafula, Selembao offer concrete cases of destruction of the surrounding forest plant cover.

---

[75] KOUAGOU RAOUL SAMBIEN (2019), KOUAGOU RAOUL SAMBIEN (2019), Dynamique du paysage de la ville province de Kinshasa sous la pression de la périurbanisation: l'infrastructure verte comme moteur d'aménagement.

Photo GKZ

Photo GKZ

Photo GKZ

Photo GKZ

Photo GKZ

Photo GKZ

Photo GKZ

Photo GKZ

Photo GKZ

Photo GKZ

Photo GKZ

Photo GKZ

Photo Gutu Kia Zimi

TITLE II: DISTRIBUTION OF TREES FOLLOWING THE YEARS OF PLANTING

REPARTITION DES ARBRES SUIVANT ANNEES DE PLANTATION					
N*	ANNEE	ARBRES	N*	ANNEE	NOMBRE
1	1954	81	33	1986	667
2	1955	2	34	1987	591
3	1956	8	35	1988	630
4	1957	18	36	1989	543
5	1958	15	37	1990	490
6	1959	21	38	1991	520
7	1960	48	39	1992	519
8	1961	86	40	1993	461
9	1962	88	41	1994	514
10	1963	125	42	1995	377
11	1964	109	43	1996	445
12	1965	209	44	1997	341
13	1966	307	45	1998	331
14	1967	311	46	1999	305
15	1968	491	47	2000	377
16	1969	502	48	2001	375
17	1970	471	49	2002	379
18	1971	510	50	2003	407
19	1972	491	51	2004	319
20	1973	566	52	2005	385
21	1974	609	53	2006	307
22	1975	557	54	2007	388
23	1976	490	55	2008	411
24	1977	544	56	2009	436
25	1978	544	57	2010	345
26	1979	645	58	2011	362
27	1980	543	59	2012	417
28	1981	615	60	2013	412
29	1982	599	61	2014	487
30	1983	735	62	2015	467
31	1984	619	63	2016	464
32	1985	674	64	2017	476
				TOTAL	25581

Table n*67; Source: Gutu Kia Zimi (2020)

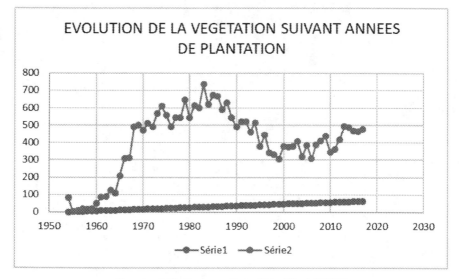

Graph n*79, Source: Gutu Kia Zimi (2020)

TITRE III: RELATIONSHIP BETWEEN YEARS OF PLANTING AND NUMBER OF TREES CORRELATION COEFFICIENT (R)

COEFFICIENT DE CORRELATION

RELATION ENTRE ANNEES DE PLANTATION ET NOMBRE D'ARBRES

ANNEES	X	Y(Arbres)	XY	X²	Y²	ANNEES	X	Y(Arbres)	XY	X²	Y²
1954	1	81	81	1	6561	1986	33	667	22011	1089	444889
1955	2	2	4	4	4	1987	34	591	20094	1156	349281
1956	3	8	24	9	64	1988	35	630	22050	1225	396900
1957	4	18	72	16	324	1989	36	543	19548	1296	294849
1958	5	15	75	25	225	1990	37	490	18130	1369	240100
1959	6	21	126	36	441	1991	38	520	19760	1444	270400
1960	7	48	336	49	2304	1992	39	519	20241	1521	269361
1961	8	86	688	64	7396	1993	40	461	18440	1600	212521
1962	9	88	792	81	7744	1994	41	514	21074	1681	264196
1963	10	125	1250	100	15625	1995	42	377	15834	1764	142129
1964	11	109	1199	121	11881	1996	43	445	19135	1849	198025
1965	12	209	2508	144	43681	1997	44	341	15004	1936	116281
1966	13	307	3991	169	94249	1998	45	331	14895	2025	109561
1967	14	311	4354	196	96721	1999	46	305	14030	2116	93025
1968	15	491	7365	225	241081	2000	47	377	17719	2209	142129
1969	16	502	8032	256	252004	2001	48	375	18000	2304	140625
1970	17	471	8007	289	221841	2002	49	379	18571	2401	143641
1971	18	510	9180	324	260100	2003	50	407	20350	2500	165649
1972	19	491	9329	361	241081	2004	51	319	16269	2601	101761
1973	20	566	11320	400	320356	2005	52	385	20020	2704	148225
1974	21	609	12789	441	370881	2006	53	307	16271	2809	94249
1975	22	557	12254	484	310249	2007	54	388	20952	2916	150544
1976	23	490	11270	529	240100	2008	55	411	22605	3025	168921
1977	24	544	13056	576	295936	2009	56	436	24416	3136	190096
1978	25	544	13600	625	295936	2010	57	345	19665	3249	119025
1979	26	645	16770	676	416025	2011	58	362	20996	3364	131044
1980	27	543	14661	729	294849	2012	59	417	24603	3481	173889
1981	28	615	17220	784	378225	2013	60	412	24720	3600	169744
1982	29	599	17371	841	358801	2014	61	487	29707	3721	237169
1983	30	735	22050	900	540225	2015	62	467	28954	3844	218089
1984	31	619	19189	961	383161	2016	63	464	29232	3969	215296
1985	32	674	21568	1024	454276	2017	64	476	30464	4096	226576
						TOTAL	2080	25581	924291	89440	12500537
						Moyenne	32.5	399.703			
						Coefficient de R = 0.42					

Table n*68; Source: Gutu Kia Zimi (2020)

Le coefficient de corrélation (r = 0.4) indique une faible corrélation entre le nombre d'arbres et les années de plantation de ces arbres dans les parcelles

$$r = \frac{n(\Sigma xy) - (\Sigma x)(\Sigma y)}{\sqrt{[\,n\Sigma x^2 - (\Sigma x)^2\,][\,n\Sigma y^2 - (\Sigma y)^2\,]}}$$

Soit R = 5.946.144: 1.182,3 x 12.068,4
= 5.946.144: 14.268.469,32 = 0,42

Le coefficient de corrélation (R= 0,42) nous indique une faible relation entre le nombre d'arbres et l'année de plantation des arbres[76].

$$a = \frac{n \cdot (\Sigma XY) - (\Sigma X) \cdot (\Sigma Y)}{n \cdot (\Sigma X^2) - (\Sigma X)^2}$$

où a représente le taux de variation
        n représente le nombre de couples de valeurs observeés
        X représente chacune des coordonnées X des points observés
        Y représente chacune des coordonnées Y des points observés

$$b = \bar{Y} - a \cdot \bar{X}$$

où b représente la valeur intiale (l'ordonnée à l'origine) de la droite
        a représente le taux de variation
        $\bar{X}$ représente la moyenne de la variable X
        $\bar{Y}$ représente la moyenne de la variable Y

a = 64x924291 – 2080 x25581: 64x89440 – 4.326.400

   = 59.154.624 – 53.208.480: 5.724.160 – 4.326.400

   = 5.946.144: 1.397.760

   = 4,3

b = 399,7 - 4,3 x 32,5

   = 399,7 – 139,8

   = 259,9

---

[76] We can also use this formula: $r = \Sigma[(x_i - x^-)(y_i - y^-)] / \sqrt{[\Sigma(x_i - x^-)^2 \cdot \Sigma(y_i - y^-)^2]}$

YEARS	X	Y(Trees)	X²	Y²	XY	YEARS	X	Y(Trees)	X²	Y²	XY
1954	1	81	1	6561	81	1986	33	667	1089	444889	22011
1955	2	2	4	4	4	1987	34	591	1156	349281	20094
1956	3	8	9	64	24	1988	35	630	1225	396900	22060
1957	4	18	16	324	72	1989	36	543	1296	294849	19548
1958	5	15	25	225	75	1990	37	490	1369	240100	18130
1959	6	21	36	441	126	1991	38	520	1444	270400	19760
1960	7	48	49	2304	336	1992	39	519	1521	269361	20241
1961	8	86	64	7396	688	1993	40	461	1600	212521	18440
1962	9	88	81	7744	792	1994	41	514	1681	264196	21074
1963	10	125	100	15625	1250	1995	42	377	1764	142129	15834
1964	11	109	121	11881	1199	1996	43	445	1849	198025	19135
1965	12	209	144	43681	2508	1997	44	341	1936	116281	15004
1966	13	307	169	94249	3991	1998	45	331	2025	109561	14895
1967	14	311	196	96721	4354	1999	46	305	2116	93025	14030
1968	15	491	225	241081	7365	2000	47	377	2209	142129	17719
1969	16	502	256	252004	8032	2001	48	375	2304	140625	18000
1970	17	471	289	221841	8007	2002	49	379	2401	143641	18571
1971	18	510	324	260100	9180	2003	50	407	2500	165649	20350
1972	19	491	361	241081	9329	2004	51	319	2601	101761	16269
1973	20	566	400	320356	11320	2005	52	385	2704	148225	20020
1974	21	609	441	370881	12789	2006	53	307	2809	94249	16271
1975	22	557	484	310249	12254	2007	54	388	2916	150544	20952
1976	23	490	529	240100	11270	2008	55	411	3025	168921	22605
1977	24	544	576	295936	13056	2009	56	436	3136	190096	24416
1978	25	544	625	295936	13600	2010	57	345	3249	119025	19665
1979	26	645	676	416025	16770	2011	58	362	3364	131044	20996
1980	27	543	729	294849	14661	2012	59	417	3481	173889	24603
1981	28	615	784	378225	17220	2013	60	412	3600	169744	24720
1982	29	599	841	358801	17371	2014	61	487	3721	237169	29707
1983	30	735	900	540225	22050	2015	62	467	3844	218089	28954
1984	31	619	961	383161	19189	2016	63	464	3969	215296	29232
1985	32	674	1024	454276	21568	2017	64	476	4096	226576	30464
						TOTAL	2080	25581	89440	12500537	924291
						Average	32.5	399.703			

Table n*68; Source: Gutu Kia Zimi (2020)

207

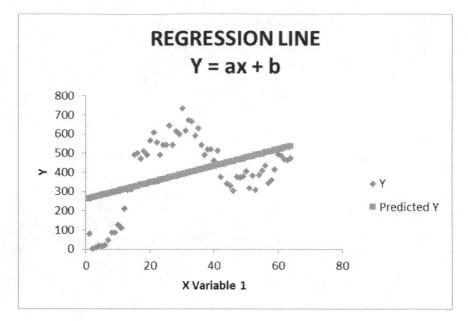

$$Y = 4,3x + 259, 9$$

Graph n*80; Source: Gutu Kia Zimi (2020)

Following the regression line above, the general trend of urban vegetation in Kinshasa would be increasing. But depending on the interpretation of this line, we must first see the annual change in the curve of urban vegetation. We know that this positive trend is very noticeable in the neighborhoods of the peripheral municipalities and in decline in the neighborhoods of the former municipalities. The regression line is obtained according to the following formula[77]:

$$Y = ax + b$$

$$b = [n(\textstyle\sum x_i y_i) - (\sum x_i)(\sum y_i)] / [n(\sum x_i^2) - (\sum x_i)^2] \; ; \; a = y^- - bx^-$$

---

[77] MICHAEL KELLEY W and ROBERT A. DONNELLY Jr, The Humongous book of Statistics Problems, Alpha Books, NY, 2009, p.390

With the regression line (Y = 4,3x + 259,9) we will estimate the future evolution of urban vegetation. Thanks to the linear regression line, it is possible to predict a trend for a given value X.

For the year 2018, (i.e. X = 65), the estimated number of trees (Y) is: Y = 4.3 x 65 +259.9 = 539.4 (trees).
−   For the year 2030, (i.e. X = 77), the estimated number of trees (Y) is: Y = 4.3 x 77 + 259.9 = 591 (trees).

Thanks to the regression line, the table below gives us the estimate of urban vegetation from 2018 to 2030.

According to our analysis, it turns out that the trend of increasing global evolution of shrub vegetation in the Kinshasa plots is statistically confirmed by the regression line. This growing development is the result of the city's rapid expansion. The peri-urban municipalities are experiencing an extension through the creation of new housing estates such as Mpasa, Bibua, Miteni, etc. The shrub vegetation in the residential plots in these new neighborhoods in the peripheral communes is still young, abundant and vigorous. The more the expansion of the city will continue, the shrub vegetation will develop in these new districts of the peri-urban municipalities (Maluku, Nsele, Mont Ngafula, Kisenso, Masina, Kimbanseke, Ngaliema). On the other hand, the shrub vegetation in the residential plots will continue to decrease in the old districts of the old urban communes (Kinshasa, Barumbu, Lingwala, Gombe, Kintambo), known as new (KasaVubu, Ngiri Ngiri, Bumbu, Ngaba, Selembao, Makala) and folded cities (Kalamu, Bandalungwa, Lemba, Limete, Matete).

Gutu Kia Zimi, PhD

ESTIMATE OF THE EVOLUTION OF URBAN VEGETATION 2018-2030					
YEARS	X	Y(TREES)	YEARS	X	Y(TREES)
1954	1	81	1992	39	519
1955	2	2	1993	40	461
1956	3	8	1994	41	514
1957	4	18	1995	42	377
1958	5	15	1996	43	445
1959	6	21	1997	44	341
1960	7	48	1998	45	331
1961	8	86	1999	46	305
1962	9	88	2000	47	377
1963	10	125	2001	48	375
1964	11	109	2002	49	379
1965	12	209	2003	50	407
1966	13	307	2004	51	319
1967	14	311	2005	52	385
1968	15	491	2006	53	307
1969	16	502	2007	54	388
1970	17	471	2008	55	411
1971	18	510	2009	56	436
1972	19	491	2010	57	345
1973	20	566	2011	58	362
1974	21	609	2012	59	417
1975	22	557	2013	60	412
1976	23	490	2014	61	487
1977	24	544	2015	62	467
1978	25	544	2016	63	464
1979	26	645	2017	64	476
1980	27	543	2018	65	539.4
1981	28	615	2019	66	543,7
1982	29	599	2020	67	548
1983	30	735	2021	68	552,3
1984	31	619	2022	69	556,6
1985	32	674	2023	70	560,9
1986	33	667	2024	71	565,2
1987	34	591	2025	72	569,5
1988	35	630	2026	73	573,8
1989	36	543	2027	74	578,1
1990	37	490	2028	75	582,4
1991	38	520	2029	76	586,7
			2030	77	591

Table n*69; Source: Gutu Kia Zimi (2020)

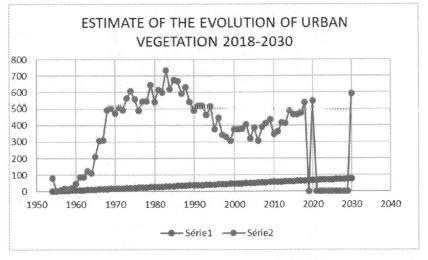

Graph n*81; Source: Gutu Kia Zimi (2020)

Following the regression line, the graph n*81 above gives us an illustration of the evolution of shrub vegetation in the residential plots of Kinshasa until 2030. The estimate of the evolution of urban vegetation following the regression line reveals us an increase (growth) in urban vegetation for the period from 2018 to 2030. As explained above, this overall change is selective depending on whether it is the shrub vegetation in the districts of the former municipalities on the one hand, or in the neighborhoods of peri-urban municipalities on the other hand. Indeed, the vegetation is regressive in the districts of the old communes of Kinshasa. In addition, it is increasing in the neighborhoods of peri-urban municipalities.

TITLE IV: WHAT FUTURE FOR URBAN VEGETATION IN KINSHASA

To answer this question, it is necessary to observe the factors that determine the evolution of this urban vegetation in residential plots. It will be necessary to highlight the fact that the shrub vegetation in the residential plots of Kinshasa depends exclusively on the sole will of the owners of the plots. But, they also do not hesitate to sacrifice the spaces available for trees in response to demographic pressure and the housing or habitat crisis in the city. Kinshasa is a booming megalopolis. Unfortunately, this expansion takes place in disharmony with its environment. For example, if you observe the urban space, which starts from the Mandela Roundabout on the former avenue November 24, Avenue Kabinda and the former avenue du Flambeau, it is plausible to observe that the vegetation of these districts of Lingwala, Barumbu, Kinshasa are in very strong decline. In other respects, urban greening is an integral part of a vast urban development program, as are socio-economic ones. On the one hand, in view of future demographic projections making Kinshasa the third largest megalopolis in Africa, and on the other hand, given the consequences of global warming, the revegetation of the city of Kinshasa is required. It must also be considered as an ecological and environmental emergency. However, major constraints: the population density in the residential plots, the size of the households of the inhabitants in continuous growth, the level of poverty of the populations constitute important constraints in the motivation of the population for the planting of new trees and the maintenance. old trees in residential plots of Kinshasa. The health risks, the discomfort of the sweltering heat and the consequences of the effects of climate change are only accelerating. Kinshasa, Africa's third largest megalopolis, like all of the country's major urban agglomerations, must adapt to the ecological characteristics of the city of tomorrow to guarantee a pleasant quality of life for city-dwellers in Kinshasa by protecting the surrounding biodiversity. As has been underlined before, to breathe new life into our neighborhoods in the various municipalities of Kinshasa, making more and better the urban space in Kinshasa is an ecological but also an environmental priority.

TITLE V: URBAN GROWTH OF KINSHASA

With nearly 400,000 inhabitants in 1960, the year of independence, Kinshasa has since seen its growth accelerate due to a sustained rural exodus and a high birth rate. Kinshasa, capital of the Democratic Republic of Congo (DRC), is one of the largest cities in Africa. Like all mega-cities, the largest Congolese city is suffering the full brunt of the urbanization of the planet. While in 1960 it had only 500,000 inhabitants, its population is now estimated at 15 million people, or 12% of the Congolese population. Moreover, this trend is not likely to be reversed. The number of inhabitants is expected to climb to 20 million in 2025[78]. This does not go without posing challenges in terms of economic growth to manage to support the additional populations. The latest report from the United Nations Habitat Organization (UN Habitat) places the DR-Congolese capital among the twenty-nine African cities in the midst of a population explosion. Leading the pack are cities like Cairo (Egypt), Lagos (Nigeria). Kinshasa (DRC), 23rd position globally. Demographic pressure is the consequence:

- from the mass rural exodus,
- the deterioration of living conditions in rural areas,
- the influx of refugees fleeing insecurity and wars that continue to ravage the east of the country,
- without forgetting an always numerous procreation,
- conflicts that undermine other parts of the country,
- the impoverishment of the countryside because of the economic crisis,

As a result, it begins to ask itself needs for basic social services (water, energy, health services, housing, etc...) in Kinshasa.

---

[78] UNITED NATIONS, op.cit

The city of Kinshasa had a population of 400,000 in 1960 and is estimated to have reached over six million in 2008; the average annual growth rate between 1960 and 2003 is estimated to be around 6.8% (Lelo Nzuzi,2008). Kinshasa developed in the plain along the Congo River. The plain, located at 300 meters above sea level, covers about 200 km2. It is the most industrialized, densely populated and formerly inhabited area; it is commonly called the "low" City. After independence in 1960, the city expanded on the hilly complex surrounding the Lower Town and culminating about 600 m above sea level; this area is mainly occupied by spontaneous neighborhoods. Kinshasa, the capital, will become Africa's largest megacity by 2030. Between 1984 and 2010, the city's annual population growth rate averaged 5.1%, compared with 4.1% nationally. Much of this population growth is attributable to factors in population-providing communities (i.e. conflict and inadequate rural services) rather than to incentives in cities (i.e. better work and living opportunities). With an estimated population of 12 million in 2016, Kinshasa is the densest urban system and has the fastest growth in Central Africa. At its current rate of growth, this city will be home to more than 24 million inhabitants within ten years and will be the most populous city in Africa, ahead of Cairo and Lagos. This perspective is an opportunity, but also a risk that the living conditions of the people in Kinshasa will become more precarious and that the city will become the largest slum in Africa if urbanization is not properly managed and the trend of exclusive urbanization as well as marginalization is not reversed. Rapid population growth comes with many challenges. It has the effect of increasing the demand for social services and education, health and basic services infrastructure to make cities livable[79]. Kinshasa is experiencing rapid population

---

[79] DINA RANARIFIDY, La Revue de l'urbanisation en République démocratique du Congo, Des villes productives et inclusives pour l'émergence de la République Démocratique du Congo,

growth, without cadastre and difficult to quantify in the absence of any census. The capital, whose population has doubled in less than twenty years, is estimated to have 10 million inhabitants. Between 2000 and 2005, the number of "Kinois" rose from 6 to 7.5 million, according to the satellite mapping of the Belgian geography magazine Belgeo[80]. The same scholarly review stated in 2009 a conclusion still valid to this day that on the Ngaliema Hills: "30% of urban growth took place on slopes of more than 15%, presenting a significant risk of erosion". According to Corneille Kanene (2017), this growth is the result of "urban planning of poverty", and "three quarters of Kinshasa are made up of slums without access to water or electricity". The spatial growth of Kinshasa (DRC) is mapped by classification of built spaces based on SPOT satellite images dating from 1995 and 2005.

According to the results, the growth of the city is less rapid than the demographic change; it is now carried out in interstitial spaces despite their steep slopes and a certain distance from the main communication routes (beyond 1 km)[81]. However, the same authors claimed based on demographic data from 1969 and 1995 that this densification of central areas would have reached its limit, resulting in the migration of some urban people from the Centre to the periphery. However, more recent studies suggest that the spatial extension of the city still coexists with the densification of the building, in particular by self-construction in interstitial spaces especially close to the main roads and by the fragmentation of the plots (Kayembe wa Kayembe et al., 2009; Sambiéni et al., 2018A). In any case, periurbanization is a clear fact in Kinshasa, with its procession of degrading effects

---

Banque Mondiale, Direction du développement, Environnement et Développement Durable, 2018, p.2.

[80] FLOURIOT, op.cit

[81] MATHIEU KAYEMBE WA KAYEMBE et all, Cartographie de la croissance urbaine de Kinshasa (R.D. Congo) entre 1995 et 2005 par télédétection satellitaire à haute résolution, Revue Belgeo, 2009, p.2

of landscape and habitats especially in an unplanned context. ... As Trefon (2004) described it, "the image of Kinshasa is often that of a disorderly world turned in on itself: confusion, crisis and chaos reign giving rise to a bizarre form of social cannibalism where society becomes its own prey", but the city of Kinshasa is also a place characterized by an order hidden in this disorder, an agglomeration where multiple initiatives and innovations despite the widespread lack of public services and even, at times, the State at large[82]. As everywhere else, the density of cities is currently a reflection of the phenomena of population growth and rural exodus. Cities are areas of high concentrations of population, human activities and communication axes. This rampant urbanism causes immense social segregation. The fragile homes of Ngaliema are a few hundred meters from the luxurious villas of "my countryside", and a few km from the towers, residences, embassies and the Presidential Palace of the Gombe. An elusive megacity, Kinshasa grows out of control. Among the popular megacities that grow larger each year without knowing how to welcome their new inhabitants, Kinshasa is the craziest. On a continent of more than 1 billion inhabitants that is expected to host a quarter of the world's population by 2050, the capital of the Democratic Republic of Congo (DRC), Africa's third largest city, is a city-state with a shadow administration, over which no one has a real control. No one knows how many people live or survive in the Congolese capital, an urban monster with no land registry or development plan[83]. The demographic situation in the capital of the Democratic Republic of the Congo is similar to that prevailing in many cities in tropical Africa; the population continues to grow rapidly since independence (Vennetier, 1991). The socio-economic

---

[82] P. KAPAGAMA, R. WATERHOUSE, Portrait of Kinshasa: A city on (the) edge, Crisis States Research Centre, 2009
[83] JOAN TILOUINE ET PIERRE BENETTI (2017), Journal Le Monde, Juillet 2017

crisis created very difficult living conditions: the development of the informal sector, the destructuring of public transport networks and the extreme spatial growth of the city, leading to longer and longer journeys to the city center, the place of concentration of all administrative and commercial activities. In Kinshasa, the average annual growth rate was about 8% between 1960 and 1980 (Mwanza Wa Mwanza, 1996); it has been estimated at 4-5% since the 1980s (Nzuzi Lelo, 1991; Luzolele et al., 1999). Such population growth has consequences on the morphology of the "kinois" space. Two processes can be observed: the growth of the population generates a spatial extension of the city; the growth of the population, in a context of scarcity of employment opportunities, insecurity, the concentration of infrastructure and growing difficulties in transport leads to the densification of existing neighborhoods ....[84]

United Nations figures indicate that in 1990 only 37% of the total population of developing countries lived in urban areas. By 2025, it is estimated that 61% of the population will be urbanized. There are many reasons for this rapid urban growth, including declining death rates, industrialization (which concentrates employment opportunities in urban areas), high fertility rates, popular perception of better opportunities in urban areas. urban areas and the political and economic problems of rural areas (UNDP 1996). Kinshasa, Africa's third largest megalopolis, is one of the cities in Central Africa with a degrading peri-urban landscape due to strong uncontrolled urbanization (Misilu Mia et al., 2010). In addition, the peri-urban communes of Kinshasa like that of Kisenso are located on erodible and floodable sites (Kayembe Wa Kayembe and Wolff, 2015). Several studies then recommend in Kinshasa various "Uses

---

[84] ELEONORE WOLFF ET VIRGINIE DELBART (2002), Extension urbaine et densité de la population à Kinshasa: contribution de la télédétection satellitaire, Belgeo, Revue Belge de Géographie, p. 45-99.

of Plant for Habitat" (UVH) for the adequate development of peri-urban plots based on vegetation (Wouters and Wolff, 2010). It has in fact been recognized since the 1990s that controlling erosion in Kinshasa should involve managing what is happening at the plot level (Miti et al., 2004). Fortunately, scattered studies report various UVH "use of plants for habitat (UVH)" in these peri-urban municipalities (Makumbelo et al., 2005).

Some studies even specify that almost all of the lush vegetation visible in aerial photographs and satellite images of these peri-urban municipalities is concentrated in inhabited plots (SOSAK, 2014)[85]. This observation is even more true as the peri-urban fabrics develop without voids and collective spaces. The sustainability of this vegetation is however compromised not only by its essentially private character but also by the current practice of cutting to, for example, supply the many informal bakeries in the city with firewood (Lelo Nzuzi, 2008), but also also and above all from demographic growth which exerts demographic pressure on urban space. It is therefore important to better conceptualize this vegetation present in inhabited plots and to properly control its determining factors to ensure its management. Reducing traffic congestion In Congolese cities, accessibility remains easy in the business center; on the other hand, it is quite good in the ring, which surrounds the business center. In the outlying districts, this accessibility is very uncertain or even poor due to a lack of good roads. Traffic congestion in Congolese cities has become an urban fact due to the narrowness and saturation of the roads, unsuitable roundabout radii, sources of traffic jams; and worse, it is especially at these points that air pollution is felt. The traffic density at the crossroads of main city roads is high. In

---

[85] KOUAGOU R. SAMBIENI (2019), Dynamique du paysage de la ville province de Kinshasa sous la pression de la périurbanisation: l'infrastructure verte comme moteur d'aménagement, Thèse de doctorat, ERAIFT, Université de Kinshasa, RDC.

Kinshasa, for example, this densification is around 2,500 vehicles per day. In addition, there is an impressive number of sedentary shops around crossroads, attracting thousands of users and contributing to vehicle congestion. These areas are then polluted by old vehicles in poor condition which use leaded gasoline and reinforce traffic jams at peak times (LELO N. 2011). Contrary to all these constraints, and in almost all the big cities the central and provincial governments with the support of the partners, modernize the urban infrastructures in order to improve the conditions of the mobility of people and goods. We note the reconstruction of urban roads, which are enlarged, gutters and collectors, crossroads, bridges; modern footbridges are planned, etc. All these actions allow a better improvement of urban congestion in Matadi, Mbuji-Mayi, Lubumbashi, Goma, Bukavu, Kisangani, and remarkably in Kinshasa the capital. In total, nearly 2,500 km of urban roads have been rehabilitated over the past ten years (Cellules Infrastructures, 2013). Eleonore Wolff et al. claim that:

- The built-up area in the hilly area of municipalities in the South and West is underestimated.
- The built-up area is overestimated in the eastern municipalities, mainly for the Mpasa neighborhoods in the municipality of Nsele.
- To limit the city's expansion to the east, the Kinshasa administration had planned basic amenities (water, electricity, etc.) in this area. The people of Kinshasa bought plots of land there, which they cleared with a view to building homes when the planned improvements were made. However, the crisis has left these adjustments in abeyance for more than ten years.

The cleared plots are characterized by a spectral signature too close to that of urbanized areas to be able to distinguish them, hence a certain overestimation of the built surface. From this identification of the building, it is possible to calculate the built-up areas per municipality, the proportion of municipal areas occupied by built and to compare it with the typology of communes of Flouriot (1975).

- Cities, whether classified as old, new or planned in Flouriot's typology (1975), are generally densely built (> 80%), with the exception of Bandalungwa and Ndjili (70%). For Bandalungwa, this can be explained by the presence of the military domain, Camp Kokolo and Camp Adoula, in which the buildings are more spaced. For Ndjili, only part of the commune is occupied by planned cities, some of which are of relatively high standing; in the latter, the density of buildings is lower and the space occupied by infrastructure is greater. The rest of the commune of Ndjili is built spontaneously. The town is also crossed by the Ndjili river.

- The South-West extensions, with the exception of Mont Ngafula, are also very densely built (> 80%). The communes of Ngaba, Bumbu, Makala, Selembao are relatively close to the city center and urbanized according to the same model as the central communes after independence.

- The municipality of Kisenso, eastern extension of the city, is 56% built. This relatively small town is partly located in the hilly area where the built-up areas are necessarily less important. Its urbanization is later than the South-West extensions.

- The municipalities of Ngaliema, Gombe and Limete have intermediate values (65-77%). The municipality of Ngaliema is close to the center, but it has luxurious accommodation surrounded by gardens and is located in the hilly area. La

Gombe is the administrative, business and commercial center, developed in the former colonial town greened up and crossed by wide avenues; it is also a high standard residential area. Limete is a high level industrial and residential municipality; in addition, a third of the town is marshy and uninhabited.

– The municipalities of Masina, Kimbanseke and Mont Ngafula appear to be sparsely built (12-26%); in reality, the frame is distributed very unevenly. Two thirds of the town of Masina along the river are occupied by swamps, the rest is very densely built. The municipality of Kimbanseke is densely built up near Boulevard Lumumba, but the further one moves away from it the more the density of the built environment decreases, the south of the municipality being almost uninhabited. The commune of Mont Ngafula is the least built (12%); The habitat is scattered in the hills with the exception of areas close to communication routes or the city center which are densely built.

Photo Gutu Kia Zimi

221

TITLE VI: EXTENSION OF THE CITY OF KINSHASA OR DENSIFICATION OF THE COMMUNES

The increase in the urban population of Kinshasa has been accompanied by a phenomenon of sprawl (urban growth), pushing further and further the limits of the city of Kinshasa. This extension of urban areas is incompatible with the principles of sustainable development advocating more economical management of areas and in particular control of space consumption (Rouxel, 1999). The collective imagination of a dense city where man is lost in the mass, where concentration is synonymous with nuisance, noise, pollution, and where exchanges are reduced to a minimum is also conveyed by many pictorial productions ... (Jonas, 2002). However, this rejection of density is not unfounded; the more populated the city, the more the living conditions are degraded. Nevertheless, according to Jacobs (1977)[86], density can also be synonymous with richness, diversity, animation and possibility of exchange[87]. However, in the case of the city of Kinshasa, is it really the density of the population that poses a problem in itself, or it is the lack of public facilities, transport, play areas that cause competition between inhabitants to access it or the lack of a social life in the neighborhoods? For example, the Matonge district in the commune of Kalamu is one of the densely inhabited districts of Kinshasa, but it is one of the busiest districts of the capital where we observe a very hectic social life and active, although lacking public facilities (green spaces, noise pollution, noise, etc.). Population growth is putting pressure on the Kinshasa area because

---

[86] JACOBS (1991), Déclin et survie des grandes villes américaines, Vintage Books, New York, Mardaga

[87] APUR (2003), Densités vécues et Formes Urbaines, https://www.apur.org/sites/default/files/documents/165.pdf

it is at the origin of the expansion of the built-up area on the outskirts and the densification of already built-up areas. These last two are closely related via intra-urban migration. In fact, the growth of the population in the outlying municipalities is mainly due to migrations from other towns in the city, not to mention the natural growth factor, which is very important in this city. The comparison between the city limits in 1969 and the extension of the built environment in 1995 makes it possible to visualize the extension of the urban spot of Kinshasa. To quantify urban expansion, we can assume that the proportion of built-up space in 1969 is identical to that in 1995 for the urban municipalities in 1969, i.e. that urban growth has taken place only by extension and not by densification. The urban patch is then estimated at 147 km² in 1969 and at 339 km² in 1995, including interstitial spaces and urban green spaces. Urban expansion would have taken place at a rate of 7.1 km² / year over 27 years. In 1967, the census counted 901,520 people in Kinshasa and mentioned an average annual growth rate of 8%. In 1969, Kinshasa's workforce can be estimated at 1,051,000 inhabitants. If Kinshasa had expanded without densification, we can estimate the population of 1995 based on the extension of the city in 1995, the population of 1969 and the extension of the city in 1969. Indeed, if we multiply population density from 1969 to the expansion of the city in 1995, the population of the city in 1995 is estimated at 2,423,735 people. In 1995, according to INS (1993) projections, there were approximately 4,787,000 inhabitants in Kinshasa. We can therefore say that the extension of Kinshasa has absorbed a little more than a third of the growth of the population while the densification of the districts concerns a little less than two thirds of this increase.

SECTION I: URBAN EXTENSION OR SPREAD

The causes and consequences of Kinshasa's urban sprawl are well known and are the subject of much analysis. One of the main consequences of the city's extension to the neighborhoods of peripheral municipalities is surely urban growth. Which leads to an increase in demand for basic infrastructure (water and electricity), schools, sanitation, roads, consumption energy, loss of agricultural land, various forms of pollution and health problems, which result from it and affect the vulnerable elements of the Kinshasa population. The expansion of the city of Kinshasa is a worrying phenomenon and remains inexorable. The city is expanding in a haphazard and rapid fashion. The border of the city of Kinshasa with the province of Kongo central has been extended several times and the southern extension of the city of Kinshasa is already on the outskirts of the province of Kongo central. Currently, the southern limit of Kinshasa, which is located in Mitendi is 5 km from Kasangulu city. It will be necessary to fear in future years its adhesion with the city of Kasangulu!. The city of Kinshasa extends above ground. This extension has enormous socio-economic consequences on the quality of life of the urban population and involves very large public and private investments. Despite everything, the expansion of the city of Kinshasa continues and accelerates day by day. The ideal would be to build a new city with new urban standards. Until before Independence in 1960, the city of Kinshasa developed mainly in the plain or lower town.

The development plans of 1950 and 1967, 1975 orient the urban expansion towards the east and prohibit construction on the slopes of hill sites ("non aedificandi" zones) because of their sensitivity to erosion. These hills were to be the subject of two types of use: residential districts and green spaces on their heights and market gardening zones in the valleys (FLOURIOT et al., 1975). However, as early as the 1950s, the city began to expand southwards due to the saturation of the space along the river; indeed, the banks of the river were sought after by settlers for their freshness. The latter (who arrived in Kinshasa in the late 1940s and during the 1950s) found two advantages in occupying the hilltops: a panoramic view of the city and fresh air, especially at night. This is how the cities of the "settlers", occupied by the Congolese ruling class after independence, were built on the heights of these hills. But after 1960, the valleys were not spared from urbanization, without a minimum of development. Indeed, in order to constitute the electorate in the perspective of the first democratic elections to take place in the DRC in the 1960s, political leaders at the national level encouraged the arrival of rural people in the city of Kinshasa (DE SAINT MOULIN, 2010). These leaders signaled to their activists that independence was synonymous with the end of tenant life. They launched the slogan "sala ngolo zako" (literally, "Make your effort or according to your abilities") which invited the militants to each take a building plot (KAYEMBE et al., 2010; LELO NZUZI, 2011).). Thus, new and old city-dwellers in central municipalities set out to find a property as close as possible to the city center, both in terms of distance and travel time. This is how the valleys close to the old cities were spontaneously taken over by these activists, despite their great sensitivity to ravine erosion in the context of the *Kinois* sandy soils and the ban on urbanization of these areas by the plans development. It turns out that urbanization continues without any notion of spatial limit to the detriment of the natural environment or the rural domain, according to the principle of low density[88]. In this way, low-income populations occupied marginal

---

[88] MORGANE COLOMBERT, JEAN-LUC SALAGNAC, DENIS MORAND ET YOUSSEF DIAB (2012), Le climat et la ville: la nécessité d'une recherche croisant les disciplines, *VertigO - la revue électronique en sciences de l'environnement* [En ligne], Hors-série 12 | mai 2012, mis

land (KAYEMBE WA KAYEMBE, 2012)[89]. The site occupied by the city of Kinshasa is particularly sensitive to environmental problems. They come from the nature of the soils and the steep slopes of the hills that surround it, but above all from human pressure on an already fragile environment. The waterproofing of soils, the anarchic constructions without retaining walls which weaken the slopes, the obstruction of river beds… have direct and indirect impacts, all too often catastrophic. We cannot intervene in one part of the city without having consequences for the surrounding neighborhoods. It is essential in the preparation of the urban planning document to take into account this fragile environment and to propose corrective or safeguard measures for the already urbanized areas, and to plan upstream the necessary developments for those, which will be urbanized in the area future. If it continues at the same pace, it is expected to cover around 86,000 hectares by 2030, almost double the area it occupies today. The city spreads very quickly on its margins, mainly to the east and the southwest, along the roads of Matadi and Bandundu, allowing access by public transport to the city center, which polarizes most of the urban jobs. However, since the beginning of the 1990s, neighborhoods have developed far from the city center and transport axes (eg: Cogelo district, Chad, Mandela, Department, Plateau); however, they do not benefit from any urban convenience. Between 1995 and 2005, on the one hand, 30% of urban growth took place on slopes of more than 15%, that is to say presenting a significant risk of erosion and, on the other hand, nearly 50% of the growth urbanization takes place more than a kilometer from major communication axes, or in interstitial spaces that are not easily accessible. If the city's population is to double in the next 15 years,

---

en ligne le 04 mai 2012, consulté le 05 septembre 2020. URL: http://journals.openedition.org/vertigo/11811; DOI: https://doi.org/10.4000/vertigo.11811.
[89] KAYEMBE WA KAYEMBE M. et WOLFFE (2015), op.cit., p. 119-138.

the area it occupies will likely have to double as well, even if dense housing is advocated. Thus, of the 450 km² occupied today, it will probably have to occupy 800. It will be necessary to find new land to expand in the years to come. Analysis of the surrounding areas is therefore essential at this stage to assess the site's capacity to absorb the expected extensions of the city. The urban authorities of Kinshasa when they intervene in the new urban subdivisions, often limit themselves to the layout of the streets, usually without foreseeing future green spaces. The streets and avenues of the districts of Kinshasa are often devoid of trees. It is generally accepted that the quality of life in an urban agglomeration depends largely on the extent and the quality of the green spaces, which it contains, or which surrounds it. Trees to which, in addition to their aesthetic value, a vital role is increasingly attributed in the protection of the urban environment generally occupy these green spaces, when they exist. With accelerated urbanization all over the world, urban forestry is likely to become an important branch of forest science.

The plain occupied today by Kinshasa is bordered by a cirque of hills, which reach an altitude of 600m in the south and in the east. The still flat part is entirely occupied to the west, and the urbanization front observed is mainly located along the Matadi road, even if the space between this road and the river tends to fill up. However, the land is on steep slopes, and the administrative limits of the province, soon exceeded. The extension of the city has always been recommended towards the east, it is the other major urbanization front that we are currently observing. With the construction of the railroad bridge and the creation of the Special Economic Zone in Maluku, this trend is expected to strengthen. However, the relatively flat space between the river and the barrier hills of the East is not unlimited. The services of the city province of Kinshasa have also expressed the wish to contain the urbanized space within the curve formed by the NSele River. The positioning of the contour lines makes it possible to identify a potentially urbanizable zone of 240 km2, and a second zone north of the river with an area of 38 km2. Nevertheless, this part is now occupied by the agricultural domain of N'Sele. Since 1960, land management has experienced serious problems. The lack of specialists in the field of land has encouraged the involvement of customary chiefs in the distribution of land for construction. This state of affairs is still felt to this day through several urban studies (DR Congo, National Workshop on Land Reform, 2012; Lelo N., 2008; Lusamba K.M., 2010). To easily access a plot of land for construction in Congolese cities, the population prefers to go see the customary chief instead of the state. Mainly the population by means of self-construction builds the cities resulting from this mode of appropriation. They also lack basic infrastructure (drinking water and electricity) and socio-community facilities (schools, hospitals, social centers, etc.) and extend over non-"aedificandi" areas or even the hillsides. To remedy this disproportionate growth of cities, the public authorities must provide them not only with Urban Development Plans (PDU) with a spatial orientation, but efforts must also focus on the establishment of Particular Plans developments (PPA) intended for establishment, enforceable against all. This tool remains one of the ways to better control the extensions of urban communes and overcome the weakness of the current chaotic evolution of the cities of the DR Congo. Control and monitoring remain essential in the effective implementation of these urban planning tools. However, the rapid increase in the urban population of Kinshasa and the other cities of the country is easily explained by the high birth rates and the migration from the countryside to the cities, a phenomenon often amplified by events such as poverty, basic infrastructure in rural areas (schools, hospitals, etc.) and above all local armed conflicts. All this contributes to the expansion of Congolese cities. However, it is not only the size of the population that matters, but also the total area affected by urbanization. If we consider this area, and not just the population, we can say that the urbanization process is continuing rapidly both in Kinshasa and in all the other cities of the country such as Matadi, Lubumbashi, Kisangani,

SECTION II: DENSIFICATION

Densification can describe very varied types of urban interventions, ranging from the insertion of buildings in neighborhoods already built to the entire reconstruction of urban wastelands. Density alone, however, is a measure that gives little indication of built form, since it relates to the number of dwellings in a given area, regardless of the shape and layout of buildings and public or private spaces. Several urban forms or types of buildings can achieve equivalent densities without providing the same benefits[90]. This is the case of the city of Kinshasa. The densification of Kinshasa does not bring the same benefits, both in terms of the quality of the urban environment and social in all the other districts of the city. As densification is an increase in existing densities, as regards the city of Kinshasa, the latter should bring benefits such as: improving the health of populations by promoting healthy lifestyles: fight against global warming (heat island) and allow adaptation to climate change; promote the economic dynamism of other neighborhoods, above all on the outskirts of Kinshasa; make infrastructure profitable and reduce distances; curb urban sprawl (extension) to preserve natural

---

[90] VIVRE EN VILLE (2014), La ville compacte, un modèle éprouvé, Compacité / Densité, Collectivitesviables.org, http://collectivitesviables.org/articles/compacite-densite. aspx#body-section

environments and agricultural land; etc… While densification can be achieved by different means (renovation, requalification, extension, raising, adding a wing, etc.) which remain controversial, in any case, densification is not a goal in self, as Antonio Da Cunha (2015) underlines. It is only one of the levers of urban quality. In fact, densification does not yet say anything about the quality of the city to be developed. It does not say anything about the organization of urban space, the "arrangement of equipment", the organization of "spatial charges", the quality of the urban composition, the quality of the relationship between the full and the "empty. », Morphological and functional diversity, building typologies, accessibility to amenities, etc.

The quality of densification must be ensured in parallel with the quantitative aspect[91]. This is not the case with the city of Kinshasa, where there is a mismatch between the quantitative aspect of densification and the quality of life of the inhabitants of Kinshasa. A good match between the built density, the quality of public spaces and urban forms is essential for the success of a project, as is respect for a balance between housing, activities and services. You cannot fill the city like an egg. The ecological imperative, the requirement of immediate access to facilities, the reduction of the costs of urbanization can be harmonized with the aspirations for a greater availability of quality "open" spaces. "Qualified densification" must be contextualized, sized, differentiated and coordinated. In fact, the challenges of qualified densification articulate a plurality of actions and actors at different scales of development[92]. However, in the case of the city of Kinshasa, the city is becoming denser in disorder without an urban planning standard. The densification is very intense

---

[91] ANTONIO DA CUNHA (2015), Densité, densification et qualité urbaine, http://www.densite.ch/fr/blog/densite-densification-et-qualite-urbaine
[92] ANTONIO DA CUNHA (2015), ibid.

in the districts of the old communes, although the phenomenon is identical in the other communes. As regards the city of Kinshasa, as Eleonore Wolff and Virginie Delbart (1995) underline, "Densification seems to have reached its limits, which is currently reflected in migrations from the city center to neighborhoods in intermediate or peripheral municipalities., with a location close to the communication axes towards the city center. It is therefore these neighborhoods located near communication routes that are becoming denser". In Kinshasa, the extreme concentration of functions and infrastructure, as well as the relative facilities for transport and connection to water and electricity distribution networks make central municipalities very attractive areas compared to peripheral municipalities. Land is therefore particularly expensive there. There is a worrying phenomenon of overdensification. "Everyone tries to get closer to the 'City' to seize opportunities or be close to areas of activity. Since land is expensive, people prefer to rent and divide their plots to make money. "According to our personal surveys, in 2020, the sale price of a plot in Kalamu amounted to US $ 85,000, while it was US $ 25,000-30,000 in Mont Ngafula, and US $ 15,000 -20,000 $ to Masina. The particularly high population densities (from 20,000 to 50,000 inhab./km² built) lead to great promiscuity; Indeed, according to our personal surveys, in Kalamu, 3 to 4 households live on the same plot, while in Mont Ngafula or Kimbanseke, there are only one or two households per plot. The densification of central municipalities since 1984 is very real, but it seems to have reached its limits, which is currently reflected in migrations from the city center to districts of intermediate or peripheral municipalities, with a location close to communication axes towards the downtown. It is therefore these neighborhoods located near communication routes, which are becoming denser. However, the urban densification of

Kinshasa does not exclude the expansion of urban vegetation and the promotion of generous green spaces. This involves the establishment of an eco-responsible management of urban public and private space (residential plots), the development of qualitative greening and the creation of multiple green spaces in the city. This in order to recreate the conditions of a city of Kinshasa where it is good to live; or a transfer from "Kinshasa la poubelle" and transfer to "Kinshasa la belle". It is therefore these neighborhoods located near communication routes, which are becoming denser. However, the urban densification of Kinshasa does not exclude the expansion of urban vegetation and the promotion of generous green spaces. This involves the establishment of an eco-responsible management of urban public and private space (residential plots), the development of qualitative greening and the creation of multiple green spaces in the city. This in order to recreate the conditions of a city of Kinshasa where it is good to live; or a transfer from "Kinshasa la poubelle" and transfer to "Kinshasa la belle". In the east, outside the rural communes of Nsele and Maluku, the buildings are not only expanding, they are also becoming denser. Urbanization towards the east of the city, encouraged by local authorities, benefited from proximity to major roads, extensive alluvial terraces and relatively inexpensive available land. Today, the communes of Masina, Ndjili and Kimbanseke are densely populated, but the infrastructure and roads have not kept up with urbanization. As a result, access to communication routes (located to the north of these municipalities) from the urbanization front (located to the south of these municipalities) is increasingly difficult. The urbanized area cannot therefore expand forever in the absence of connecting roads. Thus we observe an extreme densification of buildings near the main roads, for example along Boulevard Lumumba and the road from Mokali to Kimbanseke, but also the urbanization of spaces previously left "virgin", for example the flood-prone and unsanitary areas of Masina. As Antonio Da Cunha (2015) asserts, at the agglomeration level, densification must be coordinated with public transport and make it possible to improve the polycentrality of the urban territory.

At finer scales, the compactness of the built forms must precisely allow the lacunarity, ventilation and permeability of the tissues, the soothing presence of water and vegetation. Densification will thus be accompanied by a supply of generous public spaces and quality local facilities ensuring the compatibility of uses (young people, not so young, women, etc.) and the harmonization of social spaces, from housing to street, from the street to the neighborhood, from the neighborhood to the city. Finally, densification needs to be coordinated globally: owners, public authorities and the population must intervene in the process according to appropriate procedures. The quality of densification often depends on strong political support, well-organized consultation and serene land control. Densification generates economic value. Sustained and acceptable densification also creates use value. This is the miracle of urban quality. It stems from the expertise of wise designers, but also from attentive listening to all of the city's stakeholders. In the imagination of urban sustainability, densification is now linked with the control of the ecological footprint, living together and the quality of the city[93].

I. FACTORS AND CONSTRAINTS RELATING TO DENSIFICATION

According to the United Nations report, human geography will seem completely unknown at the turn of the century. According to the list of the 20 largest mega-cities planned for 2,100, the city

---

[93] ANTONIO DA CUNHA (2015), op.cit.

of Kinshasa, the capital of the Democratic Republic of Congo is expected to be the second largest city in the world with a population of 83 million inhabitants[94]. Kinshasa had only 20,000 people in 1920. In 1940, it housed around 450,000 people. Today, it has perhaps 12 million inhabitants and is expected to be the second largest city in Africa with 75 million inhabitants in 50 years. By Western standards, it is a dysfunctional and sprawling megalopolis, surrounded by vast slums of informal settlements, their infrastructure non-existent or collapsing. "When you go there today, you see the disarray and the congestion," says Somik Lall, the World Bank's chief economist for Africa. "Yes, it will be one of the largest cities in Africa by 2050, but I don't think it's the model for the future Africa, nor do I think it will have a population of 70 million." He argues that Kinshasa's current situation is not necessarily indicative of its future status. "There is no way to tell what the cities will look like in 2,100. Seoul in 1980 could never have predicted how it is today. It was a dirty industrial town. Africa has a young workforce. Places like Kinshasa are among the most dynamic places in the world"[95]. In 2020, the population of the city of Kinshasa is estimated at 14,342,000 inhabitants. People who come to cities like Kinshasa add no economic benefit. Investments in infrastructure in African cities are insufficient[96]. Projections suggest that cities will swell at an astonishing rate, but that this means that our salvation or an eco-disaster is not certain. However, the "COVID 19" coronavirus pandemic is a warning to humanity.

---

[94] PETER FISK (2018), https://www.thegeniusworks.com/2018/08/the-worlds-megacities-of-2100-lagos-kinshasa-dar-es-salaam-a-mind-blowing-growth-in-the-urban-populations-of-africa/

[95] JOHN VIDAL (2018), The 100 million city: is 21st century urbanization out of control? https://www.theguardian.com/cities/2018/mar/19/urban-explosion-kinshasa-el-alto-growth-mexico-city-bangalore-lagos

[96] WORLD BANK, United Nations, Population Stat, 2017-2020, Data sources, World Bank, United Nations, Census, GeoNames. https://populationstat.com/democratic-republic-of-the-congo/kinshasa

EVOLUTION OF THE KINSHASA POPULATION

YEAR	POPULATION	GROWTH RATE
2020	14,342,000	4.36%
2019	13,743,000	4.34%
2018	13,171,000	4.33%
2017	12,624,000	4.33%
2016	12,100,000	4.33%
2015	11,598,000	4.34%
2014	11,116,000	4.33%
2013	10,655,000	4.34%
2012	10,212,000	4.34%
2011	9,788,000	4.33%
2010	9,382,000	4.34%

Source: United Nations - World Population Prospects[97]

The first period covers the 20 years after independence (until 1981). It is characterized by very strong demographic growth and rapid spatial expansion. During the second period, the population growth rate slows down very markedly, even if it remains high, going from 9.26% between 1960 and 1981 to 5.07 between 1981 and 2005. Spatial expansion is growing at a rapid pace less sustained and went from 5.31% between 1960 and 1981 to 3.25% between 1981 and 2005[98]. Unfortunately, this development in demographic growth has serious consequences. It seriously affects the level of household poverty in Kinshasa but also the urban space in general and residential in particular. One of the consequences of population growth is also the increase in the size of households in Kinshasa.

---

[97] UNITED NATIONS, Kinshasa, Republic of Congo Metro Area Population 1950-2020
https://www.macrotrends.net/cities/20853/kinshasa/population
[98] MATTHIEU KAYEMBE WA KAYEMBE, MATHIEU DE MAEYER ET ELEONORE WOLFF, Cartographie de la croissance urbaine de Kinshasa (R.D. Congo) entre 1995 et 2005 par télédétection satellitaire à haute résolution, Revue Belgeo, 2009, p.439

1. Household size and vegetation

The increase in household size also has an impact on urban vegetation. In fact, the more the household size increases, the more it puts a strain on the space in the plot. This obliges the owners either to undertake new constructions known as the "annexes" or to extend the old constructions on the spaces formerly occupied by vegetation to contain the number of family members.... This also has a corollary between the size of households and the level of poverty in the plots. The quality of life in these plots is diminishing. During the survey, we counted a plot with 32 people with a single toilet and a single *"Kikoso"* (place to wash) and a single yard. In fact, the average size of households is a determining factor in the living conditions of households. The smaller the household size, the less it is exposed to poverty and vice versa. In Kinshasa province, the average size of poor households is 7.3 while that of non-poor is 5.0.

2. Level of Poverty

In Kinshasa, poverty is more prevalent in households headed by women (45.7%) than in households headed by men (40.7%). This configuration of poverty according to the sex of the head of household is not surprising, given the precarious status of women in the labor market and their social status, which limits their access to productive assets. The level of poverty among female-headed households could be explained by the fact that in general women have less physical and human capital than men do. Household size is an important criterion in the analysis of living conditions (Houyoux (1973), but its composition is more so. Considering these two elements sometimes makes it possible to understand the mechanisms and logics, which are not always easily perceptible. In addition to the still high fertility, the size of households in Kinshasa is also magnified by hospitality. The average number of individuals per household, which was 4.8 and 5.7 respectively in 1967 and 1975 (Houyoux and Kinamvwidi, 1975), rose to 6.7 in 1984 (INS, 1990) and to 7.7 in 1995 (Lututala et al 1996). The 1-2-3 Survey, DHS 2007, estimates the average household size in Kinshasa at 6.0 (UNAIDS). The ECOSEX study (2003) estimates it at 8.1 people (Kalambayi, 2004a). From 1995 to 2003, the relative importance of nuclear family members (spouse and their children) increased from 82.7% to 74.3% in Kinshasa. This decrease seems to concern the children of one of the spouses for the benefit of the couple's brothers, sisters, cousins, nephews and nieces. From 16.1% in 1995, the proportion of children with only one spouse rose to 8.7% in 2003 (Ngondo, 1996; Kalambayi, 2004a). We are therefore witnessing a restructuring of the household by reducing the family unit and enlarging the social unit, thus increasing the size of the household. Unfortunately, this expansion, which testifies to the hospitality and attachments to the traditional values of the extended family, is not however accompanied by the expansion of the living environment or housing, which leads to an over densification of households and therefore to the promiscuity (Ngondo, 1996).

3. Demographic pressure

Faced with this continuous growth in the size of households in Kinshasa, demographic pressure is amplifying in the urban residential space of housing mainly in the plots. Unlike his traditional conception, this author indicates that hospitality as currently practiced in Kinshasa is no longer expressed in the old way. In the new formula, households offer housing to their relatives of the extended family who, due to a lack of formal employment, carry out informal activities and contribute to the survival of the households. Since efficiency is a function of numbers, housing a large workforce justifies the increase in the relative importance of members other than the nuclear family. This workforce is generally made up of young people who have dropped out of school, but also children in care (Lututala et al., 1996).

CHAPTER VI

IMPORTANCE AND ROLE OF VEGETATION IN THE URBAN ENVIRONMENT

———— ❋ ————

TITLE I: ROLE OF URBAN VEGETATION ON THE URBAN ENVIRONMENT

Referring to the Bible, the original home of man, which is paradise, is represented as a wonderful garden bordered by trees and flowers in which to live. This biblical picture of paradise would simply like to invite us to a clean and healthy human habitat fitting in with nature because indeed, there is no better place to admire the wonders of God than in nature. According to Hubert Reeves "Man is the most insane species. He worships an invisible God and destroys a visible nature. Unaware that this nature he is destroying is this God he is worshiping". This is why; everywhere and always associating green space with habitat is not only in good taste but also in common sense. It is about preparing for man a harmonious living environment where he can fully develop (Parrot, 1973). Furthermore, it is undeniable that a natural environment plays a fundamental role in the development and maintenance of physical and mental balance. That is why we say it is good to live in nature. On the other hand, plant nature realizes and maintains the biological and social conditions essential to human life. It humanizes the surrounding environment, meets the permanent needs of man, to live in contact with nature and plays an important role from the aesthetic, hygienic and sanitary, economic, educational, biological and nature conservation points of view (Nyakabwa, 1982). It turns out that over time, economic and urban development has resulted in an increasingly significant decrease in urban vegetation and green spaces, especially in developing countries. With hindsight, we are now able to sound the alarm and see that the quality of urban life is suffering heavily from the consequences of deforestation. The city of Kinshasa is suffering a high rate of deforestation with urban and demographic growth, especially in the districts of the former communes. We have unfortunately forgotten the many advantages that trees provide in urban areas, especially in this period of global warming. Vegetation is a key element in our life cycle for breathing, eating and even healing. The benefits of vegetation are numerous in social, aesthetic, economic, ecological terms, etc. On the other hand, while being an element of decor and urban planning, the tree seems to have in some civilizations been strongly associated with the image of the expected and / or lost paradise, with nevertheless the ambiguity of the tree sometimes valued as a "tree of life" but also sometimes associated with the "forbidden fruit" of knowledge. This ambiguity seems to have its source in the Book of Genesis according to which God planted in the Garden of Eden two trees, which have elicited many comments "The Lord God planted a garden in Eden, in the east, and placed man there. That he had trained. The Lord God made sprout from the ground every tree of attractive appearance and good to eat, the tree of life in the middle of the garden and the tree of the knowledge of happiness and misfortune"[99]. Kinshasa's urban vegetation must not only meet the needs of all city dwellers, but they must also participate fully. Kinshasa is a cosmopolitan city. It brings together many ethnic, tribal and regional communities that make up the population of Kinshasa. Nevertheless, how does urban vegetation

---

[99] https://fr.wikipedia.org/wiki/Arbre_urbain

fit into their varied lifestyles and livelihoods? The accelerating pace of urbanization is worsening the serious environmental problems that already exist in the city of Kinshasa. The urban poor, generally residing in marginal and ecologically sensitive neighborhoods, are often the most exposed to urban environmental risks. This is the case for the districts of the communes of Kisenso, Mont Ngafula, Selembao, Bumbu, Ngaliema, etc. or floodplains in various neighborhoods such as Mombele in the municipality of Limete.

Despite the fact that it is the poor who are most often the hardest hit by these environmental risks, air, water and noise (noise) pollution, which affects people from all socioeconomic strata. The social and ecological costs of urban pollution will continue to affect the growing urban populations of the city of Kinshasa in particular and Congolese cities in general, unless the cycle of degradation and poverty can be broken. Very often, we witness ecological tragedies, which affect the urban areas of Congolese cities. This is the case of floods, erosions, epidemics ... Other cases of soil, air and water pollution, as well as other environmental problems, are to be deplored in Kinshasa and in n 'any city in the country. For example, of the tons of waste produced each day in the city of Kinshasa, only private and municipal companies collect a small amount of waste. The rest ends up in landfills or underground rots in vacant lots in the city or around the city or in rivers and other gutters in the city.

The cases of erosion most often occur on the steep slopes surrounding the neighborhoods of the peri-urban municipalities of Selembao, Ngaliema, Kisenso, Mont Ngafula, Lemba, which are often inhabited by poor populations.

Water pollution in the city is particularly widespread and frequent. For example, it is common for the people of Kinshasa and industries in the city to discharge untreated wastewater into municipal sewers or discharge it directly into urban rivers or gutters. Another major source of contamination is human excreta, which is often poorly managed or often dumped in gutters. Infectious and parasitic diseases are thus spreading among the main causes of morbidity and mortality in the city of Kinshasa. In addition, the use of charcoal and wood as fuel for cooking contributes to air pollution in the city. As a reminder, some main physical functions of the tree[100]:

- a mature tree would provide the necessary quantity of oxygen for 4 people;
- a mature tree in an urban environment can intercept up to 20 kg of dust per year;
- a mature tree can capture up to 7,000 suspended particles per liter of air;
- a tree near the house can reduce air conditioning needs by 30%;
- a small tree 8 to 15 cm in diameter and which grows slowly can sequester 16 kg of CO_2 / year; this number increases to 360 kg for a large tree at its maximum growth level;
- a mature tree can absorb 450 liters of water, then transpire it in the form of water vapor, which refreshes the ambient air;
- a difference of 4 to 8 * C can be observed between an open site and a site located under the treetops.

This is particularly the case with the seeds of pollen from certain species of trees and flowers which, spread in the air, are responsible for certain allergic diseases such as respiratory diseases (colds, asthma, etc.). This observation deserves to be taken into account

---

[100] MELANIE BEAUDOIN et all (2017), INSPQ, Verdir les villes pour la santé de la population, https://www.inspq.qc.ca/sites/default/files/publications/2265_verdir_villes_sante_population.pdf

when introducing into the urban flora certain species of trees or flowers harmful to the population.

TITLE II: ADVANTAGES OF URBAN VEGETATION

Urban vegetation provides improvements in air, water and land resources by absorbing air pollutants, increasing water uptake and floodplain surfaces, and stabilizing soils. Urban vegetation acts as temperature buffers providing shade in summer and windbreaks in winter in addition to reducing noise pollution and CO_2 levels and providing habitat for urban flora. The economic benefits include timber and marketable agricultural products, as well as a variety of products such as handicrafts. Finally, the overall benefits to the urban community, particularly to low-income residents, are significant. They include the contribution of trees and vegetation to the mental and physical health of the population, and the provision of recreational opportunities, for example, outdoor walking. In addition, they bring aesthetic improvements to an artificial environment, otherwise dominated by asphalt and concrete. The vegetation in the urban environment of Kinshasa is quite simply essential to us and we must reintroduce it as soon as possible. All of the current urban living conditions disrupt the living environment and the health of residents. Indeed, stress, discomfort, fatigue, allergies are among the recurring ailments for city dwellers Kinois.

1. **ECONOMIC ACTION**: Urban and peri-urban agriculture support the city's economic activity. In Kinshasa, the development of market gardening activities means that most of the city's needs for certain vegetable products are produced in the city itself. This is the case of vegetables like Amarante (*bitekuteku*), Sorrel (*Ngai*

ngai), sweet potato leaves (*Matembele*), spinach, etc. Certain species, in addition to their aesthetic or hygienic role, are also of definite economic interest. One example is the flower trade in Kinshasa. However, it should also be noted that it is possible to develop in the city a factory for fruit compost (mangoes, maracuja and others) from the urban flora of these trees. We were surprised during our investigation to find that some owners have managed vegetable gardens in their plots, one of them on Public Force avenue has found no better than to exploit part of the public road to develop its flourishing vegetable garden. We will also say that with the number of palm trees growing in the city, their exploitation could favorably fuel the trade in wine and palm nuts. It would be enough for the wine-drawers to decide to do it.

SECTION I: ENVIRONMENTAL BENEFITS

1. **ACTION ON URBAN CLEANING**: Recent work has demonstrated the bactericidal effect of substances emitted by the leaves of certain forest species. This role deserves to be elucidated given the interest it presents in the fight against mosquitoes in our cities, especially in Kinshasa. It would be unwise not to reveal here some negative aspects of the urban flora. This is particularly the case with the pollen seeds of certain species of trees and flowers which, spread in the air, are responsible for certain allergic diseases such as respiratory diseases (colds, asthma, etc.). This observation deserves to be taken into consideration when we introduce into the urban flora certain species of trees or flowers harmful to the population.

Photo Gutu Kia Zimi

2. ATMOSPHERIC POLLUTION

The flora has the property of capturing airborne dust, retaining them and reducing them to the ground, also playing a role of very effective natural filter (Boyer and Al (1977) state that plants can retain 30 to 40 % of dust, which is deposited on the surface of the ground. It is known that vegetation contributes effectively to the depollution of the air of certain harmful gases such as SO_2, CO_2. For example, reducing the concentration of SO_2 (Sulfur dioxide) is obtained by the dilution effect of which it is important to point out that the vegetation does not offer direct protection against this gas because it does not absorb it unlike CO_2. In addition, CO (carbon monoxide) very dangerous gas having a harmful effect on health by reducing visual activity and intellectual activity, its concentration is reduced by 28% in the atmosphere by vegetation. It is also necessary to point out that the phytocenosis, which is the grouping of plants linked by a reciprocal dependence, eliminates 50% of nitrogen oxides, which are generally formed at the level of all combustion sources, including in particular automobile engines. These oxides have the particularity of binding to hemoglobin competitively with oxygen (Boyer et al). Carbon monoxide, which is a pollutant mainly due to the action of light on vehicle exhaust gas, can be absorbed and reduced by plants, as are certain pollutants including fluorine and lead.

Photo Gutu Kia Zimi

Vegetation is a material of choice by making its contribution to cleaning up the urban atmosphere through the action of its foliage, including:

– By fixing dust: this therefore indicates that pollution increases with the increase in the vehicle fleet in our urban areas.

–   By bacterial purification: the process of capturing bacteria on the leaves follows the same mechanism as that of dust, only many bacteria are destroyed by the ozone which is emitted by the leaves.

–   By the chlorophyll function: we know that chlorophyll photosynthesis in sunlight absorbs CO_2 and releases oxygen and ozone, by performing biological syntheses, the basis of all animal and plant life. At night, leaf activity picks up oxygen and releases CO.

–   By thermo-hygrometric regulation: the drying out of the urban climate has the consequence of making the air unhealthy, the action of the tree offers a valuable contribution to this problem. Hygrometric regulation is achieved by an emission of water vapor by the foliage in the form of direct physical evaporation of rains or dews, physiological transpiration of the plant, chloro-vaporization of water vapor during chlorophyll assimilation of atmospheric CO_2 under the action of solar radiation.

All these evapo-transpiration phenomena absorb calories, which causes a decrease in the temperature of the local microclimate during the hottest hours.

–   By fixing toxic gas: the arrangement of trees approximately sources of nuisance would constitute a screen, which would attenuate their effects and their spread. Thus, it is undeniable that woody or herbaceous vegetation helps to purify and regenerate the urban environment and consequently to restore the psychosomatic balance of man. Let us not forget that where the tree suffocates its death, it is a signal of danger to the human organism. To realize this, it would suffice to examine the characteristics of the trees that grow around the sources of nuisance.

Photo Gutu Kia Zimi

3. IMPROVEMENT OF URBAN AIR QUALITY

The atmosphere above Kinshasa is particularly interesting as emissions from the rainforest mix with urban pollution (ISAB, 2018)[101]. Air pollution in the city of Kinshasa sometimes exceeds the tolerated threshold. It circulates in the air of Kinshasa, 63.2 micrograms / m3 of fine particles (PM 2.5), dangerous for health. These WHO data taken in Kinshasa reveal a worrying situation for many Congolese cities[102]. The main causes of this air pollution are urban transport and the way of cooking in Kinshasa. Kinshasa has more than two

---

[101] ISAB (2017), Belgian Institute for Space Aeronomy, https://www.aeronomie.be/fr/rapport-annuel/qualite-lair-kinshasa.
[102] DIDIER MUKALENG MAKAL (2017), L'inquiétante pollution de l'air en RDC, https://earthjournalism.net/stories/linquietante-pollution-de-lair-en-rdc

million cars in circulation, and several are estimated to be dilapidated and poorly maintained. The May 2016 World Health Organization (WHO) study notes 63.2 micrograms / m3 of fine particles (PM 2.5), which circulate in the air of Kinshasa. The carbon dioxide released by cars is important there. Accused of polluting, 10-year-old vehicles are also banned from importing into the DRC according to regulations. There is also another source of gas: it is the proliferation of electric generators, an alternative to untimely cuts in electricity and load shedding. Indeed, only 15% of Congolese are connected to the national electricity grid, according to the National Electricity Company (SNEL). With regard to urban household waste, everyone therefore manages this waste as they wish, many preferring to burn it. This is without counting also the dust raised by the wind in the city of Kinshasa. In such an environment, it can get worse. According to climatologist Jean Pierre Ndjibu *"air plays a role of transport. The moisture we have in the atmosphere transforms chemicals: sulfur dioxide, for example, can easily become sulfuric acid when it combines with water vapor. We then understand that* "what was a primary pollutant becomes a secondary pollutant, and therefore much more dangerous". The impact of all these practices on health is significant. Alfred Ntumba, who also worked on air pollution, indicates, *"That in Kinshasa, carcinogens are detected in the urine, in particular lead. Some doctors think it comes from unburned diesel fuel in cars,"* he explains. Dirty fuel, the one that contains lead, in fact, does not burn enough in the engine. It all ends up in the air. The mining industry is identified as the main source of air pollution in Lubumbashi in Katanga. In 2015, according to climatologist Jean-Pierre Ndjibu, following the taking of surprising measurements in the west of the city, he declared: *"We are practically over 290 MG per m3 of fine particles. These particles, MP10, carry away sulphate and nitrate, particles that reach the lungs and the cardiovascular system. We just do not realize it,"* he worries. In addition, the reduction of trees in the Lubumbashi belt would worsen the deterioration of air quality. Now, with the air moving at 18km per hour, polluted air spreads very quickly. However, Lubumbashi, Kinshasa knows a weak establishment of industries. Nevertheless, *"the few that exist pollute more. On 7ʰ Street, in the town of Limete,"* explains an inhabitant of Kinshasa anonymously. *"A match factory pollutes every day from 4 a.m. Unfortunately, a law on polluter pays remains blocked in the Kinshasa provincial assembly. No one is stalking them"[103].* The demography of Kinshasa, the largest city in the DRC, has exploded in recent years[104]. Traffic congestion with the widespread use of motorcycles as well as vintage cars coupled with poor maintenance, inadequate infrastructure and poor fuel quality is a major source of outdoor pollution. The main source of indoor air pollution is the burning of wood, charcoal, crops, residual oils and wastes for heating and cooking in open fires or poorly functioning stoves. Thanks to a study carried out to assess the exposure to trace elements in the urine of the population of Kinshasa, showed high levels of Al, As, Cd, Pb and Hg compared to other databases. Nevertheless, there is little documented information regarding the different sources of exposure to trace oligo-elements in Kinshasa[105]. Kinshasa suffers from poor air quality, characterized by large amounts of nitrogen oxides ($NO_x = NO$ and No_2) and particulate matter (PM). This pollution is linked to the widespread use of domestic biomass fuels for cooking and to the obsolescence of its vehicle fleet. As in other

---

[103] DIDIER MUKALENG MAKAL, op.cit
[104] UNITED NATIONS (2008) World urbanization prospects. Department of Economy and social affairs, Population Division, New York, USA.
[105] AFFAIRS, Population Division, New York, USA.

growing African mega-cities, we expect air pollution in Kinshasa to deteriorate further[106]. With regard to air quality in Kinshasa, the main pollutant are fine particles (Pm2.5). The uncontrolled combustion of waste is one of the practices, which contributes to the deterioration of air quality in urban centers and rural areas.

Photo Gutu Kia Zimi

Due to the composition of the waste (plastics, used tires and other organic / inorganic materials), the combustion of unregulated waste can be a source of harmful emissions to health such as dioxins and furans[107]. In 2009, around 11.1% of the country's population had access to the electricity grid. The vast majority (over 95%) of

---

[106] ISAB (2017), Belgian Institute for Space Aeronomy, https://www.aeronomie.be/fr/rapport-annuel/qualite-lair-kinshasa
[107] NSOKIMIENO, CHEN S, ZHANG IQ (2010) Sustainable urbanization's challenge in Democratic Republic of Congo. Journal of Sustainable Development 3: 242-254.

the population continue to use traditional biomass-based fuels for domestic energy needs[108]. In addition, air pollution has a significant health impact, including a reduction in life expectancy. In accordance with World Health Organization guidelines, the air quality in the Democratic Republic of the Congo is considered hazardous. The most recent data indicate that the annual average concentration of PM2.5 in the country is 45µg / m3, which exceeds the recommended maximum of 10µg / m3. Poor air quality in the Democratic Republic of the Congo contributes in particular to waste combustion, mining, mineral processing, forestry and the cement industry. Available data indicates that Kinshasa has consistently high levels of air pollution. Outdoor air pollution is a mixture of chemicals, particles and biological materials, which react with each other to form dangerous tiny particles. It contributes to respiratory problems, chronic disease, increased hospitalization and premature mortality. Particulate matter (PM) concentration is a key indicator of air quality, as it is the most common air pollutant that affects both short and long term health. Two sizes of particles are used to analyze air quality; fine particles with a diameter of less than 2.5 µm or PM2.5 and coarse particles with a diameter of less than 10 µm or PM10. PM2.5 particles are of greater concern because their small size allows them to penetrate deeper into the cardiopulmonary system. The World Health Organization's air quality guidelines recommend that annual average concentrations of PM2.5 do not exceed 10µg / m3 and 20µg / m3 for PM10[109]. While air pollution indices in many cities in developed countries have declined over the past twenty-five years, levels of air pollution have increased

---

[108] UNEP (2015), Democratic Republic of the Congo Air Quality Policies, https://wedocs.unep.org/bitstream/handle/20.500.11822/17179/DemocraticRepublic_Congo.pdf?sequence=1&isAllowed=y

[109] KABAMBA M ET ALL, Toxic Heavy Metals in Ambient Air of Kinshasa, Democratic Republic Congo, Journal of Environmental Analytical Chemistry, 2016

in cities in much of the developing world. Children, the elderly and people with respiratory problems are most affected by these harmful air contaminants. Using urban vegetation to reduce air pollution is an effective technique, which also offers other benefits such as beautifying the city. Urban vegetation can reduce air pollutants to varying degrees. Air pollution is directly reduced when dust and smoke particles are trapped by vegetation. In addition, plants absorb toxic gases, particularly those from vehicle exhaust, which are a major component of urban smog (Nowak et al. 1996). High temperatures accelerate the formation of smog. The moderating effect of urban vegetation on a city's climate can reduce temperature extremes and thus reduce this phenomenon to some extent. Carbon dioxide (CO_2) is also a major component of air pollution and is one of the main causes of the greenhouse effect. Urban vegetation can reduce carbon dioxide levels in two ways. First, all plants, through photosynthesis, take up carbon dioxide directly in their biomass and release oxygen in return. Second, when extensive plant cover reduces the heat island effect in an urban area, residents use less fossil fuels to cool buildings, thereby reducing carbon dioxide emissions from power plants (McPherson, E. Gregory et al., 1994). Trees and other plants can also have a big impact on the energy budgets of buildings and, in turn, entire cities. This effect is most visible in urban centers with little or no vegetation and large paved areas. Large paved areas dissipate heat from the sun only very slowly. This results in the urban heat island effect where a city heats up quickly and then maintains a high temperature. In addition, as city temperatures rise, so do air pollutants and smog (Kuchelmeister 1991).

Photo Gutu Kia Zimi

4. FIGHT AGAINST AIR POLLUTION IN URBAN AREAS

Air pollution is another major cause of environmental concern. The increasing number of vehicles with untreated exhaust fumes, expanding industrial sectors and poor natural ventilation in many cities have combined to create serious smog problems. Congolese urban air is often polluted by industrial, hospital and household waste and gases ejected by vehicles. Faced with this problem of air pollution, the country lacks an adequate policy to reduce the risks of air pollution due to industrial and hospital waste. However, an effort is still being felt in some cities, particularly in Kinshasa, Lubumbashi and Bukavu where the provincial governments are organizing themselves in the collection of household waste. Regarding the waste ejected by vehicles, the Government has taken salutary measures to prohibit all imports of vehicles over ten years old. Also, by putting all old buses over ten years out of circulation, the Government had granted buses on credit, called "spirit of life" to the informal operators of these old buses called "spirit of death". One of the preventive measures for combating air pollution is the obligation of all vehicles to pass a technical inspection each year. In addition, used vehicles increase air pollution in Kinshasa. Indeed, the number of cars has increased in recent years in Kinshasa. In 2010, this metropolis had around 500,000 vehicles or 1 car for every 20 inhabitants, in a city with an estimated population of over 10 million. Compared to 2009, this figure represents an increase of 12.5%. However, many of these second-hand vehicles are imported from Europe, Asia being worn out, and good for scrap. They increase air pollution, experts say. A study reveals[110] that air pollution caused by car exhaust can be a health hazard and reach high levels, especially during frequent traffic jams in Kinshasa. With the rehabilitation of the main arteries, huge traffic jams are observed when the roads are blocked or diverted because of works in the capital. According to experts from the University of Kinshasa (UNIKIN), nitrogen dioxide (No2) is a gas, under normal temperature and pressure conditions, molecules are made up of oxygen (O) and d atoms. Nitrogen (N). Nitrogen dioxide participates in various mechanisms generating various pollution. According to the same sources, cars are the source of 32% of nitrogen dioxide emissions into the air: its average concentration inside a vehicle is well above the limit recommended by that which World Health Organization (WHO). The latter estimates that air pollution is responsible for around 2 million premature deaths per year, more than half in developing countries. In many cities, the annual average

---

[110] Study conducted in February 2010 by a group of Congolese environmental experts from the University of Kinshasa (UNIKIN).

concentrations come mainly from the combustion of fossil fuels or other fuels. This concentration, according to the WHO, exceeds 70 micrograms / m3. To do this, the new guidelines state that in order to avoid harm to health, these concentrations should be below 20 micrograms / m3. Data from the Ministry of Health show, in 2010, cases of bronchitis, asthma and respiratory diseases in the DRC, especially among children. According to Jean Marie Kayembe,[111] a few years ago, one in ten children suffered from respiratory problems. However, today, around three in ten children suffer from respiratory illnesses in the city of Kinshasa. This expert attributes this slight increase in respiratory illnesses to the city's lack of sanitation and the excessive number of vehicles in Kinshasa[112].

Photo Gutu Kia Zimi

[111] JEAN MARIE KAYEMBE, pulmonology specialist and professor at the faculties of medicine at University of Kinshasa (UNIKIN)
[112] RADIO OKAPI (2011), MONUSCO, https://www.radiookapi.net/environnement/2011/03/02/les-vehicules-uses-augmentent-la-pollution-de-lair-a-kinshasa

5. ENERGY SAVINGS IN URBAN HOUSING

Various elements of an urban greening program can go a long way in reducing a city's overall energy budget. As mentioned earlier, the concentrations of paving and concrete in the city center produce an urban heat island effect, which causes discomfort and health problems, especially for the poor, who cannot afford the air conditioning. In contrast, cooling air-conditioned buildings requires considerable amounts of energy. Regarding the relationship between density and urban climate, it turns out that the larger the size of cities, the more they are prone to the urban heat island phenomenon. A high demand for electricity during the hot months can often cause voltage drops, a very common phenomenon in Kinshasa. This can be greatly reduced by planting substantial amounts of vegetation in dense urban areas. In Kinshasa, construction materials seem to be unsuitable for the tropical climate. This is the case with galvanized sheets for the roofs of houses, cement bricks or stone blocks.

Photo Gutu Kia Zimi

These materials greatly contribute to the propagation of heat in homes often without air conditioning. A plot entirely paved with cement, as is often the case in certain plots of Kinshasa, is a source of strong heat. Shrub vegetation in residential plots can significantly help reduce heat in homes. A study in Chicago shows that increasing tree cover by 10% in the city can reduce the total energy used for heating and cooling by 5-10% (McPherson et al. 1994). The densification of residential and work buildings, as well as the centralization of activities, lead to significant heat emissions and high-energy consumption. The relief formed by the building has other impacts on the climate, in particular in terms of humidity and aerology, creating specific climatic conditions grouped together under the term "urban climate".

Photo Gutu Kia Zimi

6. PROTECTION OF WATER SUPPLY BASINS

Regarding the purification and regulation of water, the roots of trees allow water to be filtered and thus obtain a better quality. The presence of trees reduces the volume of runoff, protects water sources, reduces flood damage and decreases soil erosion. The shadow created by trees on the water reduces the warming of water, especially of shallow ponds or lakes. Contaminated water sources and water-borne illnesses cause a high percentage of illness and death, especially in infants and young children. In general, the poorest urban communities are the hardest hit by the problems associated with unsafe water supplies. One of the major challenges for the urban authorities of Kinshasa is to provide drinking water to the entire population of the city.

Photo Gutu Kia Zimi

Considering the importance of maintaining a quality water supply, it is imperative that the city of Kinshasa adequately protect the watersheds. Unfortunately, this is not the case in Kinshasa. Water catchment areas, for most cities in the country tend to be close to their location and are often found in the suburbs, defined as areas of urban sprawl on the perimeter of urban centers and sometimes referred to as peri-urban. In Kinshasa, with the expansion of the city, the water catchment areas of Lukunga, Ndjili…, formerly outside the city, are currently subdivided and invaded by buildings and other dwellings. In addition, other towns in the country such as Mbanza-Ngungu, Inkisi ... have implemented a variety of strategies to protect suburban or rural areas, which serve as a source of water supply. Since many of these watersheds are quite close to the outskirts of the city, some of them have inevitably been depleted or polluted, and these cities now have to carry water quite a distance away. One of the main functions of the urban vegetation of Kinshasa is to control the sites of erosion and to protect the watersheds from the urban supplies of clean and regular water for the urban area.

Photo Gutu Kia Zimi

7. **ACTION ON SOIL CONSERVATION**: In the fight against soil erosion, the role of trees is to stabilize the soil by retaining the soil. Nevertheless, we know that vegetation plays an important role in protecting the soil; bare ground is exposed to the sun's radiation due to the absence of a protective cover and the impact of radiation. In the case of dry soils, heating will occur. Hill (1966) in his study in Singapore recorded soil temperatures at depths between 3 and 50 cm in bare soil, prairie and under forest. Findings showed that temperatures were higher in bare soil, lower in prairie, and significantly lower and less variable under forest.

Photo Gutu Kia Zimi

These high soil temperatures increase the rate of mineralization of organic matter; which reduces the structural stability of the soil (aggregation). Soil resistance decreases and the risk of erosion increases. The harmful exposure of soils leads to hardening of the latter and therefore a reduction in infiltration, that is to say an increase in runoff and erosion. The loss of vegetation marks the beginning of aridity; this is the current drama of the SAHEL. Note also that the loss of vegetation also favors the detrimental effect of wind and rain on soil conservation. The studies of Pereira (1954, 1956) HENIN et Al, (1958) and MONNIER (1965) confirm that the soils of tropical regions only pose structural problems in the event of the disappearance of plants or of the savannah that protects them from the phenomena sudden and altered desiccation caused by high temperatures and humidification due to heavy rains. The soil structure is generally good under vegetation and maintains a good level of infiltration.

Photo Gutu Kia Zimi

8. **ACTION ON SOUND POLLUTION**: The theory of interpretation of the role of vegetation on noise attenuation considers that each plant element breaks the waves, which lose their energy by resonance (Boyer, 1978). The effectiveness of plants in this fight against nuisances depends on the density of plantings, their thickness and the methods of planting. Boyer et al in his example say that a properly constructed 6cm wide green screen can lower the noise level of automobile traffic by 50%; on the other hand, alignment trees can reduce noise measured in the street at human height by 5 times. Noise pollution is a serious problem in the city of Kinshasa. The main sources of noise pollution, we cite: revival churches, music from "Nganda" bars and clubs, motorists. Noise nuisance at night and during the day disturb many citizens. Bar owners and church leaders are often arrested by the authorities. Loudspeakers broadcast decibels all day and night, disturbing the tranquility of neighbors. Noise is considered by 58% of professional actors as a major nuisance to the quality of life. The inhabitants questioned also cite the fight against noise pollution caused by automobile traffic among the three priorities for quality of life. According to Kaumbu and all (2015) in a study carried out in Kinshasa confirms that: *More than half of those exposed to loud noises especially from mechanical appliances and bars had hearing impairment. In view of the Congolese culture and dysfunction of the regulations of noise pollution in urban areas, it is essential to implement an education program for the prevention of auditory effects due to noise in the workplace and social environment[113]*. More than half of those exposed to loud noises, especially from mechanical

---

[113] KAUMBU IM ET ALL, Nuisances sonores et recherche des déficiences auditives dans quelques milieux socioprofessionnels de la Lukunga, Kinshasa. Annales Africaines de Médecine, Articles originaux, Vol.8 N*3, Juin 2015

devices and bars, had a hearing impairment. Given the Congolese culture and the dysfunctional regulation of noise pollution in urban settings, it is essential to implement an education program for the prevention of hearing effects due to noise in the workplace and the social environment. In Kinshasa, the atmosphere or the celebrations last until very late at night. It is a habit already ingrained in the mores of many Kinshasa. Thus, restricting the opening or closing hours of bars is quite simply declaring war on "ambianceurs". A measure according to which "bars can only open from 6 p.m. to 11 p.m. weekdays, from 6 p.m. to midnight on Saturdays and from 11 a.m. to midnight on Sundays throughout the capital". This measure does not appeal to bar owners or fans of the "atmosphere" of the capital. The "Kinois" likes to be happy all day and sometimes all night[114]. Noise pollution produced by bars is a very serious problem in the capital Kinshasa. It was more than urgent that the authorities get involved. However, it would be better to lighten the measure so that these bar keepers who are only resourceful cannot suffer financially. "Article 15: get by", say the "Kinois". On the other hand, churches are not to be outdone. Repeated rumors, thus undermining the serenity of the entire population, saw their perpetrators, in this case their pastors, being punished and, even, musical instruments seized by law enforcement officials. Several measures in the fight against the noise at night are already in force in Kinshasa. They particularly target revival churches, but are never respected or applied by the authorities. "Prayer cannot upset the neighbors". In their occupations, these revival churches, like bars elsewhere,

---

[114] Action taken by Kinshasa's provincial environment minister, Didier Tenge Litho. According to edict 005 of October 9, 2012 on daytime and night noise, failure to observe the opening and closing times of bars is punishable by the payment of a fine of 300,000 Congolese francs. In addition, for repeat offenses, the fines go up to 1 million Congolese francs.

which no longer limit the hours of activities, generally orient their baffles outwards, thus covering the entire environment with decibels, to the chagrin of the neighbors. "Playing music is not prohibited. What the law prohibits is going beyond that, "said a lawyer. According to him, the difficulty of concentration due to excess noise causes dryness of intellectual production and disturbs sleep. Whatever the source of the music, noise pollution is not a concern of those who are entertained or of neighbors and even less of passers-by, while the noise, especially at night, is a ticket in the DRC. Today, especially in Kinshasa, music is played all day long on every street corner, either directly by "artists" or from magnetic multimedia media. The phenomenon is more important in working-class areas of the city where there are a large number of idle young people, who are entertained with music. These gather either in places commonly called "fan clubs" or in "Nganda", that is to say dancings, clubs or private clubs. We often observe in these environments conversations or incessant tugging between individuals or groups of individuals around musical controversies (Shomba, 2004). In Kinshasa, there is at least one "Nganda" on each street. Besides the "Nganda", music is played in coaches, kiosks where records are sold, rental houses of music equipment, shops, markets, hairdressing salons, gas stations. Fuel, residences, revival churches,… (Shomba, 2004) to a volume breaking the eardrums. "When it comes to noise, it's like the sun. When there is more sun, there is more drought".

9. FLOODS

Floods cause considerable damage every year in the city of Kinshasa. The damage included the destruction of roads, bridges, canals, drainage systems, dikes, water and sewer systems, electrical networks, factories, residences and commercial establishments. In addition, there were the additional costs of interrupted economic activity, loss of income, and cleanup expenses. For example, the Kalamu, Makelele, Ndjili rivers and a number of their natural sources of food flow through the various communes of the city of Kinshasa. When the city of Kinshasa was smaller, the annual flooding of these rivers during the rainy season was less severe and manageable. With a rapid growth rate and a population of over 16 million, the city of Kinshasa has started to experience severe flooding problems. The expansion and development of the city, and the encroachment on flood-prone areas and neighborhoods put the lives of the population in danger. Using wetlands and parks as important parts of a city, the flood control system is not only recommended but also quite achievable. By locating municipal parks and green spaces in floodplains of rivers, streams or other drainage systems, planners can increase the permeable area available for catchment, reduce water flows compared to non-vegetated areas such as asphalt and avoid damaging urban infrastructure. Urban vegetation and green spaces can also mitigate flood damage simply by increasing the permeable area of a watershed, thereby decreasing runoff flows and reducing peak flow levels. The floods in Kinshasa are "linked to overpopulation, to the occupation of floodable land, which should not be occupied". Many other watersheds are just smaller streams. This is the case of Lubudi, Lukunga, Binza, Mampenza, Makelele, Yolo, Matete, Bandalungwa, Tshangu and Ikusu, which have low flow rates and seasonally. Their waters overflow after heavy rains and dry up during the dry season. These rivers originate in the hills with steep or medium slopes. Before flowing into the river, they cross the plain part where the slopes are weak, even very weak. This means that in this part of the plain a lot of sediment and other trash is deposited. These deposits block the natural flow of water and raise the level of rivers. Thus, in the event of rain, rivers overflow and cause often significant flooding, especially along streams. We also observe a backflow of water from rivers upstream, due to the flooding of the river into which they flow This phenomenon causes or aggravates flooding. This backflow is also observed in rivers that receive tributaries, for example at the level where the Matete flows into the NDjili, causing flooding in the lower quarters of the Kingabwa area. Some seasons floods turn into natural disasters. According to testimonies and the archives of the Kinshasa newspapers, one day there were around thirty dead, nearly a hundred injured and significant material damage with seriousness in Limete-Mombele, Ngaliema, Kinseso, Ngaba, Kimbanseke, Bumbu and Selembao. In the event of a flood, several homes are destroyed, bridges are cut, preventing traffic and isolating certain neighborhoods, pipes are destroyed, causing water cuts in certain neighborhoods, etc.

Photo Gutu Kia Zimi

10. **NOISE REDUCTION**

Urban vegetation contributes to the mitigation of noise pollution. Who says urban environment, says traffic and noise of all kinds. Urban vegetation acts like a sponge, absorbing this noise and suffocating it. Sound screens are useful along roads where traffic is particularly heavy and noisy. The rustling of the leaves of the trees, added to the song of the birds that nest there, also help to mask the sounds of the city[115]. Noise often reaches consistently unhealthy levels in the city of Kinshasa. Urban populations living near trade corridors, churches, bars and major thoroughfares (avenues) of traffic are often exposed to the highest levels. To make matters worse, the rules which prohibit and protect the population against noise are not observed by the "Kinshasa" population itself. In this regard, the city of Kinshasa is ranked among the worst cities in the country. Trees and vegetation can help reduce noise pollution in five important ways:

- by sound absorption (the sound is transferred to another object),
- ionic deflection (the direction of the sound is changed),
- reflexion (the sound is returned to its source),
- refraction (sound waves bend around an object) and
- masking (unwanted, so that it is covered with more pleasant sounds).

So leaves, twigs and branches will absorb sound, just like grasses and other herbaceous plants. The barriers of trees or plants will deflect the sound of the listeners and, if they are perpendicular to the

---

[115] MARIE JOËLLE SAUCIER (2018), Les bienfaits de la végétation en milieu urbain. https://mjsaucierpaysagiste.com/les-bienfaits-de-la-vegetation-en-milieu-urbain/

source, will reflect it towards that source. If the noise passes through and around vegetation, it is refracted and thus dissipated.

Urban vegetation can also mask sounds as people filter out unwanted noise by selectively listening to nature sounds (birdsong, leaf rustling, etc.) over city sounds (Miller 1988). Particularly beneficial to humans is the fact that plants absorb high frequency noise better than bass, since high frequency noise is the most distressing for humans. The optimum design of the plantation to reduce noise pollution is dense plant cover in a range of heights. Such green barriers can be established throughout the city of Kinshasa, along major traffic arteries and at the edges of noisy industrial and commercial corridors. Which is not the case.

Photo Gutu Kia Zimi

11. EROSION CONTROL

With the exception of desert areas where wind erosion predominates and Polar Regions with permanent frost, land is subject to water erosion. This very specific phenomenon in our tropical regions is better identified today. The Wischmeier and Smith (1969) erosion prediction equation: $E = R * K * SL * C * P$ also helps to better define the relative influence of erosion factors and conditions.

This equation means that soil losses (E) are a function of five factors and conditions including climate (R), soil resistance (K), topography (SL), soil cover (C) and practices. anti-erosion (P). Note that in tropical regions, climatic aggressiveness (R) is very high (200-1500-2000) in semi-arid areas of Africa (Roose, 1975). However, it is important to say that in our tropical regions, the ground cover by vegetation remains the conditional factor of erosion, the importance of which outweighs all others. Where vegetation exists, erosion remains minimal because it counteracts the action of the factor that creates the phenomenon. We cite the rain and the conditions that regulate its intensity. The role of vegetation is very evident and it is not surprising that the land devoid of vegetation is the most eroded. n certain districts of Kinshasa such as KISENSO, MONT NGAFULA, BINZA, SELEMBAO, the phenomenon of erosion requires enormous means of control. The main cause at the origin is the uncontrolled urbanization, which caused the destruction of the vegetation cover of the districts of these communes. Ravines do not develop everywhere in the urban space of Kinshasa, and this including if we consider only the districts built on the hillsides of the peripheral districts of Kisenso, Mont Ngafula, Selembao, Makala, Bumbu, Selembao, Ngaliema. Analysis of the spatial distribution of ravines in urban areas shows that the heterogeneity of the physical factors of ravine erosion is not the only cause. There would be human dimensions, which accentuate or slow down this phenomenon. BUSNELLI et al. (2006) indirectly acknowledge this when they say that spontaneous urbanization worsens the situation when combined with environmental fragility.

Intra-urban gully erosion can be qualified as an anthropogenic natural fact (METZGER et al., 2011), that is to say that it would result from the meeting between the natural event and the social organization of the space (LEONE et al., 2010). The factors of gully erosion in Kinshasa are no exception to this rule[116]. There are around 600 areas of frontal erosion in the city; induced by the soil ... Some neighborhoods in the outlying communes of Kinshasa are located below, on or above steep hills, or on slopes. The lack of urban vegetation cover and the heavy seasonal rains experienced by the city of Kinshasa, erosion and landslides have become common phenomena in the city of Kinshasa. The numerous anarchic constructions in the city of Kinshasa are particularly affected by erosion or landslides, because they are most often built on marginal slopes of the outlying districts. The built-up area in the hilly area of the municipalities of the South and West is underestimated. To retain the sandy soil, which tends to erode during heavy rains such as landslides leading to housing and infrastructure, the inhabitants plant tree vegetation, made up of fruit trees (mango trees, avocado trees, palm trees, etc.) and bamboos from China; this urban vegetation sometimes disturbs the spectral response of the "building". In Kinshasa, few scientific studies have been devoted to intra-urban gully erosion. The available studies fall into six groups. The first defines the categories of slopes likely (from 12%) to trigger gully erosion (VAN CAILLIE, 1997). The second group identifies some human causes of intra-urban gully erosion based on field observation (MITI TSETA & ALONI., 2005; LELO NZUZI, 2008) or on a diachronic series of Google Earth images (OZER, 2014). It has in fact been recognized since the 1990s that erosion control in Kinshasa should involve managing what is happening at the level

---

[116] KAYEMBE WA KAYEMBE M* & WOLFF E, Contribution de l'approche géographique à l'étude des facteurs humains de l'érosion ravinante intra-urbaine à Kinshasa (R.D. Congo), Géo-Eco-Trop., 2015, 39, 1: 119-138.

of the plots (Miti et al., 2004). Fortunately, scattered studies report various UVH in these peri-urban municipalities (Makumbelo et al., 2005). Some studies even specify that almost all of the lush vegetation visible in aerial photographs and satellite images of these peri-urban municipalities is concentrated in inhabited plots (SOSAK, 2014). It has in fact been recognized since the 1990s that erosion control in Kinshasa should involve managing what is happening at the level of the plots (Miti et al., 2004). It thus appears that the practice of UVH is generalized in the peri-urban area studied. These results confirm the observation made of the presence of lush vegetation in inhabited patches in the areas (Makumbelo et al., 2005; Wouters and Wolff, 2010; SOSAK, 2014).

The great importance given to plants in the development of plots in the area studied comes, among other things, from the recommendations for plant management resulting from studies reporting the high erodability of sandy and inconsistent soils in the hills of Kinshasa such as that of Kisenso., the municipality studied (Miti et al., 2004)[117]. For the human causes of intra-urban gully erosion we can mentioned: the unfinished construction, the poor sizing and lack of maintenance of the collectors, the lack of maintenance of retention basins, the lack of roof water management; the tracks laid out in the direction of the greatest slope (WOUTERS & WOLFF., 2010), and the waterproofing of slopes to the detriment of woody vegetation due to unplanned urbanization on vulnerable sandy soil (OZER, 2014). The third group defines a visual interpretation key to identify on a very high spatial resolution satellite image not only active and inactive ravines but also their origin (WOUTERS & WOLFF., 2010). The fourth group illustrates the speed of the gullying phenomenon in the hilly areas of southern Kinshasa from a diachronic series of Google Earth images

---

[117] KOUAGOU RAOUL SAMBIENI, op.cit.

(OZER, 2014). It is a phenomenon with significant socio-economic consequences: isolation of certain neighborhoods, disruption of neighborhood life, destruction of homes and roads. The fifth group studies the relationship between the distribution of mega ravines and urbanization in the city of Kinshasa and makes an inventory of the anti-erosion control techniques implemented in the south of the city of Kinshasa or describes them (MAKANZU IMWAGANA and al., 2015; KAYEMBE WA KAYEMBE, 2012; VAN CAILLIE, 1983, 1990). The last group emphasizes the money spent by donors within the framework of international cooperation to fight against the intra-urban gully erosion in Kinshasa (STEVENS, 2006; LELO NZUZI, 2008; KAYEMBE WA KAYEMBE, 2012). While the mere consideration of physical factors in the fight against erosion has not stopped the ravines, they swallow up several million US dollars of erosion control work in Kinshasa every year. However, few scientific studies on intra-urban gully erosion combine both physical and anthropogenic factors in a geographic, holistic and multi-scalar approach. The objective is to show that intra-urban gully erosion is not a natural calamity by using a holistic and multi-scalar geographic approach of physical and human factors combining the interpretation of very high-resolution satellite images, a fieldwork (observations, interviews, DGPS surveys) and the use of a geographic information system[118]. Mainly sandy and with some coarse features (UNDP / UNOPS, 1998). Due to this texture, the soils are very sensitive to erosion even on a slight slope and are not intended for agriculture. Nearly 600 heads of ravines identified destabilize the city of Kinshasa and, which result from serious erosion due to the accelerated runoff of rainwater. The intense development of the land, without any real control on the part of the authorities responsible for development, as

---

[118] KAYEMBE WA KAYEMBE M* & WOLFF E, op.cit.,

273

well as the lack of knowledge by the latter of effective actions that can be taken against soil degradation by regressive gullying, are currently not taking place, that aggravate the situation of instability and danger in the hills. The customary chiefs distributed the latter, considered in colonial times as unsuitable for construction, without taking into account their sensitivity to erosion and the potential risks. Some of these ravines, like that of Mataba located in the municipality of Ngaliema, continue to take on more than alarming proportions, reaching imposing sizes (about 1 km long, 10 m deep and 300 m wide) and reducing the more often to nothing any attempt to stabilize the sites. This gullying causes significant material losses (houses, roads, school buildings, dispensaries, etc.) and human losses (deaths during landslides). While the local population knows where the ravines are, there is no comprehensive picture at this time.

Photo Gutu Kia Zimi

The most important ravines of the city of Kinshasa are the following:

– Ravine de Mataba: it actually encompasses the entire district around the Delvaux market to the large ravine in front of the

Saint Sacrament Church in the Municipality of Ngaliema. Several branches or heads compose it. Currently, it threatens or progresses at the level of avenues Mbekama, Matadi, Kinsuka, Kilambo and Kinsiona.

- Ravin Maternité: It is located on the extension of the Maternity Route between avenues Pumbu and Avenues of Christian Schools in Binza Delvaux. To this are added two other heads in the extension of this avenue towards the valley of the Laloux district. Currently, there is total degradation of the road, which has become impassable following the influx of water from the Pigeon slope. At the rate of this erosion, it risks sweeping away the homes along this avenue if nothing is done.
- Ravine du Campus de Kinshasa: The university site alone has 20 ravines over an area of less than 5km2. One of these ravines is due to the bursting of a retention basin which was storing wastewater from one of the Homes.
- Manenga Ravine: It is located in the Binza Village district to the west of the Veterans Affairs district between the Matadi road and the Binza river (Ngaliema municipality). More than 15 erosion heads are linked to this ravine.
- Ravine de Okapi: This ravine is located in the Punda district (municipality of Ngaliema) between the main avenue Laloux and the road to Matadi. It extends to the valley of the Lubudi river. It houses the equestrian center called Etier de Binza, the Congo district which is behind the Hotel Okapi and extends to the cemeteries in the Kintambo valley. The lack of a competent and capable drainage system, the lack of maintenance of the one that existed there make this site one

of the most erosive and dangerous in the city of Kinshasa. It has more than 30 heads of erosion

- Ravine de Dreve de Selembao: Located in the Binza Pigeon district on Yandonge Avenue on the side of the Lubudi river (Municipality of Ngaliema). More than 9 heads of erosions are already listed.

- Ravine Lolo la Crevette: it is located on the slope 150 m from Saint Luke Church and Nguma Avenue. This ravine was due to the overflowing of the waters of the Mapenza river at the level of the Hotel Lolo la Crevette. The Saint Luc site is currently under threat, including Nguma Avenue, the main access road to the Kintambo shopping center, the school avenue that connects the Matadi road to Nguma Avenue as well as the entire neighboring block the Church.

- Ravin de Kingu / UPN: Located in front of the UPN Market. The road to Matadi, the avenue de la Liberation and the Madiata district limits it. The reception basin built some 250 meters from the Matadi road is completely silted up due to lack of maintenance. This is the origin of the birth of new erosion heads, 2 of which are particularly threatening.

- Ravin Ngafani: it is located in the Ngafani district (Municipality of Selembao), next to the By Pass Route. This erosion, which progresses towards Gemena Avenue with 13 branches, has swept away the Catholic Church of Saint Maximilian. Other branches are advancing towards Parc Avenue.

   The silting up of its 3 basins at the level of the Catholic primary school, threatens the By Pass road while other heads are heading towards Salongo, Kisanga and Kipati avenues.

- Ravine Bolikango-Santé: It is located in Binza Delvaux (Municipality of Ngaliema) in the presidential concession.

The basin built in 1991 in the enclosure of the fence and which constituted the valve of the safety of the district was washed away by the rain. The non-maintenance of this basin is the basis of its destruction. Indeed, from its installation until its rupture, all the elements of the cleared soil (eroded products) have accumulated in the basin. These made it waterproof. Unable to retain the critical volume of water, the basin gave way and evolved, subdividing itself into several erosion heads. Various works were carried out there without real success to stabilize the district.

– Kindele ravine: the ravine is located in the municipality of Lemba and is the result of diffuse runoff of rainwater, associated with the non-servicing of neighborhoods and the lack of maintenance of some existing drainage structures.

– Ravine Top: The ravine is located next to the Matadi road, at the entrance to Masikita Avenue between the Binza Delvaux and UPN districts.

Due to the numerous cases of loss of life and property represented by erosion, the urban authorities in the city of Kinshasa long ago enacted legislation to prevent urban development on too steep hills or in flood-prone areas.

Nevertheless, with the demographic growth, the population in complicity with the cadastre services granted themselves documents of title deeds and erected constructions there. Subdivision on high-risk sites, combined with poor vegetation cover, increases susceptibility to erosion and landslides, which often follow heavy rains (Bernstein, 1994). Much of this risk can be reduced by planting hardy species to hold back eroded soil on steep slopes. The population without first installing basic infrastructure (water, electricity, roads, wastewater evacuation systems, etc) has anarchically occupied the hill areas. This occupation destroyed all the vegetation cover stripping the soil, mostly sandy. Thus, the runoff has notched the slopes of these hills giving rise to ravines with multiple dimensions causing enormous human and material damage of the communes strongly affected by erosion are as follows: Bumbu, Kisenso, Lemba, Makala, Mount Ngafula, Ngaliema and Selembao.

Photo Gutu Kia Zimi

12. WILDLIFE HABITAT AND URBAN BIODIVERSITY

Urban vegetation and urban green spaces have been found to provide habitats for a surprising number of species and for large populations of birds and animals. Most urban residents are familiar with at least some local species of birds and animals, which have adapted to urban conditions. Where there are more parks and urban vegetation, local and migratory species can find suitable habitats. In particular, suburban wetlands can provide some of the world's most productive natural ecosystems as transition zones between terrestrial and aquatic environments (Bernstein, 1994). Wetlands, which are integrated into urban greening projects, including those designed or maintained for flood control and sewage settling ponds, provide particularly important habitats for local and migrating flora and fauna contributing to the maintenance of healthy biodiversity in urban areas. On a larger scale, urban greening can create or restore biological diversity, which will reconnect a city to its surrounding urban space. Cities are built into an existing ecosystem and often destroy it. This is the case of Kinshasa where the original urban vegetation has been destroyed. The urban flora and fauna, which once lived in this ecosystem are destroyed, either displaced or must adapt to the new urban environment. This process seriously depletes the genetic diversity (plant and animal) of a region and can threaten with extinction certain species essential to the natural ecosystem of the urban space and, consequently, to the resident urban population.

Photo Gutu Kia Zimi

To safeguard urban biodiversity, trees provide habitat (shelter, protection and food) for several species of birds, insects and small animals. Numerous fruits of trees attract and feed several species. Plants also provide them with protection against certain predators. The integration of urban vegetation and green spaces in a city like Kinshasa can reverse the trend towards biological destruction. For example, green belts and greenways can provide biological corridors for many species of plants and animals from the surrounding urban space, allowing them areas large enough to disperse their genetic material, a process crucial for survival some change. Urban agriculture can also provide biodiversity on a small but important scale. Ecological and biological diversity protects wild and domestic species from adverse conditions, including natural and economic fluctuations, and thus ensures the survival of plant and animal species. Foreign plants that urban populations have introduced may grow very well, but their flowers or fruits and seeds or foliage may not be useful as food, nest-building material, or shelter for local birds or insects. Moreover, without their natural enemies, many introduced species grow rapidly, reproducing through extensive seed production and dominating native flora. Although birds use the available trees and shrubs for cover and nesting, they need insect protein to breed and feed their young. Sometimes very specific plants and animals cannot exist without each other; for example, the yucca moth is the only pollinator of common yucca[119]. However, some species can be problematic in the domestic urban environment and you should give them special attention before planting them in your plot. We know the case of the species "*Chromolaena Odorata*", an invasive species accidentally introduced into Congolese plant flora. Although fertilizer, this species has the disadvantage of destroying forest vegetation. *Chromolaena Odorata* is considered an environmental weed in many parts of the world. It has been named one of the 100 of the "world's worst invaders" by the IUCN Invasive Species Specialist Group. It has been classified as a noxious weed in South Africa as a prohibited plant, which must be combated. It has no economic purpose and has characteristics that are harmful to humans, animals or the environment. *Chromolaena Odorata* forms dense stands that prevent the establishment of other species, both due to competition and allelopathic effects, and interfere with natural ecosystem processes. This species has the disadvantage of modifying the integrity and diversity of natural plant communities. Unfortunately, this invasive species is present in some residential plots of Kinshasa.

---

[119] HELEN HAMILTON and GUSTAVUS HALL, Wildflowers and Grasses of Virginia's Coastal Plain, Brit Press, 2013.

It must be fought, because it constitutes a danger for the urban flora of Kinshasa and the country. It is also the case of another invasive species *"Eichhornia Crassipes"* Water hyacinth, or *Camalote* of origin of South America, commonly called "Congo ya Sika", which constitutes a real danger which obstructs the courses of the country's waters. Its rapid growth and the changes in ecosystems it generates are problematic. It has become a scourge for the freshwater bodies, rivers and lakes of the tropics where it has become naturalized. The edges of the river in Kinshasa are invaded by this plant, which covers the length of the river with an impenetrable sheet.

Photo Gutu Kia Zimi

13. CLIMATE IMPROVEMENT

Climate projections predict an amplification of global warming, potentially exacerbated in urban areas due to the urban heat island phenomenon. The resurgence of extreme events such as heatwaves can have dramatic ecological, health and economic consequences at the scale of the cities, which concentrate the population. Climate change is a major driver of change on a global scale. Many extreme weather events are beginning to be experienced from climate change, including extreme urban heat waves. Heat waves are projected to increase in frequency, intensity, and duration in the future. The number of cities like Kinshasa exposed to extreme temperatures with average summer highs of 35*C or greater will almost triple over the coming decades (UCCRN, 2018)[120]. Beyond these average summer highs, heat waves will produce temperatures at which many human health, social, and ecological problems occur. Increased green infrastructure can help increase urban resilience to extreme heat by decreasing the urban heat island effect. Adequate tree cover can reduce temperatures by several degrees, which can be lifesaving. Green space and increased tree cover will be much more important in the future (David N. Bengston, 2019)[121]. Among the adaptation measures aimed at improving climatic comfort and energy demand, air conditioning and urban greening constitute two levers of action with sometimes antagonistic effects[122]. One of the most important benefits of urban vegetation is its impact on the climate. Two distinct influences can be identified. First, there is a direct effect on human comfort. Second, there is an effect on the energy budget of buildings in cities where air conditioning is used. These two effects can be significant or negligible, depending on the size, spacing and design of the vegetation zones. The direct impact on human

---

[120] UCCRN, Impact 2050, The future of cities under climate change. Urban Climate Change Research Network Technical Report, February 2018

[121] DAVID N. GENGSTON, Scanning the Horizon for the future of arboriculture, ISA, Vol.28, N*4, p.30

[122] DE MUNCK, CECILE. Modélisation de la végétation urbaine et des stratégies d'adaptation au changement climatique pour l'amélioration du confort climatique et de la demande énergétique en ville. Thèse de doctorat, PhD, Institut National Polytechnique de Toulouse, 2013.

comfort is a phenomenon that everyone is familiar with although it is difficult to quantify. Anyone who has walked down a city street on a rainy, hot or windy day knows from personal experience that trees can greatly increase human comfort by influencing the degree of solar radiation, air movement, humidity and temperature, air and providing protection against heavy rain. Wind speeds 2 meters above the ground in a residential area have been shown to decrease by 60% or more in areas of moderate tree cover compared to open areas (Heisler 1990). At the microclimate level: it is obvious that vegetation has a direct influence on the climate of both urban and rural areas. The function of bioclimatic regulator of urban vegetation consists of humidifying the ambient air by trees, which absorb water through their roots and release it through the phenomenon of evapotranspiration. It also helps regulate temperature, which can decrease in hot periods. This, by the release into the atmosphere of water by summer sweating. In this way, plants influence thermal regulation and the humidity of the air. This role that vegetation plays is considerable in improving the urban living environment and largely justifies the need for green spaces in our urban neighborhoods. Vegetation masses correctly established in the urban fabric would stem certain consequences of urban activities on the climate. Urban dwellers are therefore more vulnerable to climate change, in the sense that it can be exacerbated by the urban heat island (Lemonsu et al., 2015; Aude Lemonsu, Kounkou-Arnaud et al., 2013). Increasing the resilience of cities, especially from a health point of view, is therefore a decisive issue for the health of populations in the future. Urban planning must offer responses that are both mitigating and adapting to these two thermal disturbances. Ventilation inside streets is one of the factors modulating excess temperature in the city[123].

---

[123] EMILIE REDON (2017), Modélisation de la végétation urbaine comme régulateur thermique, Thèse de doctorat Université de Toulouse, Document inédit, https://tel.archives-ouvertes.fr/tel-01922348/document

Photo Gutu Kia Zimi

14. URBAN VEGETATION AND WARMING OF THE PLANET

It is important to clarify here that climate change and global warming are two distinct, albeit interdependent, phenomena. Since the dawn of time, the planet's climate has still not been the same. The planet has experienced several changes and other climatic variations (ice age, etc.). The climate has fluctuated since the earliest ages and geologists have been able to reconstruct certain climatic parameters that prevailed during the Precambrian, Primary and Secondary eras (i.e., the Archean, Paleozoic and Mesozoic periods). The Earth's climate has evolved between very contrasting regimes, ranging from extreme cold during widespread glaciations up to the equator to an atmosphere overheated by the greenhouse effect during the time of the dinosaurs[124]. Climate change is a natural phenomenon. On the other hand, the current global warming is a phenomenon of anthropogenic origin due mainly to the economic activity of man, one of the consequences of which is the production of greenhouse gases, including carbon dioxide. (CO_2). Climate change underway since the Industrial Revolution results from a modification of the composition of the Earth's atmosphere by greenhouse gas emissions generated by human activities. The current climate change is a consequence of global warming. For the first time in the history of humankind, through his economic activities, man is threatening life on the planet and his own survival through the imbalance of the biogeochemical cycles, which maintain life on earth. Of course, global warming has consequences for climate change. According to numerical simulations of the future climate, we anticipate a drastic increase in the occurrences of extreme weather events such as intense episodes of precipitation and high heat, caused by climate change (Tebaldi et al., 2006). In August 2020, extreme temperatures of 56 * C - 66 * C were recorded in "Death Valley" in California (USA) for the first time on the planet. Added to this global warming is a thermal signature of cities, characterized by a positive temperature anomaly between urbanized areas and their periphery (Tim R Oke, 1982; T. Oke, 1987). Indeed, the urban fabric is a matrix made up of buildings and roads made of impermeable materials, often dark, which capture solar and IR energy from the sky during the day and store it. Artificial walls limit the cooling of the air at night by releasing heat and emitting IR radiation. The three-dimensional urban form also acts as a trap for the energy received and exchanged on the street. This urban air warming, characteristic of the micro-climate of cities,

---

[124] EDOUARD BARD, Les variations climatiques du passé et de l' avenir, https://www.college-de-france.fr/media/edouard-bard/UPL62252_Bard07ENSG.pdf.

is referred to as the urban heat island phenomenon[125]. A country's climate is one of its basic natural resources. Indeed, all climatic factors are ecological factors. However, it is the latter that determine a given ecosystem. However, with the entry of the earth into the so-called "Anthropocene" era, human activities or the "Technosphere" are causing climate change, including global warming. The impact of global warming on climate change is convincing more than one, even the most skeptical of humans, that the effects of climate change are indeed real and noticeable[126]. In the DRC, the projection of variation in climatic parameters due to the effects of global warming indicates temperature variations (* C) for the following years: 2010 (0.45-0.52); 2025 (0.91-1.03); 2100 (2.69-3.22). For precipitation (%), it is estimated for 2010 (0.3-2.5); 2025 (0.4-4.2); 2100 (0.8-11.4)[127]. According to the DRC projection[128], mean temperature is projected to substantially increase in the future independent of the scenario, with a stronger increase under the high emission scenario; not only mean temperatures are projected to increase but also extremes. Therefore number of cold days and nights are projected to decrease and number of hot days and nights are projected to increase; Only a very moderate change in total precipitation is projected to occur in the future for both scenarios, with a slight tendency for a precipitation increase. This is also true for the rainfall during the rainy season; Rains are likely to be less uniformly distributed in the future, as dry spells in

---

[125] EMILIE REDON (2017), Modélisation de la végétation urbaine comme régulateur thermique, Thèse de doctorat Université de Toulouse, Document inédit, https://tel.archives-ouvertes.fr/tel-01922348/document.

[126] US President Donald TRUMP is among those who do not believe in global warming.

[127] Ministère de l'Environnement, Conservation de la Nature et Tourisme, Seconde Communication Nationale à la Convention Cadre sur le Changement Climatique, 2009, http://unfccc.int/resource/docs/natc/rdcnc2.pdf

[128] CSC (2020), Fact-Sheet - Climate - Democratic Republic of the Congo (DRC)- Zone 4, https://www.climate-service-center.de/imperia/md/content/csc/kongo/fact_sheet_climate_drc.pdfwww.giz.de and www.comifac.org

the rainy season are projected to substantially increase; the intensity of rainfall extremes is projected to increase, but almost no change in their frequency is projected. For that, ggreening is an effective strategy to fight against global warming because it offers social, economic and environmental benefits that go beyond the regulation of the micro-climate in the city.

Urban vegetation like any other forest or savannah vegetation contributes in the fight against global warming. The perception of the problems of climate change, a consequence of global warming, by the Congolese population in the DRCongo has been the subject of two series of surveys[129]. Initially, only the city province of Kinshasa was targeted in 2004 by interviewing 1,600 people, taking into account the period 1980-2004. With regard to the perception of climate change by the "Kinoise" population:

- 94% attest that climate change is noticeable in their environment
- 83% mention a "shortage" in water resources
- 90% have already experienced at least one natural disaster of climatological origin in their living environment
- 81% say that climatic events affect health
- 74% speak of an increase in the frequency of heavy rains or tornadoes / hurricanes
- 52% speak of a decrease for rain per season
- 73% say the number of rainy days in the rainy season is decreasing
- 93% find that the rainy season starts late but ends too early.
- 94% attest to an increase in temperature (sensible heat)

---

[129] https://www.thegef.org/sites/default/files/ncsa-documents/375_0.pdf

- 94% want to drink with cooled water
- 94% deplore the lack or interruptions of the electricity supply, which makes their nights painful, especially during the rainy season[130].

Global warming and its consequences is an undeniable reality among the "Kinshasa" people. It is increasingly hot in Kinshasa and torrential and torrential rains have become chronic and recurrent.

Overall, among the effects of climate change, we can cite:

- Reinforcement of temperature inversions, especially in the dry season
- Increase in thermal forcing; hence the heat wave
- Disruption of the rainfall regime:
- Shortening of the rainy season and lengthening of the dry season;
- Scarcity of rains;
- Reduction in the number of rainy days;
- Increase in heavy rains (hence flooding);
- Reduction of water in aquifers;
- Intensification of runoff;
- Land degradation;
- Ravine erosions;
- Siltation of the hydrographic network
- Disruption of the hydrological cycle
- Increasingly pronounced low water;
- Drying up of rivers.

---

[130] Les changements climatiques en République Démocratique du Congo: état de lieux et perspectives dans le cadre de l'ANCR, https://www.thegef.org/sites/default/files/ncsa-documents/375_0.pdf

- Disturbance of ecotopes (Consumption of forest fires);
- Intensification of extreme weather phenomena (hurricane, tornado, typhoon, etc.)

Photo Gutu Kia Zimi

SECTION II: MATERIAL ADVANTAGES OF URBAN VEGETATION

The effects of climate change over the last decades on global surface temperature have been quantified by the IPCC (Edenhofer et al., 2014). The magnitude of the observed increase cannot be explained on its own by the variability of the climate system or natural forcing. It is considered extremely likely that anthropogenic greenhouse gas emissions have altered the composition of the atmosphere to the point of causing global climate disruption. However, the metabolism of cities generates more than 75% of anthropogenic carbon emissions, because they are places of intense consumption of fossil energy and electricity, of materials and of the production of synthetic substances (Brown, 2001; Svirejeva -Hopkins, Schellnhuber and Pomaz, 2004). No one can ignore the various environmental services that trees provide, especially since they are above all a vital resource for society. The sad reality is that urban development has for some time made itself a real and formidable enemy against trees. The various roles that trees are called upon to play in urban settings have been relegated to the background. In Kinshasa for example, the various forest belts, which once surrounded the city, have disappeared, giving way to residential houses. This is how avalanches of bad news keep reaching us from the city. Erosion, floods, high heat, strong winds, torrential and destructive rain, this is what everyday life looks like in urban areas, which have not thought of giving an important place to trees. This is why it is important to watch and demonstrate the ecological, environmental and economic benefits of trees and green spaces, which must remain the center of our concerns. In some cases, depending on their planting density and morphology, trees can alter airflow, which slows down the dispersal of pollutants and even leads to an increase in pollutants, which therefore concentrate in certain places. This may for example be the case in steep streets. Although it can help improve air quality, vegetation also presents negative aspects such as the emission of CO_2, which will be more or less important depending on the species of trees. In addition to these emissions, we must consider those of CO_2 and methane linked to the decomposition of plant biomass. Finally, it is necessary to favor the least invasive and non-allergenic species in the development of green spaces or the planting of rows of trees in the city. The greening of cities is presented as a strategy of adaptation to climate change "without regret" (de

Munck, C. and Lemonsu, A., 2014; Mills, Wilson and Johansson, 1991) with multiple benefits for the environment and society (M. Musy, 2014). When the urban form and the orientation of the streets cannot be changed, this is the most effective cooling strategy. In addition, it brings many social and economic benefits, by creating heritage value for example, and spaces for social cohesion, sports and leisure activities. Shading provided by trees has been shown to be effective in reducing energy consumption for air conditioning in summer. The choice of deciduous species (which fall in autumn) avoids additional heating demand in winter. Vegetation also regulates the climate (production of O_2 and storage of Co_2), air quality (absorption and retention of pollutants), water (phytoremediation) and a reduction in the thermal amplitude observed on a daily cycle, so as to prevent long exposure to very high heat stress in the middle of the day. Evapotranspiration is a unique heat dissipation phenomenon, which consumes 99% of the solar energy absorbed by plants and humidifies the air. Restoring a sufficient fraction of natural cover in the city is an appropriate response to effectively combat the deleterious effects of the urban heat island. Nature in the city not only supports the effort to adapt to climate change by improving the conditions of thermal comfort for city dwellers, the reduction of anthropogenic emissions of heat and greenhouse gases through energy savings, and the attractiveness of urbanized poles for various sociological reasons, among others in connection with the image of "viability" of the living environment. The fraction of vegetation present in contemporary cities is not negligible. It takes various forms such as alignment trees, public parks, private gardens, but also plant envelopes covering buildings (Anquetil, 2010). It directly influences the urban climate through its radiative, thermal, hydric and aeraulic properties; this from the scale of the street to the entire city. Few urban climate models today take into account vegetation (C. Grimmond, Blackett et al., 2010), and in particular trees, in an urban environment while they modify the radiative and energy balances by intercepting and absorbing part of the incident solar radiation, create shade, dissipate energy and increase the humidity of the air by evapotranspiration and also modify the flow of air masses in the canyon[131].

Photo Gutu Kia Zimi

1. FOOD AND AGRICULTURAL PRODUCTS

Urban agriculture is an activity that sustains many families in Kinshasa (Democratic Republic of Congo). It can therefore contribute to the sustainable development of African cities under

---

[131] EMILIE REDON (2017), op.cit.

certain conditions, notably through its professionalization, the non-use of chemical inputs and the equitable distribution of arable land. The case of Kinshasa clearly illustrates that this agriculture remains a palliative solution to the social constraints of survival, absence of remunerative wages and lack of sustainable jobs ... This case shows that there is no shame in practicing urban market gardening, because even academics do it (only 5% do so by family tradition); there is the problem of the choice of sites and supervision. In fact, poorly supervised, market gardeners cultivate along roads with intense motorized traffic, thus exposing vegetables to various contaminations, in particular lead. The urban market gardening sector has developed in many districts of Kinshasa, either out of necessity or under the impetus of changes in living standards and eating habits. Although its usefulness is recognized, the sector is neglected, supply systems are not well known. In the absence of an adequate strategy and supervision, we are witnessing uncontrolled development, which is however closely linked to the management of urban space, water resources, and the protection of the supply of consumers with quality products. In view of the positive and negative aspects of the market gardening sector in Kinshasa, particular attention deserves to be paid to it by the municipal authorities. In addition, in order to properly manage the attraction sites for market gardeners, it involves securing them in favor of the many functions they perform by delimiting those that can accommodate economic activities. The extension of these urban agricultural perimeters will have to be included in future urbanization plans and the dynamics of evolution of this urban agriculture will have to be supported according to strategies relating to urban development. In this regard, Smith et al. (1996) cite surveys, which have found that 28% to 80% of urban households in developing countries practice some form of urban agriculture. Urban farmers maintain open spaces and turn urban waste into food and biodiversity, saving the municipality the cost of landscape maintenance and waste management. The market gardening sector contributes somewhat to the sustainability of the city of Kinshasa. That is to say, it allows a better quality of life through the employment created, the income generated and the social integration caused, for socio-economic development; partial control of its waste by recycling biodegradable waste. Of all the waste produced in some nine markets in Kinshasa (54,385 m3 per year), the market gardening sector devotes 42,617m3 per year to the recovery by burying this waste (green manure) and by composting for the compost needs. This corresponds to 78.4% of recycled waste to produce 14,516 m3 of compost required per year. This recycling constitutes an upstream contribution to the sanitation of the intra- and peri-urban environment by garbage collection, and downstream an agronomic advantage due to the availability of fertilizers, given the low texture and structure of Kinshasa's soils. As a risk factor for the environment, waste in constant increase, invades the city and often dumped in vacant lots, gutters and in rivers, they generate an increasing cost of disposal and treatment and therefore constitute a growing problem pollution (Pichat, 1995). When available, small garden plots can help urban farmers, especially the poor, provide food for their own families, thereby reducing the burden on their already scarce financial resources or on government subsidy programs limited. Container horticulture (in boxes, gutters, pots, used tires and even plastic bags) is also a popular alternative for low-income families without access to land. In Kinshasa, for example, the town's agricultural service helps and supervises gardeners and market gardeners to produce cash crops (UNDP, 1996). Studies have shown that these home-farming systems can provide between one-tenth and one-third of a family's annual vegetable consumption. In addition, these gardeners eat more vegetables and their families are healthier than other comparable low-income families. There are various markets in the city of Kinshasa (Zikida Market, UPN, Cecomaf,…) where local producers can sell their products to the general public. Many of these farmers grow their products in urban or suburban areas and contribute significantly to the diet of the urban population. Their proximity to markets gives them a competitive advantage thanks to reduced transport and storage costs. Additionally, farmers can tailor their production to meet market demand for perishable items of great value (UNDP 1996).

Photo Gutu Kia Zimi

1. URBAN FOREST PRODUCTS

Urban greening can bring significant material benefits in areas where firewood and construction wood are in high demand. The tree species that produce fence posts are highly valued, especially in arid regions where low-cost fence materials are scarce. This is especially true in suburban areas and small towns where fence posts are more commonly used to surround livestock or cultivated plots. Poles are also used in construction, furniture making, and crafts. There are many tree species suitable for urban and suburban growing conditions, such as *Leucaena leucocephala*, which provide high quality fodder for livestock. Likewise, a large percentage of city dwellers, especially the poor, use firewood as their primary cooking and heating fuel and depend on nearby green spaces for their source of wood. Urban greening can provide sustainable fuelwood plantations to meet the needs of these urban residents. Fruits, nuts and fibers are part of other forest products, which are valued and harvested in urban and suburban green spaces. Most of the trees that provide these usable products are found in private patios and gardens, not in public. Traditionally, species selection criteria for standard horticultural plantations in urban areas have emphasized ornamental value versus the value of material products that could be harvested from vegetation. While fruit trees and other species that provide material benefits are often highly valued in private lots, the vast majority of species selected for use on public lands are ornamentals. Their products are rarely taken into account in their selection. Often, the ornamental and statutory value of a landscape plant appears to be enhanced by the fact that the plant is useless for practical purposes and of exotic origin. In practical terms, ornamentals are less prone to damage and theft than fruit trees or other beneficial species and there may be an element of cost reduction targets by municipal planners when choosing which species to use plant in public green spaces.

Photo Gutu Kia Zimi

Photo Gutu Kia Zimi

1. THE IMPROVEMENT OF FOOD PRODUCTION IN URBAN AREAS

As a source of Income, the agricultural land within the city can of course be used for the production and sale of fresh vegetables and fruits, seeds and ornamental plants. Another economic dimension of agricultural space concerns self-consumption. According to Raki (1991), the incomes of urban farmers are determined not only by the size of the means of production, but also by the importance of resources outside the farm, its physical environment, and the choice of crops. This income from urban farmers plays a determining role in the economic balance of the family farm. They cover current consumption needs (food, clothing, housing, health and education expenses), but also the financing of production capital. Th Many households derive income from the sale of these products, often as a supplement when wage income does not allow them to be self-sufficient. Several authors, including Kabanga (1992), have also stressed the role of urban agriculture in environmental management. Urban agriculture through market gardening helps reduce pollution in the city (urban and peripheral districts). It makes it possible to recycle household waste and urban waste, especially municipal markets, breweries, etc. as Fleury et al. (1997). The revenues derived from the sale of market garden products are an important complement to other revenues. The question of the "urban green belt" has always been taken into account by the governors in the various urban development plans to preserve agricultural green spaces. The public authorities are keen on it, for obvious reasons of both food security and jobs for city dwellers. However, the poverty that rages in Congolese cities is a real dilemma for the populations, who are confronted with both food and housing difficulties. Indeed, the rapid demographic evolution of cities influences urban sprawl and agricultural areas are swallowed up by the sprawl of housing. Much more, as Lelo Nzuzi points out. (2010), "this demographic and spatial growth is taking place against a backdrop of poverty and serious crises in housing, employment, transport and recreation, etc. ". Thus in the Congolese cities, the rulers find it difficult to make the choice between feeding the population and housing them, especially in large cities like Kinshasa. It is not uncommon to see fields of cassava, corn and other vegetable crops razed by the municipal authority under the pretext of sanitation against mosquitoes or to fight against banditry, but in reality these are housing projects, which are projected onto these sites by urban managers. The case of the Bandalungwa nursery (Cité Oasis), and of Gombe currently subdivided, of the riparian districts of Kingabwa and Masina in Kinshasa are typical cases. Urban and peri-urban cultivation areas are strongly under pressure from housing and yet, faced with the poverty of urban households, urban agriculture deserves improvements because it provides jobs. This motive certainly justifies the importance of this type of agriculture. Of course, the efforts of the government and the partners can be seen in these activities: supervision of market gardeners and training them in production techniques, etc. But the results generally seem mixed in the eyes of practitioners, because they live in uncertainty about land tenure and the state can evict them at any time, as is the case of the market gardeners of the nursery of the commune of Bandalungwa and Gombe. The results of urban habitat surveys (2014) clearly show the importance of market gardeners, the number of which is estimated at 950,000 in large cities, the majority, 73% of whom are women. Despite the many harassments to which urban farmers are victims: spoliations, nibbling, land pressure, lack of supervision and the absence of an active political will to modernize urban market gardening belts, the central government, the provinces and other partners (FAO, CTB, etc.) are working with these market gardeners. They provide them with working tools (hoes, cuffs, rakes, wheelbarrows, etc.), improved seeds, fertilizer, training, credits, etc. The question of urban agriculture sufficiently shows that improving food production requires good urban planning. Municipalities should have "Agricultural Plan and Program" to protect market gardening areas in a sustainable manner. It is a question of strengthening interactions between market gardeners and urban development stakeholders. The green belt, the city's nurturing mother, will still have to keep its peri-urban place intact in order to supply the city with market garden products, create jobs and help alleviate the food crisis and malnutrition, which are rampant in Congolese cities (Mpuru MB 1998; Lelo N. 2011; Risasi M. et al. 2014).

Photo Gutu Kia Zimi

SECTION III: SOCIAL BENEFITS

1. FROM A HEALTH POINT OF VIEW

The urban environment is generally denatured in various forms including in particular noise, air pollution, sensory stimuli, promiscuity, nervousness, the monotony of the landscape, the absence of tranquility and calm, all of this plunges the individual into permanent or chronic stress. The natural environment provides an adequate framework for improving the physical and mental health of the individual, which provides invaluable social benefits. On the other hand, if the population of the air can affect respiratory and circulatory functions just as noise can exert influences on many negative functions and even affects growth and mental development, the flora constitutes an antidote to this of these negative influences, which are characteristic of the urban environment and a means conducive to improving its quality. We know that plants purify and renew the atmosphere by absorbing the carbon dioxide released by humans and their activities and regenerate oxygen. Through this process, the air is thus renewed. It should also be noted that in many cases of illness, patients are sent to breathe clean country air for better convalescence. Urban vegetation can play a role in the circulation of air in the city, especially during the dry period during which a low-pressure zone is created compensated by a demand for air from the periphery, this is a corridor wind, the air, which rises, is loaded with impurities as it reaches the center of the city. Tree-covered surfaces in the direction of this corridor stream obstruct stale air towards the center. Through their shade, some tree species very popular in the neighborhoods of the Kinshasa municipalities, such as *"Terminalia Catappa"*, effectively reduce the degree of sunstroke. In the case of eddies and other strong winds, vegetation plays a protective role by protecting dwellings, crops, vehicles by acting as a screen to modify the circulation and the direction of the wind. Although they can be difficult to quantify, the health benefits of urban greening can be substantial. Certainly, the improvements in air quality due to vegetation have positive effects on physical health with obvious benefits such as the reduction of respiratory diseases. However, the fact that urban vegetation also reduces stress and improves health by contributing to an aesthetic and relaxing environment (Nowak et al. 1996) is perhaps less evident. Ulrich (1990) found that convalescing hospital patients recovered much faster when placed in rooms with a view of trees and exteriors than patients without sight. Urban forests provide a link between people and their natural environment that would otherwise be lacking in a city. This link is important for daily pleasure, worker productivity, and general mental health (Nowak et al 1996). Shade from the trees and the resulting cooler temperatures, especially in summer, is why people tend to flock to the city's parks and green spaces to spend time together on weekends and during the week. Thus, they also fulfill a very important social function. Shade also reduces exposure to ultraviolet light, thereby reducing the risk of adverse health effects such as skin cancer and cataracts (Heisler et al. 1995). In summary, urban forests provide many direct and indirect physical and mental health benefits for the people of a city. However, some plant species can be harmful to people with allergies to pollen. So that the vegetation in cities does not have a negative impact on respiratory health, it is therefore necessary to carry out an integrated analysis of the impacts in the choice of plant species. The use of phytosanitary products must also be a point of vigilance because exposure to these products endangers human health and the environment. This can result in more or less long-term health problems such as neurological or immune damage, cancer or fertility problems.

Photo Gutu Kia Zimi

Photo Gutu Kia Zimi

2. LEISURE

Green spaces provide venues for recreation, especially for low-income residents, who tend to frequent city parks more than wealthier citizens due to financial constraints and restrictions on recreation. This, of course, depends on two conclusions: first, the park must be within an affordable travel distance for the individual or family; and second, it must have the facilities that these people prefer. The urban poor generally have few affordable leisure options and therefore place a high value on green spaces. However, their favorite recreational activities may vary from city to city, or even neighborhood to neighborhood. Therefore, research or social surveys on their preferences should be seen as a tool to help city planners design appropriate new green spaces. It is unfortunate that green spaces for the leisure of city dwellers have disappeared in Kinshasa. With population growth, these leisure areas such as "Mbudi Nature chez le Conseiller", Safari Beach, Picasso, Mayalos, Cité des Bolobo, Lac de Ma Vallée, Espace Ngindu, Jardin D'Eden ... are accessible outside the city. In Kinshasa, the absence of green spaces means that the life of "Kinshasa" is more in residential plots. The town of "Kinshasa" have developed all kinds of activities in residential plots. This is how we find bars, "Nganda", churches ... in the various residential plots of Kinshasa.

Photo Gutu Kia Zimi

Photo Gutu Kia Zimi

3. EDUCATION

As man has to live in harmonious association with nature, his life is intimately linked, hence the need to ensure his education in relation to it (Nyakabwa, 1982). Green spaces are an important educational means of observing nature; the combination of homes and green spaces (parks, children's play areas) would constitute an ideal environment for the psychological development of children. The lack of development of green spaces in our neighborhoods is a prejudice that borders on the irresponsibility of those who are called upon to defend them. Note that in Kinshasa almost all the land reserved for green spaces has been distributed to wealthy individuals. Therefore, it is a sad reality. A few trees or a few flowers are enough to give children the first idea of what is natural, true, and beautiful and calm their nervousness caused by the aggressive conditions of today's life, especially in urban areas. Parks and other green spaces also provide educational opportunities for urban residents. Many towns have botanical gardens, zoos, nature trails, and even visitor information centers that can educate residents and tourists about the flora and fauna of the area. Individuals, families and school groups can take advantage of a city's green spaces to learn about the environment and natural processes. For urban children, as well as adult students, the learning experiences available in urban parks may be some of the few opportunities they have to learn about nature through first-hand experience. In addition, by involving the public in educational activities associated with urban green spaces, planners can raise public awareness of the importance of these spaces. Another way to educate the public about the importance and benefits of urban greening is to involve people in the greening process itself.

Photo Gutu Kia Zimi

Photo Gutu Kia Zimi

4. FROM THE POINT OF VIEW OF THE BEAUTY AND AESTHETICS OF THE HABITAT

Plants and flowers give the habitat a certain beauty. To do this, it would suffice to admire a plot with a beautiful flowered and well-kept garden. This is why we will have to strive for a harmonious association of the architectural and plant element through the choice of ornamental plants. Vegetation can easily become established in the components of the urban landscape. Urban art is a matter of taste and measure. This is why the architect may be led to marry the architectural design of the habitat with the vegetation through the effects of contrast and harmony. Its foliage can highlight the aesthetic element of the plant, by the coloring of its flowers or by its habit in general. In principle, plants in houses, verandas, balconies are acclimatized in hanging or stable pots or tubs for interior decoration. This very regular practice in European homes is beginning to manifest itself in a certain category of the Kinshasa population in general. It is a question of culture and taste. Some people prefer to have a garden or flower pots in the plot out of snobbery, out of a real taste of nature or even out of imitation or even out of curiosity without any deep feeling. While not considered as important as meeting basic needs such as food and shelter, the aesthetics of green spaces can also be very meaningful to many urban residents. There are many examples of civic groups sponsoring the planting of trees to improve the aesthetics of key parts of their cities to increase civic pride. Vegetation reduces glare and reflection from the sun, complements architectural features and alleviates the harshness of large concrete surfaces. Areas of a city with sufficient greenery to be aesthetically pleasing are attractive to residents and city dwellers. For example, the beautification of Singapore and Kuala Lumpur, Malaysia, was one of the factors that attracted significant foreign investment, which helped these cities to rapid economic growth (Braatz 1993). Another advantage of aesthetic green spaces is their positive effect on property values. When vacant lots or unsightly landfills are replaced with attractive parks, not only does the quality of life of residents improve, but also the value of their property increases. In addition, rehabilitating land with vegetation is often more attractive and profitable than building new buildings on it. This is the case with Kinshasa. Indeed, the value of houses in the municipality of Gombe is greater due to the aesthetic aspect of this municipality. On large areas of municipal land, these boundaries can be maintained through the community efforts of nearby residents who value green spaces and work together to protect them. The range of benefits of urban greening is both practical and comprehensive, and addresses many of the social, environmental and economic issues that most cities face. While not the panacea for all current urban ills, urban greening can nonetheless significantly address many of them and create a much more attractive and desirable environment in which to live.

Photo Gutu Kia Zimi

TITLE III: CONSTRAINTS RELATING TO ECONOMIC EVALUATION URBAN GREENING

Several recurring obstacles hamper the planning and execution of more green spaces in cityscapes. The first major challenge is to get municipal authorities, businesses and the public to include the real benefits of urban greening or revegetation when making capital investment decisions based on cost-benefit analyzes. Although the benefits described in the previous section are very real, they are often overlooked when considering the benefits of urban communities. Building institutional capacity, using appropriate technologies and securing sustainable finance from various sources are also critical but elusive goals. Another important challenge is to maximize public participation at all levels of the implementation of the urban reforestation or reforestation project and to remove the obstacles, which prevent this, including lack of land tenure, inequality in distribution gender and outdated land legislation. Finally, planners face the obstacle of green areas, which have suffered moderate or severe environmental degradation. It can also be difficult to avoid double counting of benefits if multiple valuation methods are used independently to estimate a variety of green space benefits. Green spaces provide a range of tangible and easy-to-assess benefits such as food, from agricultural plots, but they also provide intangible but valuable amenities such as aesthetics, noise reduction, etc. How can municipal authorities value these multiple and diverse benefits, then compare them to the benefits of other projects with more easily calculable costs and benefits? Overcoming this problem may require a multi-level approach involving cooperation with other government sectors to reduce disastrous effects, land reclamation and strict monitoring procedures. Another constraint and difficulty is that relating to the economic evaluation of an action or project for urban revegetation. Putting a value on the city's green resources is one of the most important challenges that urban planners can face when implementing an urban greening or revegetation program. While there are obvious costs associated with creating and maintaining green spaces, it is difficult to calculate the value of all the benefits associated with this area. How do you assign an economic value to something intangible like aesthetics and landscape? Can non-market benefits and ecological services be measured in the same units as market goods? If the government were willing to nominate land in green spaces, with the restriction that, they could only be used for urban greening purposes, the higher bid could be used as the economic value of green spaces. Likewise, if the government acted as if it were a private developer, it could expect the same result by calculating the monetary result of using the land in different green activities and choosing the most profitable one. These procedures would be reasonable if the government's offers or calculations reflected all the costs and benefits. Unfortunately, this is probably not the case. With the exception of goods produced by urban agriculture, many of the goods and services provided by urban greening or revegetation activities do not generate any cash income. They produce public goods like: cleaner air, prettier view, calmer environment, which are appreciated by many city dwellers, but which cannot be billed to every user because people cannot be excluded from benefit. If nature in the city provides answers to certain development issues, it is important to take into account the limits and constraints necessary for its proper development in the planning of urban vegetation. Indeed, the urban environment remains a stressful environment for plants; their lifespan is shorter in the city and differs according to the area where they are located. In addition, plants also breathe, resulting in CO_2 emissions. Finally, the cost of setting up and maintaining urban vegetation can also be a brake on the implementation of an urban greening or revegetation policy[132].

Photo Gutu Kia Zimi

---

[132] The "MillionTreesNYC" program aimed at planting 1 million trees in New York City, by planting 100,000 trees each year over a period of 10 years, would lead, according to calculations, to capture 15kg of CO_2 / tree / year, i.e. 1,500 tons of CO_2 / year, Document APPA Nord-Pas de Calais - 2014.

GENERAL CONCLUSION

Over time, economic and urban development has led to an increasingly significant reduction in green spaces in the city of Kinshasa. With hindsight, we are now able to sound the alarm bell and see that the quality of urban life is suffering heavily from the consequences of the deforestation of peri-urban space. Unfortunately, we have forgotten the many advantages that trees provide in an urban environment. Vegetation is a key element in our life cycle for breathing, eating and even healing. The benefits of vegetation are numerous: social, aesthetic, economic and ecological. The importance of urban trees is well-established (Nilsson and Randrup, 1996; Kuchelmeister, 2000). They are an essential element of urban infrastructure for a livable and sustainable environment[133]. In view of our study, we insisted on the fundamental role of trees and urban vegetation on our physical and human environment. The function and the role of vegetation in our existence are fundamental; it should challenge us to a collective awareness. The association of the tree in our urban habitat would contribute to the improvement of urban living conditions by providing an effective natural means of combating atmospheric and other pollution without forgetting effective protection of the soil. The study allowed us to understand that the urban vegetation of Kinshasa has been declining over the years, especially in the neighborhoods of the old municipalities and a slow progression in the new neighborhoods of the peripheral municipalities. This general downward trend should bring us awareness so that we can maintain and protect the existing urban vegetation. This downward trend can

---

[133] NZALA D. (2003), L'arbre en ville, étude de foresterie urbaine à Brazzaville /Congo, XIIe congrès forestier mondial, Québec, Canada

be explained by the fact that the area occupied by the constructions in the plots becomes larger and larger, that is to say that over the years, the old constructions from the beginning during the the acquisition of the plots disappear in favor of new larger and more comfortable constructions in the plots. Moreover, at the beginning of the birth of the district, the owners are mainly interested in planting the trees in the plot, but as the district ages, the urban vegetation becomes dense and the interest of planting other trees are no longer justified. It is also a regrettable fact to note that no tree has been detected in the streets of African neighborhoods and this because of the narrowness of the streets or a simple omission of the town planner, who has not made the relevant arrangements during the development of these districts. Planting a fruit tree in your plot is a profitable initiative as the fruits are an important source of nutrients. In this case, the fruit tree not only provides fruit but also provides shade and also improves the living environment in the plot. For our part, we believe that planting a tree in its plot does not require any significant financial means except that of will and taste. On this, it would be beneficial if the public authorities encouraged the population to plant trees in their respective plots. What could be better to live in a shady plot? It is true that trees dramatically change the urban landscape as they dominate single-level buildings. If at the time of the establishment of the plot all the vegetation is destroyed, as soon as the houses are built, the trees are planted again, but they are mainly fruit trees as we observed in our study. Another observation is that one can read the chronology of urban growth by observing the urban vegetation of the neighborhoods. By its afforestation, one can notice a recent subdivision without trees or a young district of an old one. Also by the size of the trees, we can distinguish young quarters composed of shrubs and old ones, which are populated with trees the size of the house or a little larger. The role of trees is fundamental in our urban and rural environment; it is a nurturer, a natural conditioner, a shade carrier, an ornament to the plots. Its leaves, seeds and roots are used in cooking and in pharmacopoeia. Planted wisely in a corner of the plot, it marks the sign of possession of the plot and the space. This is why we say that the tree in the city does not have the same perception as in the rural environment. In urban areas, it is of anthropogenic origin while in rural areas, it is of natural origin with a few rare exceptions. Finally, the study also revealed to us that the ornamental trees very common in the "European" residential districts of Gombe, Limete ... are somewhat rare in the districts of the "city" inhabited by Africans. At the end of this study, the observation of the predominance of fruit trees in the urban vegetation of Kinshasa and the predominance of dominant species such as mango and oil palm is obvious. In general, the urban vegetation in the residential plots of Kinshasa is in very strong decrease or regression in the districts of the former communes of Kinshasa, Kintambo, Barumbu, Gombe, Lingwala. And also in the districts of the communes of East and West extension called "new cities" such as Limete, KasaVubu, NgiriNgiri, Ngaba, Bumbu, Ndjili, Makala, Selembao. Finally, in the districts of planned cities such as the commune of Bandalungwa, Matete, Lemba, Kalamu. However, the urban vegetation is young, flourishing and growing in the neighborhoods of the peripheral or peri-urban municipalities of Nsele, Maluku, Mont Ngafula, Ngaliema, Ndjili, Masina, Kisenso, etc.

These two trends are explained graphically according to the evolution of trees by year of plantation. As reported by Kouagou Raoul Sambieni's results[134] in his study "The diversity and abundance

---

[134] La végétation arborée domestique dans le paysage urbain et périurbain de la ville de Kinshasa, République Démocratique du Congo.

of domestic tree vegetation are relatively greater in the peri-urban area than in the urban one. In addition, this domestic tree vegetation is made up mostly of exotic species and edible species. These results clearly reveal the green potential that domestic tree vegetation represents and the need for its conservation and diversification for better resilience of urban and peri-urban ecosystems". Statistically, there is a strong correlation between population density and the number of trees. We also note the impact of urban growth on urban vegetation through densification and extension. The coexistence of these two trends in Kinshasa can be explained by its high rate of demographic growth, much higher than that of the built-up area (Kayembe wa Kayembe et al., 2009). Another explanation and consequence of this coexistence is also the development of the phenomenon of parceling out, which is detrimental to domestic tree vegetation (Sambiéni et al., 2018). Obviously, population growth remains a determining factor in the evolution of urban vegetation in residential plots of Kinshasa. Faced with the problem of global warming, the promotion and safeguard of urban vegetation remains an important challenge, hence the need for an urban reforestation program for the city of Kinshasa. May this study, like so many others, contribute to a better practical knowledge of shrub vegetation in residential plots of Kinshasa? Finally, what to say, Kinshasa remains a dynamic city with its myths and its realities. His daily life is characterized by the following: *"Kinshasa is a unique city in the world, you live, you survive, you love it or you curse it, but you are never bored".*[135] The different graphs mentioned above show us:

- – An increase in urban vegetation in residential plots between 1954-1984

---

[135] VERO TSHANDA BEYA, Main actress of the film "Félicité", quoted by JOAN TILOUINE AND PIERRE BENETTI, Journal Le Monde, July 2017

- A decline in urban vegetation in residential plots between 1984-2002
- An upward trend fluctuation from 2003

This observation leads us to the following analysis:

- The urban vegetation in the residential plots is in very strong regression especially in the plots of the old districts of the communes of Kinshasa, Kintambo, Barumbu, Gombe and of the districts of the so-called "new" communes such as Bumbu, Ngaba, Makala, Ngiri Ngiri, Selembao, Lemba, Matete,... where there is very strong demographic pressure.
- On the other hand, the tendency for the increase or growth of urban vegetation observed in residential plots after 2002 is very visible in the new districts of outlying municipalities such as Nsele, Mont Ngaliema, Maluku, Ngaliema.
- In these municipalities, we can see new subdivisions and neighborhoods such as Bibua, Matadi Kibala, Benseke, Mitendi, etc. where the vegetation is still young and flourishing.
- In conclusion, the urban vegetation in the residential plots of Kinshasa will continue to decline in the districts of the former communes. On the other hand, it will continue to grow and increase in the new neighborhoods of peripheral or peri-urban municipalities as shown by the regression line. This positive trend will diminish when these new neighborhoods reach the saturation point following the demographic pressure linked to population growth.
- Actions to be taken such as: educational action to raise awareness of the population to safeguard urban vegetation to reduce the effects of climate change due to global warming;

a city reconstruction project (urbanization plan) especially for the most affected municipalities such as the former municipalities of Kinshasa, Lingwala, Barumbu, Kintambo; improvement of shrub vegetation in residential plots in Kinshasa. This study on shrub vegetation in residential plots in Kinshasa requires another study, which will aim to assess the ecosystem services of urban vegetation in Kinshasa that can substantially mitigate the adverse effects of urbanization and climate change. The ecosystem functions targeted are the reduction of the urban heat island, the energy consumption of buildings and the carbon footprint of cities, the improvement of air quality, water management and quality pluvial, as well as the functions of habitats and biological corridors, etc.

I end with this sentence of Franklin Roosevelt « A nation that destroys its soils destroys itself. Forests are the lungs of our land, purifying the air and giving fresh strength to our people». I think we have all interest to protect our urban environment.

BIBLIOGRAPHY

1. AFFAIRS, Population Division, New York, USA
2. BILA EGONDA, Ecosystème urbain de Mbandaka: Les arbres du quartier Mbandaka II, Mémoire fin Licence en Biologie, ISP/ Mbandaka, Document inédit, 1989
3. BOLIA IKOLI Bienvenu, Kinshasa: Ma ville, ma capitale, Ed. L'harmattan, 2014
4. CRABBE M., Le climat de Kinshasa, Bruxelles, 1980
5. DINA RANARIFIDY, La Revue de l'urbanisation en République démocratique du Congo, Des villes productives et inclusives pour l'émergence de la République Démocratique du Congo, Banque Mondiale, Direction du développement, Environnement et Développement Durable, 2018
6. ELEONORE WOLFF et VIRGINIE DELBART, Extension urbaine et densité de la population à Kinshasa. Contribution de la télédétection satellitaire, Belgeo, Revue Belge de Géographie, 2002,
7. FLOURIOT J., Atlas de Kinshasa, BEAU, Kinshasa, 1975
8. GRIMM N.B, FAETH S.H, GOLUBIEWSKI N.E, REDMAN C.L, WU J, BAI X, BRIGGS J.M (2008) "Global change and the ecology of cities [archive]", Science, Vol.319, 756-760.
9. GUTU KIA ZIMI, Naissance d'une arboriculture urbaine au Zaïre (Congo), in DES FORETS ET DES HOMMES, Environnement Africain N*33-34-35-36, Vol. IX, 1-2-3-4, ENDA, Dakar, 1993, pp.221-247
10. HABARI M. JP., Etude floristique, phytogéographique et phytosociologique de la végétation de Kinshasa et des bassins moyens des rivières Ndjili et Nsele en République Démocratique

du Congo, Thèse de doctorat en biologie, Faculté des Sciences, Université de Kinshasa, 2009

11. ISAB, Belgian Institute for Space Aeronomy, https://www. aeronomie.be/fr/rapport-annuel/qualite-lair-kinshasa, 2017

12. JOAN TILOUINE ET PIERRE BENETTI, Mégapole insaisissable, Kinshasa croît hors de tout contrôle, Journal Le Monde, Août 2017

13. JOHN VIDAL, The 100 million city: is 21st century urbanization out of control?, 2018 https://www.theguardian.com/cities/2018/mar/19/urban-explosion-kinshasa-el-alto-growth-mexico-city-bangalore-lagos

14. KABAMBA M ET ALL, Toxic Heavy Metals in Ambient Air of Kinshasa, Democratic Republic Congo, Journal of Environmental Analytical Chemistry, 2016

15. KAYEMBE, Institut Panos Paris et DFID, 2004

16. KOUAGOU RAOUL SAMBIEN, Dynamique du paysage de la ville province de Kinshasa sous la pression de la périurbanisation: l'infrastructure verte comme moteur d'aménagement, Thèse de doctorat, ERAGIFTT, Kinshasa, 2019, https://www.researchgate.net/publication/340342911

17. KOUAGOU RAOUL SAMBIEN La végétation arborée domestique dans le paysage urbain et périurbain de la ville de Kinshasa, République Démocratique du Congo, Revue Afrique Science: Revue Internationale des Sciences et Technologie, Abidjan, 2018, pp.197-208, http://hdl.handle.net/2268/228882

18. KUCHELMEISTER G., Des arbres pour le millénaire urbain: le point sur la foresterie urbaine. Unasylva 200: 49 - 55 16, 2000

19. KAPAGAMA, P et R. WATERHOUSE, Portrait of Kinshasa: A city on (the) edge, Crisis States Research Centre, 2009

20. KAUMBU IM ET ALL, Nuisances sonores et recherche des déficiences auditives dans quelques milieux socioprofessionnels de la Lukunga, Kinshasa. Annales Africaines de Médecine, Articles originaux, Vol.8 N*3, Juin 2015

21. KAYEMBE WA KAYEMBE, M. et all, Cartographie de la croissance urbaine de Kinshasa (R.D. Congo) entre 1995 et 2005 par télédétection satellitaire à haute résolution, Revue Belgeo, 2009

22. KAYEMBE WA KAYEMBE M* & WOLFF E, Contribution de l'approche géographique à l'étude des facteurs humains de l'érosion ravinante intra-urbaine à Kinshasa (R.D. Congo), Geo-Eco-Trop., 2015

23. OLADIPO ADEJUWON James et all, « KINSHASA », *Encyclopædia Universalis* [en ligne], consulté le 6 juillet 2020. URL: http://www.universalis.fr/encyclopedie/kinshasa/

24. LELO NZUZI Francis, Les bidonvilles de Kinshasa, L'Harmattan/RDC, 2017

25. LEON DE SAINT MOULIN S. J., Kinshasa, ma ville... état des lieux et perspectives, Magazine LA JAUNE ET LA ROUGE, 2001, https://www.lajauneetlarouge.com/wp-content/uploads/2013/03/565-page-035-038.pdf

26. LOKAKAO ILEMBA THEODORE et all, Monographie de l'eau de la ville de Kinshasa, Document Inédit,

27. LUTUTALA et all (2008): « Etat des lieux des données du recensement scientifique de 1984 en République Démocratique du Congo » dans *Mémoires et démographie – Regards croisés au Sud et au Nord*, sous la direction de Richard Marcoux en collaboration avec Jennifer Dion, Québec: Les Presses de l'Université Laval, pp 98-101. (avec P. Kapagama et K. Ngoie).

28. LUTUTALA et all 1996: Dynamique des structures familiales et accès des femmes à l'éducation au Zaïre - Cas de la ville de Kinshasa, étude réalisée dans le cadre du Programme "Priorités dans la recherche sur l'éducation des filles et des femmes en Afrique" de l'Académie Africaine des Sciences (AAS), 114 p. + annexes (avec Ngondo a Pitshandenge et Mukeni Beya); financement: AAS/Fondation Rockefeller.

29. LUTUTALA et all (1991): Mouvements démographiques de Kinshasa (MODEKIN), Département de Démographie, Université de Kinshasa (avec Boute, J.; Nzita Kikhela et Tambashe Oleko); financement: CRDI.

30. MARC PAIN, Kinshasa, Ecologie et organisation, Thèse de doctorat, Université de Toulouse, Institut de Géographie, 1979

31. MARC PAIN, Kinshasa: la ville et la cité, mémoire O.R.S.T.O.M. d'études urbaines, Vol.105, Éditions IRD, 1984

32. MARIE JOËLLE SAUCIER, Les bienfaits de la végétation en milieu urbain., 2018; https://mjsaucierpaysagiste.com/les-bienfaits-de-la-vegetation-en-milieu-urbain/

33. MELANIE BEAUDOIN et all (2017), INSPQ, Verdir les villes pour la santé de la population, https://www.inspq.qc.ca/sites/default/files/publications/2265_verdir_villes_sante_population.pdf

34. MONUSCO, Radio Okapi, 2011; https://www.radiookapi.net/environnement/2011/03/02/les-vehicules-uses-augmentent-la-pollution-de-lair-a-kinshasa

35. MUKALENG MAKAL Didier, L'inquiétante pollution de l'air en RDC, 2017; https://earthjournalism.net/stories/linquietante-pollution-de-lair-en-rdc

36. MUKANIA BULEMBUE, L'élément végétal dans les parcelles résidentielles du Quartier Petro-Congo, Mémoire de 3*cycle

Diplôme Spécial en Gestion de l'Environnement, UNIKIN/Fac. Sciences, Document Inédit, 1986

37. NILSSON K. ET RANDRUP T. B., Urban forestry in the Nordic Countries. Actes d'un atelier nordique sur la foresterie urbaine, Reykjavik, Islande, du 21 au 24 septembre 1996. Danish Forest and Landscape Research Institute

38. NSOKIMIENO MME, CHEN S, ZHANG IQ, Sustainable urbanization's challenge in Democratic Republic of Congo. Journal Sustainable Development 3: 242-254, 2010

39. ONU, The World's Cities in 2018

40. PAULUS JACQUES s.j., Rapport d'enquête Projet JEEP, UNIKIN, Fac.Sciences, Document Inédit, 1988.

41. RENE DE MAXIMY, Kinshasa, Ville en suspens, Ed. Orstom, 1984

42. Rigaud Christophe, RDC: Kinshasa, plus grande ville d'Afrique en 2020, 2010, www.afrikarabia.com

43. SAMBIENI et al, La végétation arborée domestique dans le paysage urbain et périurbain de la ville de Kinshasa, République Démocratique du Congo, in Tropicultura (2018), 36(3), p.478-498, also in Afrique SCIENCE 14(2) (2018) p.197 - 208; ISSN 1813-548X, (http://www.afriquescience.info).

44. SHOMBA KINYAMBA S. et all, Monographie de la ville de Kinshasa, ICREDES, Kinshasa, 2015

45. SYS, C., La cartographie des sols au Congo. Ses principes, ses méthodes, INEAC, Série Sciences. Techniques, N°66, Bruxelles, 1961.

46. UNEP, Democratic Republic of the Congo Air Quality Policies, 2015 https://wedocs.unep.org/bitstream/handle/20.500.11822/17179/DemocraticRepublic_Congo.pdf?sequence=1&isAllowed=y

47. United Nations - World Population Prospects, Kinshasa, Republic of Congo Metro Area Population 1950-2020

48. UNITED NATIONS, World urbanization prospects. Department of Economy and social affairs, Population Division, New York, USA, 2008

49. WORLD BANK, United Nations, Population Stat, 2017-2020, Data sources, World Bank, United Nations, Census, GeoNames. https://populationstat.com/democratic-republic-of-the-congo/kinshasa

INTERNET

1. https://www.un.org/en/events/citiesday/assets/pdf/the_worlds_cities_in_2018_data_booklet.pdf

2. https://blog.courrierinternational.com/afrikarabia/2010/12/15/rdc-kinshasa-plus-grande-ville-dafrique-en-2020/

3. https://www.congovirtuel.com/page_province_kinshasa.php

4. www.congo2000.net/musiquecongo.html

5. https://dial.uclouvain.be/pr/boreal/en/object/boreal:4845/datastream/PDF_09/view

6. https://www.macrotrends.net/cities/20853/kinshasa/population

7. https://forrestgroup.com/en/achievement/anti-erosion

8. http://www.dknews-dz.com/article/52454-trois-morts-et-des-milliers-de-sans-abri-a-kinshasa-suite-aux-intemperies.htm

9. http://www.cheikfitanews.net/2017/12/kinshasa-sous-eau.html

10. https://www.depeche.cd/kinshasa-progression-de-lerosion-de-kindele-a-mont-ngafula/

11. http://www.appanpc.fr/_docs/7/Fichier/23-150324044906.pdf

12. https://doi.org/10.4000/vertigo.11869

THE AUTHOR

Gutu Kia Zimi, PhD

Professor

Doctorate (PhD) in sciences and techniques of development (Economic development)

M.A in Economic & Development

M.sc in Environmental Management

Special Diploma (B.A) in Economic and Development

Bachelor (B.A) in Personnel Management and Work Organization

Graduate (A.A) in Business Administration

Diploma in Police and Security Sciences

Diploma drug and alcohol counseling

Graduate Certificate intelligence studies

Certificate Leadership

PUBLICATIONS BY THE SAME AUTHOR

1. Le Développement Conscient. Un autre regard de Développement, Ed. Authorhouse, IL, USA, 2012
2. Le modèle monade de développement. Le développement des communautés en Afrique, Ed. Authorhouse, IL, USA, 2012
3. Comment sortir du sous-développement en Afrique. Diversités des problèmes et diversités des solutions, Editions Universitaires Européennes (EUE), Saarbrücken, Germany, 2013
4. Etude Economique et Développement de la région Nekongo en RDCongo, Ed. Authorhouse, IL, USA, 2014
5. Conscious development. Another approach to sustainable development, Ed. Authorhouse, IL, USA, 2014
6. Kinshasa. Une Mégapole verdoyante en crise
   Défis de gestion urbaine et environnementale, Ed. Authorhouse, IL, USA, 2020
7. Growing trees in urban Kinshasa.
   Shrub vegetation in residential plots in Kinshasa, Ed. Authorhouse, IL, USA, 2020

SUMMARY/EXTRACT

The study allowed us to understand that the urban vegetation of Kinshasa has been declining over the years, especially in the neighborhoods of the old municipalities and a slow progression in the new neighborhoods of the peripheral municipalities. This general downward trend should bring us awareness so that we can maintain and protect the existing urban vegetation. This downward trend can be explained by the fact that the area occupied by the constructions in the plots becomes larger and larger, that is to say that over the years, the old constructions from the beginning during the the acquisition of the plots disappear in favor of new larger and more comfortable constructions in the plots. Moreover, at the beginning of the birth of the district, the owners are mainly interested in planting the trees in the plot, but as the district ages, the urban vegetation becomes dense and the interest of planting other trees are no longer justified. It is also a regrettable fact to note that no tree has been detected in the streets of African neighborhoods and this because of the narrowness of the streets or a simple omission of the town planner, who has not made the relevant arrangements during the development of these districts. Planting a fruit tree in your plot is a profitable initiative as the fruits are an important source of nutrients. In this case, the fruit tree not only provides fruit but also provides shade and also improves the living environment in the plot.

Printed in the United States
By Bookmasters